PATTON'S GHOST CORPS

PATTON'S GHOST CORPS

CRACKING THE SIEGFRIED LINE

NATHAN N. PREFER

PRESIDIO

Published by Presidio Press
505 B San Marin Drive, Suite 300
Novato, CA 94945-1340

Library of Congress Cataloging-in-Publication Data
Prefer, Nathan.
    Patton's ghost corps : cracking the Siegfried Line / Nathan N. Prefer.
       p.   cm.
    Includes bibliographical references and index.
    ISBN 0-89141-646-3 (hardcover)
    1. World War, 1939–1945—Campaigns—Western Front. 2. Siegfried Line (Germany) 3. Patton, George S. (George Smith), 1885–1945.
    I. Title.
D756.3.P74   1998
940.54'21—dc21   97-40407
                                 CIP

Printed in the United States of America

CONTENTS

It will probably be a nasty business, breaking through the fortified lines, but once this is accomplished losses should not be great and we should capture another big bag of prisoners.

—General Dwight D. Eisenhower
Letter to General George C. Marshall, March 12, 1945,
referring to the attack of XX Corps in the Saar-Palatinate

FOREWORD

Patton's Ghost Corps could not be more timely, even though it's about a battle that took place more than a half century ago.

Recently, I held in my hand three jagged, rusted chunks of Krupp steel that were removed from an armored infantryman whose introduction to combat had been at Nennig, in the Saar-Moselle Triangle. Staff Sergeant (now Lieutenant Colonel, U.S. Army, Retired) Jim McDonald, like his buddies of the Eighth Armored Division's 7th Armored Infantry Battalion, wondered when and if anyone would publish an account of the accomplishments of the various U.S. Army units that participated in this attempted penetration of a particularly strong section of what they called the Siegfried Line. (Germans called it the *Orscholz Enz-Stellung,* an adjunct of the *Westwall.*) After all, other than the unavoidably dry official chronicles, no one had yet published anything about the bloody days of the bitter winter of 1944 when American GIs and German *Landsers* ferociously battled back and forth near Nennig, Berg, and Wies. Although he is in first-class shape for a man of seventy-two years, his company veterans' group newsletter is sadly filled with the names of Company A's veterans who have died or are too sick to attend their annual reunions.

Like most of the combat veterans of his generation, he doesn't complain or whine or even write letters to the editors of publishing houses, popular history magazines, or military professional journals to decry their seemingly endless deluge of articles about the same old subjects. Even the works that are published about American forays in World War II focus overwhelmingly on paratroopers, rangers, Marines, or the same old battles in Normandy and the Ardennes. No, Jim and his ilk don't complain, but their battalion lost more men in two days near Nennig than were killed or wounded in Grenada in 1983, or Somalia a decade later, so they do wonder.

They wonder because they know that they accomplished important, even crucial missions during their crusade to liberate Europe and Asia, yet they are ignored. At their unit reunions, in conversations with their dwindling circle of wartime pals, or alone in the dead of night, they remember the sacrifices, frustrations, excruciating disappointments, and final victory. But they often wait in vain to see anything about them in print or on film. Like their comrades of the unheralded infantry division of the Seventh and Ninth Armies in the ETO, or those of the Fifth Army which fought north of Rome, or practically any army units that fought in the Pacific. Jim and the other infantrymen who fought to penetrate the defenses of the *Orscholz Enz-Stellung* understand that while commando raids, fighter dogfights, and amphibious assaults are important, wars are ultimately decided by ground maneuver, by tankers and artillerymen and, most of all, infantrymen who brave a storm of fire to "pry the other guy out of his hold and make him sign the peace treaty." It has ever been so, and shall be as long as humans live on land.

Much is being made today about the future of warfare, and of military forces. Major military forces everywhere are seeking solutions to their nations' security and defense concerns that will minimize expense and manpower requirements through reorganization of their force structures, adjustment of their operation and tactical doctrines, and optimization of technological advances. In the United States, there is fierce competition among the respective armed services for their share of rapidly evaporating fiscal resources. Appealing to the post-Vietnam public intolerance for casualties, the air force publishes papers about bloodless victory from 80,000 feet. The navy presents elaborate scenarios depicting the total destruction of enemy forces by missiles delivered from "arsenal ships" steaming in serene safety, hundreds of miles offshore. The marines publicize their idea of directing the decisively decimating fires of their nautical half-siblings with small, clandestine teams of forward observers, dashing with impunity from position to position in helicopter and in airplanes capable of vertical flight. Even as a growing body of evidence emerges that indicates that enormously expensive "smart" weapons are not nearly as effective as claimed by their combatant users, chiefs of these services also claim that the days of protracted conflict are forever over, that wars of the future will be won at little or no cost by high-tech cyberwarriors, and the army will be needed only to gather the dazed prisoners at war's end.

Spurred to action by the seductive claims on Congressional heart-strings by their sister services, some army "intellectuals" embrace bizarre ideas proclaiming the arrival of "Third Wave" or "Information Age" warfare, in which wars will be fought principally against banking and telecommunications systems by killer computers. Fortunately, most mainstream army thinkers understand that even in the "Information Age" the army will still win wars by fire and maneuver, and must be prepared to do so against adversaries more formidable than untrained third-world militias and police forces, or the poorly-led and badly equipped peasant-soldiers of an utterly isolated rogue dictatorship. While some of the army's leaders (too many) are overly infatuated with an inaccurate and naive view of the German Wehrmacht and would make the U.S. Army over in its image, most are rightly focused on winning the decisive land war against the resurgent major competitor(s) that will appear in the next ten years. They perceive information and other advancing technologies to be important, but as only one of a range of avenues for maintaining dominance across the wide spectrum of military endeavor essential over the coming decade. They refuse to be beguiled by the allure of easy victory, and hone their perilously thin swords for success in future battles which will no more resemble the weird vision of practically bloodless "infowars" than some 1950s futurists' vision of nuclear battlefields resembled Vietnam rice paddies. The army's most discerning visionaries may call the patterns of future war things like "shaping the battlespace" and "conducting decisive operations," but for all the modern terminology and useful high-tech advances, Jim McDonald and his World War II infantryman buddies would recognize them as based on the fire and maneuver that wins wars.

Dr. Nathan Prefer's book is indeed timely. *Patton's Ghost Corps* documents and finally recognizes the important contributions made by the victors of the Saar-Moselle Triangle. Like other emerging works on the lesser-known battles of World War II, *Patton's Ghost Corps* chronicles another of the long-ignored actions of the Second World War, gives the veterans their belated due, and provides an heirloom for them to pass on to future generations. It enhances the reader's awareness of the great legacy of the U.S. Army. Its rich, multi-level perspective and incisive scholarship should inspire more authors, editors, and film moguls to research and produce more fine history of neglected World War II campaigns, before the war disappears from living memory.

This book also illustrates the utter inadequacy of airpower and seapower as substitutes for ground maneuver forces. In the *Orscholz Enz-Stellung,* more than 220 miles from the nearest ocean, the defenders of the maze of hundreds of impenetrable pillboxes fired their machine guns over vast minefields, protected behind thousands of virtually indestructible steel-reinforced concrete tank traps. Even though the U.S. Army Air Force had absolute mastery of the skies by the time of the assault, there were not enough bombs and rockets in the European theater to destroy the fortifications and obstacles in the Westwall, even if the weather had allowed it. Dr. Prefer tells of pillboxes so perfectly camouflaged that assault troops did not recognize them until they stood on top of them and heard the voices of the defenders inside. Even modern aircraft equipped with the most sophisticated thermal sensors would be extremely hard-put to locate such positions, and there would never be enough precision guided projectiles in the inventory to destroy the myriad blockhouses infesting a two mile-deep band of such defenses. Airpower and seapower are essential, but one of the great lessons taught by studying the battle for the Saar-Moselle Triangle is that landpower is decisive. Even when conducting limited objective attacks (in this case, discrete penetrations of the Siegfried Line) designed to "shape the battlespace" for an ensuing "decisive operation" (crossing the Rhine and conquering Germany), ground maneuver forces are indispensable. Superbly trained combined arms teams, centered around tough, well-disciplined, and well-led infantrymen competently wielding reliable, state of the art weapons—in World War II, small arms, explosives, and even bayonets—have been the key to success against similarly well-trained and motivated enemies since well before the time of Christ, and will continue to be so. Our military and political leaders would do well to read this book.

Patton's Ghost Corps hammers another nail in the coffin of the sometimes infantile, often inane, inevitably simplistic, and always dangerous tendency among far too many history buffs and self-styled defense "experts" to idolize the Wehrmacht, disparage the U.S. Army of World War II, and attribute Allied victory to overwhelming numerical and materiel superiority. Dr. Prefer's work follows closely in the train of such scholarship as Mike Doubler's outstanding book *Closing With the Enemy,* and other recent books that reexamine the roots of American victory in Europe in 1945. In the words of three-war infantry combat veteran General Frederick J. Kroesen, works like these establish the American soldier as "a formidable opponent, not to the discredit of a valiant foe, but rather to the recognition of the fortitude and determination of Americans trained, motivated, and well-led, following well-conceived and executed doctrine."

—Keith E. Bonn, Lieutenant Colonel, U.S. Army (Ret.)

ACKNOWLEDGMENTS

I wish to acknowledge the assistance of the following people and organizations for their significant contributions that made this book possible:

The 94th Infantry Division Association, and most particularly Douglas LaRue Smith (M/302d Infantry), Donald E. Mulry (F/301st), Robert K. Adair (I/376th), Col. (Ret.) Wallace M. Gallant (M/302d), Walter F. Oelschlaeger (F/302d), Eugene T. Hack (3d/302d), Robert U. Cassel (1st/301st), Robert E. Trefzger (C/376th), John L. Hoerber (1st/301st), William C. Warren (3/301), Edmund H. Lessel (Orscholz).

Particular appreciation is due James L. Malony, son of Maj. Gen. Harry J. Malony, for his comments on his father's view of the battle and his providing General Malony's notes and logs from his service with the 94th Infantry Division. Keith Bonn's expertise on the campaign is gratefully acknowledged.

Thanks to Douglas L. Smith, Donald E. Mulry, Prof. Robert K. Adair, Walter F. Oelschlaeger, and Robert U. Cassel for spending free time to travel many miles to visit with me.

The efforts of the National Archives and Records Service are gratefully acknowledged, for providing records research and photographs as are the many responses to my inquiries by the Office of the Chief of Military History, U.S. Army.

Finally, a special note of thanks to the women, all born after the end of the war, who have put up with the Second World War for so long: my wife Barbara and my daughters Hollie and Amy.

INTRODUCTION

There exists in the study of American military history, and most particularly in the history of the Second World War, a tendency to concentrate on the most fiercely contested, publicized, and costly battles or campaigns of the war. Desperate struggles such as Normandy, the Ardennes, Anzio, Tarawa, Iwo Jima, Cassino, and Leyte have been studied repeatedly. Each presented a situation where the might of the Allied, usually American, forces overwhelmed a stubborn defense or defeated a massive counterattack. These studies are valuable in learning the abilities of the American soldier in such situations, as well as understanding the methods by which nations conduct their wars. Yet there is a danger inherent that is not usually recognized.

It lies in the comments heard about the abilities of the American as a soldier. One may hear, particularly from European historians, that the American soldier fought well only when he had overwhelming material superiority, too often given the major share of the credit for the particular victory being studied. Because the U.S. Army entered the Second World War comparatively late, and because most of its campaigns were offensive in nature, the tendency to concentrate on the massive battles, where material superiority was very much in evidence, is understandable. There were lesser known campaigns and battles, however, where American soldiers fought on relatively equal terms with their opponents and prevailed. If the study of history is to seek the truth, then additional studies are needed of lesser known battles that display different conditions than those most commonly studied.

Some historians have begun this process. Lieutenant Colonel Keith E. Bonn's recent work on the Vosges Mountains campaign of late 1944 and early 1945, *When the Odds Were Even,* makes this point at the field-army level. Colonel Bonn points out the three major areas too often accepted as truth, which were not, in fact, always present. The matter of tactical air superiority, an efficient and satisfactory logistical system, and a superior manpower situation are the points used to discount the performance of the American soldier in the European Theater of Operations. As Colonel Bonn shows, the Seventh U.S. Army did not enjoy those advantages in the Vosges campaign.

Usually accepted as reasons for discounting the performance of the U.S. Army in Europe were the quality and quantity of the opposition. The drafting of both young and old men into the German army as its fortunes dwindled in the last months of the war are taken as standard and applied to all campaigns in which they were engaged. The poor equipment of the German army in this phase of the war is also cited, but this was not always the case. The training quality of U.S. Army infantry divisions is also often used as a reason for supposed poor performance. These and other negatives make the historians conclude that it was only material and numerical superiority that enabled a fumbling American army to win its World War II campaigns.

This ignores the many situations in which the advantages taken for granted did not exist. The Seventh U.S. Army, as studied by Colonel Bonn, prevailed when "the odds were even." There were other situations when the odds, at least in the beginning, were actually against them. One occurred in a least likely organization, Gen. George S. Patton's Third U.S. Army. Long accepted as a dashing commander, swift to exploit advantages while deceiving his superiors who hindered his progress by their pedantic decisions and delays, Patton and his troops are usually depicted as smashing into and through enemy opposition and racing on to the next obstacle. This is a good example of an incomplete study of military history.

In at least one instance, units of the Third Army faced an enemy that outnumbered them, as well as having more and better armored support and better individual equipment. To compound the difficulties, Third Army, the headquarters commanding the operation, imposed serious restrictions upon the operation. Had those same restrictions been applied to it by higher headquarters, one of the famous Patton outbursts would have ensued. Despite all this, the units involved in the battle, the XX Corps and the 94th Infantry Division, prevailed. The campaign not only succeeded, after a costly infantry battle not typical of Third Army, but it opened the way for the massive sweep into Germany for which Patton later received considerable credit as a thrusting armor commander.

By the end of the first week in January 1945, the Battle of the Bulge had officially ended. The First U.S. Army under Lt. Gen. Courtney Hodges stopped the enemy attack, albeit with considerable difficulty, and was soon joined by Patton's Third Army in pushing the enemy back. By January the Allies had a solid front line facing the German heartland, running some 450 miles from the North Sea to the border of Switzerland. Because the Allies were not strong enough to make serious efforts all along that line, new alternatives for future advances had to be considered. Plans to resume the offensive interrupted by the Ardennes counteroffensive had to be postponed once again when a second, less powerful, offensive hit the southern end of the allied line on New Year's Day 1945. As soon as Lt. Gen. Alexander M. Patch's Seventh Army repelled that attack, known as Operation Nordwind, the Allies could themselves return to the offensive.

Before doing that, however, the commanders had to determine how best to conduct that offensive. The original plans, as approved by General Eisenhower, had envisioned a secure base established in France, and two powerful thrusts into Germany, one north of the Ardennes, the other south, to seize the Ruhr and Saar industrial areas, thus further crippling her war effort. Events had repeatedly forced alterations to these plans. The initial tenacious German defense of France had delayed the planners' timetable considerably. Then the rapid and unexpected collapse of that resistance placed the Allies ahead of their preinvasion schedule. Finally, the recently concluded Battle of the Bulge once again altered the timetable.

Beset by constantly changing events and priorities, Eisenhower now found himself buffeted by his subordinates' priorities. Each pressed his own scheme on the supreme commander. Foremost among these was British Field Marshal Bernard Law Montgomery, who demanded that his northern group of armies be allocated massive personnel and material resources to drive into northern Germany. Montgomery commanded the 21st Army Group, which included British, Canadian, Polish, and American units. Already assigned an entire American army, Lt. Gen. William Hood Simpson's Ninth Army, he insisted on more.

Not to be outdone, Lt. Gen. Omar Nelson Bradley, commanding the 12th Army Group, argued his own case with Eisenhower, urging that a southern thrust, under his command, be undertaken to sweep the Saar basin and enter Germany via the shortest route. He, too, demanded augmentation of personnel and logistical support to the exclusion of other commands. About the only subordinate not pressing General Eisenhower was Lt. Gen. Jacob L. Devers, commanding the 6th Army Group of American and French forces. Not a close associate of General Eisenhower, a relative latecomer to the European Theater, and with internal problems over French cooperation plaguing him, he had no immediate objectives other than those already agreed to with Supreme Headquarters.

Eisenhower had his own thoughts on the progress of the campaign. He was determined that all of his forces establish a firm base along the Rhine River before any additional operations were begun, thus putting pressure on all of the subordinate commands. In early January none were firmly on the Rhine except the 6th Army Group, which itself faced a major German enclave on the river's western side around the town of Colmar, making control of the Rhine in its sector incomplete.

As to future actions, Eisenhower held firmly to the plans made prior to the actual invasion of the continent. There would be three thrusts, one northern, one central, and the other southern. This pleased none of his subordinates, and rather than settling matters, it led only to additional argument. The British chiefs of staff disagreed with the decision, supporting Montgomery, and raising the issue with the combined chiefs of staff of the Allied Forces. Eisenhower soon found himself responding to an inquiry from his next superior, General George Catlett Marshall, as to the reasoning behind his decision. The embattled supreme commander replied that he desired a firm defensive line before making any thrusts forward into Germany. He had selected the Rhine River, a natural defensive position, as that line of defense. Once firmly along the Rhine, Eisenhower advised Marshall that he would then consider the various proposals and decide on the best course to follow.

The supreme commander was also aware that the issue over the best axis to follow into Germany was the cause of another proposal then under consideration. The British chiefs of staff, citing the pressures of the post, suggested that a deputy commander be appointed to control ground-forces operations for General Eisenhower, relieving him to concentrate on other vital matters. Knowing that proposing Field Marshal Montgomery would be self-defeating given the severity of the feeling against him at this time in the American camp, they suggested instead Field Marshal Sir Harold R. L. G. Alexander for the post. Having come from the Mediterranean Theater, where he had commanded American troops without difficulty, he appeared to be a good candidate.

Eisenhower replied that given the situation as it looked in January, the main thrust would still be from the north, thus giving the British and Montgomery the opportunity they sought. He added that a subsidiary thrust, from the south and made by American forces, would be expected. He stated that no deputy could better coordinate the many factors of his position than he could himself. Matters of ground forces needed to be coordinated with political, logistical, communications, and personnel issues. Debating for several days, the combined chiefs of staff accepted General Eisenhower's plans on 2 February 1945.

Although now the formally accepted scheme of maneuver, the plan would undergo many changes and adjustments caused by the course of events over the next few months. Having squelched, if not appeased, the many egos of his generals and field marshals, General Eisenhower could now turn to the American, British, Canadian, French, and Polish soldiers to accomplish what it had taken so much argument to decide.

CHAPTER 1
STARTING A CATASTROPHE

In order to close up to the Rhine and thus fulfill the first phase of General Eisenhower's plan, most of his subordinate armies had to push forward. This resulted in four major thrusts. The 21st Army Group in the north under Field Marshal Montgomery pushed its Second British, First Canadian, and Ninth U.S. Armies toward Germany. The 6th Army Group of General Jacob L. Devers was recovering territory it had surrendered on order of Supreme Headquarters, Allied Expeditionary Forces, during the now defeated Operation Nordwind. In the center, General Hodges's First U.S. Army was still cleaning up the penetrations made during the German Ardennes Offensive, assisted by Patton's Third U.S. Army. General Patton, however, was also seeking a quicker way to the Rhine. That search would result in one of two great catastrophes for the German war effort in the west.

It was none other an authority than Reichsmarschall Hermann Goering, leader of the German Luftwaffe, and second only to the Führer for most of the Second World War in Germany, who pointed out the importance of the Saar-Moselle Triangle campaign. In an interrogation after his capture in 1945 he remarked "When the first break in the Siegfried Line was made near Ockfen, der Führer was very irritated. After that came the breakthrough near Trier, and that was wholly incomprehensible. We could not believe that these fortifications could be penetrated. The breakthrough near Trier was particularly depressing. That breakthrough and the capture of the Remagen Bridge were two great catastrophes for the German cause."

The Reichsmarschall would have been more depressed to learn that the entire operation was done as a footnote to what the Americans considered more vital operations elsewhere. Had it not been for General Patton's refusal to sit still while others carried on the main effort, the Saar-Moselle Triangle might never have annoyed Hitler and Goering.

Lieutenant General George Smith Patton Jr. was a warrior. He often commented how he would have preferred to have lived in an earlier age, when he would have been a Roman consul, or Napoleon's marshal. Born in 1885 in California, he was raised on stories of his Confederate soldier ancestors. He entered the Virginia Military Institute as soon as he could, and from there transferred to the United States Military Academy at West Point, where he graduated, after academic difficulties, with the class of 1909. Here he revealed to his parents the intensity that would characterize his military career when he wrote them shortly before graduation, "I have got to, do you understand, got to be great. It is no foolish child dream. It is me as I ever will be. . . ." One noted historian who has studied Patton described him as "first and foremost a man of enormous ambition."

Commissioned in the cavalry, he quickly earned a reputation as a hard-driving and fearless soldier. He rode with Pershing in the American expedition against Pancho Villa in 1916, seeing his first combat. Sent to France when America entered the First World War, he was assigned to develop an American tank force. He first established the American Expeditionary Force Tank School, then, as a temporary lieutenant colonel, he commanded the first U.S. tank unit in the battles of Saint-Mihiel and Meuse-Argonne. Wounded while commanding the 304th Tank Brigade, he survived and brought the unit home after the war's end. He briefly remained with the tank corps, working with another officer he befriended, Maj. Dwight David Eisenhower.

Between the world wars Patton had an ordinary career for a regular-army officer. He spent much of the interwar years with the mounted cavalry, his personal favorite. In 1940 he was promoted to brigadier general and given command of the newly formed 2d Armored Division. His success in molding the division into an effective fighting force earned him another promotion and command of the western portion of the North African invasion in November 1942. During this and subsequent operations, he would be closely thrown together with old friends now in influential positions. Among these were future generals of the army Eisenhower and Bradley. The latter considered Patton "one of the most extraordinary fighting generals the army had ever produced" while at the same time expressing concern over his lack of attention to details, particularly logistics.

General Patton was next called upon to improve the American effort in the North African campaign, when he took command of the II U.S. Corps after the debacle at Kasserine Pass, and quickly redeemed the reputation of American arms in the eyes of Washington, if not in the eyes of his British allies.

Replaced by Omar Bradley, Patton next was assigned to command the Seventh U.S. Army, and to lead that force in the invasion of Sicily. Once again his drive led to success for American forces, much to the chagrin of certain British officers who earlier had criticized both Patton and his troops. His unfortunate conduct, while visiting a front-line hospital, became public knowledge and raised cries for his dismissal from command. General Eisenhower did, in fact, relieve him from command of the Seventh U.S. Army and sent him into temporary obscurity. However, after a suitable time, Eisenhower asked the Army chief of staff, General Marshall, to let Patton have a chance to redeem himself by posing as the commander of a fictitious invasion force scheduled to open the second front in France in the area of the Pas de Calais. Marshall, always a shrewd judge of men, agreed and Patton took command of a force that existed mainly on paper. Using his reputation with the Germans as the most respected American commander, he purposely made himself known around England to deceive the German command as to the time and place of the second-front assault.

Meanwhile General Bradley was assigned to command the assault force destined to invade Normandy. As a reward and a form of redemption for his reputation, General Patton was to be given command of the Third Army, the major follow-up force for the American part of the Normandy invasion. At the end of July 1944, with the First U.S. Army breaking out of the Normandy beachhead, Patton and his Third Army were committed to action. Patton, driving hard as always, pushed his troops east, north, and south against collapsing German resistance. He quickly earned back all his old fame as a battle leader, both with the media and the enemy. His earlier fear, that "the war would end before I got into it," no longer nagged him, but restoration of his reputation was still a concern.

Leading his Third Army through the remnants of the German forces that had held the Allies at bay in Normandy for two months, he began a rampage across France that endeared him to the media, which quickly latched on to him as a ready source of stories for the hometown papers. Throughout August and September 1944, Third Army covered ground and crossed battlefields of the First World War, much to the pleasure of Patton and his supporters. General Marshall, who had monitored his progress closely, remarked to an associate that he was pleased that Patton had "come rushing out of a dog-house." General Eisenhower, whose patience Patton had tried more than once in recent years, was later to remark that Third U.S. Army was "a fighting force that is not excelled . . . by any other of equal size in the world."

It was during this race across France that Patton and his loyal staff developed a belief, later fostered in their memoirs, that they repeatedly outfoxed their own high command by moving unexpectedly, stealing supplies meant for other armies, and acting without orders to defeat both the enemy and their own leadership, particularly SHAEF. Eisenhower, who still viewed General Patton with suspicion after his repeated falls from grace, had arranged with Bradley to keep a close watch on the Third Army. Patton's abilities as an army commander were appreciated by his superiors, but they agreed that he would never rise above army command, and that even in that capacity, he would need to be watched closely. In fact, as General Bradley would explain in his memoirs, in every case but one his 12th Army Group headquarters was fully aware of what Patton and his army were doing, and often allowed them to relish their belief in their deception when the entire scheme was known in advance of implementation. This false belief on the part of Third Army would play a prominent role in the battle of the Saar-Moselle Triangle.

The race across France ended abruptly at the German border. The German army, resilient as always, managed to stop the allies short of German soil in most areas. This, combined with a problem of supplies, slowed the advance of the Allied armies to a crawl. Third Army bogged down in the mud before the fortress city of Metz, and spent much time and effort in finally seizing the city. Meanwhile the other American armies, the First and the Ninth, north of the Third Army, were equally bogged down in front of the Siegfried Line, the German major defensive line. As the Americans were resting and regrouping, the German army, ordered by Adolf Hitler, took a hand in events, launching a major offensive in the Ardennes that soon became known as the Battle of the Bulge.

When the Germans came storming out of the forest of the Ardennes, the Third Army had three corps attached to it. Both the III Corps and the XII Corps were ordered by Patton to divert northward to assist in containing, and later reducing, the enemy penetration in the First Army area. This left only one corps, the XX Corps, to man the line formerly held by all three. Even that unit was ruthlessly stripped of all possible infantry and armored units to assist in the drive north. Ordered on the defensive, the XX Corps manned the line with only a minimum of troops and equipment to perform its assignments.

By January of 1945 it became clear to all concerned that the German offensive had run its course, and that it was now the Allies' turn to attack and reduce the invasion salient to its former lines. Most of the attention was centered on this goal, but for General Patton it was not sufficient, due in large part to the fact that his Third Army would have a subsidiary role. Besides, Patton had plans of his own that did not include following any other army into Germany. Patton's resources were largely tied up in reducing the Bulge, but he did have one force facing Germany directly, and at the Siegfried Line. That force was Maj. Gen. Walton Harris Walker and his XX Corps. The part of the line they faced was known to the Germans as the Orscholz Switchline, while the Americans called it the Saar-Moselle Triangle.

It was at this time, the second week of January 1945, that Col. Oscar W. Koch, the Third Army's chief intelligence officer, evaluated the situation in the Bulge as mopping up, and offered the opinion that an attack by American forces, particularly the Third Army, would have a good chance of success. Koch had earned Patton's confidence in the months since July 1944, and in any case it was the kind of advice the general wanted to hear at this time.

But Third Army was under orders to participate in the continuing reduction of the German Bulge salient. Indeed, three of its four corps, the III, VIII, and XII, were fully engaged in that task. Only the XX Corps under General Walker faced directly toward the Rhine River and Germany. Even XX Corps had been stripped of nearly all its mobile troops, and had no armored division assigned to it. Plans written in December, before the German counteroffensive, had called for the entire Third Army to penetrate the Siegfried Line, cross the Rhine, and advance into the Palatinate area of western Germany. The strength planned for that drive had envisioned some three corps, with several armored divisions, much field artillery, and a dozen or more infantry divisions.

To the south Seventh Army, General Patton's old outfit, now under the command of Lt. Gen. Alexander M. Patch, had come ashore in southern France in August of 1944, and had then fought its way northeast to link up with the southern flank of the Third Army. The Seventh Army had joined with the Third at the Siegfried Line and then, under Eisenhower's orders, had withdrawn to shorten their lines in order to allow reserves to be held to counter more German attacks. Sure enough, New Year's Day 1945, brought another German counterattack, Operation Nordwind, in the sector of Seventh Army. After heavy fighting every bit as difficult as that just concluded in the Battle of the Bulge, Seventh Army restored its positions and began planning for future operations.

One of these was code-named Operation Undertone, and as originally conceived placed Seventh Army attacking across the front of Third Army into Germany. It was this concept, subsequently modified, that disturbed General Patton. Once again, he feared that Third Army would be given a subsidiary role. To the warrior Patton, it was unacceptable to allow his former command, led by a West Point graduate four years his junior, to lead him anywhere.

Finally, there was an old rival plaguing General Patton. British Field Marshal Bernard Montgomery, commanding the northernmost group of armies, was planning a massive attack into the heart of Germany as directed by General Eisenhower. With his usual aplomb, Montgomery was demanding massive reinforcement with American divisions while the remaining U.S. units sat in defensive postures awaiting his anticipated victory. As far back as North Africa in 1942, Patton had felt himself in competition with Montgomery, whose skills he often derided, particularly the British commander's insistence on a set-piece attack, with massive supply and manpower superiority. General Patton chose to ignore, or was perhaps unaware of, the manpower crisis in the British forces where divisions were being disbanded to provide reinforcements for those still capable of combat. Patton now learned that the Supreme Commander was considering a plan advanced by Montgomery in which some thirty-five U.S. divisions would be attached to his 21st Army Group for his planned offensive. Coming in addition to the fact the entire Ninth U.S. Army had already been "loaned" to him as a result of the Battle of the Bulge, this information signaled to Patton that his own Third Army was to be left out of the coming conquest of Germany. As Patton viewed it, Montgomery was just another competitor for fame and glory, as Patton understood those concepts, and it was imperative to him that the Field Marshal did not overshadow his own efforts. All these self-imposed pressures led Patton to seek out the one remaining available force by which he could get his foot in the door of the German homeland. Looking toward Walker's XX Corps, he was pleased to learn that he and his subordinates were thinking along the very same lines: attacking into Germany proper.

CHAPTER 2
THE GHOST CORPS

Major General Walton Harris Walker commanded the XX Corps from its inception as the IV Armored Corps in September 1942, through its conversion in October 1943. He brought it overseas to England, landing in France in July 1944.

General Walker's early career was similar in many ways to that of his commanding officer, General Patton. Born in Texas on 3 December 1889, Walker also attended Virginia Military Institute before entering West Point. Graduating with the class of 1912, he was commissioned in the infantry. He also served in Mexico, during the occupation of Veracruz in 1914. Again like Patton, he was sent to France in World War I, serving as a machine-gun officer with the 5th Infantry Division at the same battles as Patton, Saint-Mihiel and Meuse-Argonne. Between world wars, he served as an instructor at West Point, attended the Field Artillery School, the Infantry School, and the Command and General Staff School. After serving with infantry troops in China, he returned to graduate from the Army War College, after which he was assigned as a lieutenant colonel to the Army's prestigious War Plans Division, where he served with such influential fellow soldiers as Eisenhower and Bradley, and was evaluated by the army's premier soldier, George Marshall.

At the outbreak of war, he was assigned to command the 3d Armored Division, and in September 1942 became the commander of the IV Armored Corps and later XX Corps. Leading this unit into Normandy behind the now rampaging First Army, Walker quickly showed just how similarly he and General Patton executed their assignments. He pushed his troops hard and seized any opportunity to move against the enemy, regardless of plans or available support.

He became one of Patton's most trusted subordinates. The XX Corps served throughout its career in the European Theater with the Third Army.

Walker's command was one of twenty-two corps that saw combat service in the Second World War. The U.S. Army in World War II considered the corps to be "the key headquarters for employing all combat elements in proper tactical combinations." The army corps is the bridge between the tactical units of which the division is the largest, and the operational responsibilities of the field army. As such, it has operational control over a variety of tactical units, which are added as the situation requires. A corps might have anywhere from one to six divisions attached to it for a particular mission. These can be rotated in or out as the need arises. The corps provides operational direction to these units in accordance with the plans it receives from field army. From its own attached group of specialized units it provides engineer, artillery, medical, and transportation support to its attached tactical units.

It was in its drive from Normandy to Metz, when XX Corps captured Reims, crossed the Moselle, and reduced the fortress complex at the city of Metz, that the corps entered the Siegfried Line. Here it earned from the enemy its most cherished accolade. During prisoner-of-war interrogations they learned that they were referred to by the enemy as the "Ghost Corps." Because they moved so fast and so often, the Germans couldn't keep track of them.

Although Walker was considered by some as "a little martinet who patterned his life after Patton's," General Patton considered him to be "a very fine soldier." Patton's chief of staff, Gen. Hobart Gay, believed that Walker was "always the most willing and cooperative" of Patton's corps commanders, and that Walker would "apparently fight anytime, anyplace, with anything that the army commander desires to give him." Walker was such a good commander that he would, before the outbreak of the Korean War, be given command of the Eighth U.S. Army and lead it after serious setbacks in one of the outstanding defensive stands in American military history. General J. Lawton Collins, a fellow corps commander in Europe, considered him "a fine, gallant field commander." Described as "unostentatious, wearing GI shoes and an ordinary webbing belt," General Walker was "approachable but it seems he was never really liked." As one historian has pointed out, there was "no General Walker popularity cult, no legends, and no anecdotes."

One of the outstanding corps commanders of the American army of World War II, Maj. Gen. Matthew B. Ridgway, described the typical corps commander of that war. "He is responsible for a large sector of a battle area, and all he must worry about in that zone is fighting. He must be a man of great flexibility of mind, for he may be fighting with six divisions one day and one division the next as the higher commanders transfer divisions to and from his corps. He must be a man of tremendous physical stamina, too, for his battle zone may cover a front of one hundred miles or more, with a depth of fifty to sixty miles, and by plane and jeep he must cover this area, day and night, anticipating where the hardest fighting is to come, and being there in person, ready to help his division commanders in any way he can." Several of these corps commanders, including Omar N. Bradley, Robert L. Eichelberger, Leonard T. Gerow, Alexander M. Patch, George S. Patton, Matthew B. Ridgway, Lucian K. Truscott, and James A. Van Fleet rose to army or army group command, as did General Walker.

At the beginning of January 1945, the Third Army consisted of the III Corps, VIII Corps, XII Corps, and the Ghost Corps. All but the XX Corps were engaged in the continuing reduction of the German penetration in the Ardennes. Walker's unit list included the 90th and 95th Infantry Divisions, holding the line, and the 10th Armored Division, in reserve and refitting after its rough time in the Battle of the Bulge. The armored division was technically not attached to the XX Corps, but was only in its area of responsibility while reorganizing. Walker could not use it without approval of both Third Army and SHAEF. Holding the flank was the corps's assigned cavalry reconnaissance squadrons, and the 3d and 43d Cavalry Squadrons of the 3d Cavalry Group (Mechanized). The 90th Infantry Division had been ordered to move to and reinforce III Corps. A unit new to Third Army, the 94th Infantry Division, was on the way to replace the 90th.

North of Third Army's zone, First Army was still heavily engaged in reducing the German penetration resulting from the Battle of the

Bulge. North of First Army, Field Marshal Montgomery's 21st Army Group of British, Canadian, and American armies were clearing their way to the Rhine in preparation for a massive air and ground assault to force a crossing. To the south of Third Army, Seventh U.S. Army was also struggling to restore its former positions along the Siegfried Line, which it had given up on the orders of General Eisenhower in preparation for the German offensive, Operation Nordwind, which hit the Seventh Army on New Year's Day 1945. Having halted the German drive, Seventh Army was beginning the process of returning to the offensive.

In the Pacific the U.S. Navy began the preparation of the Lingayen Gulf area for the coming invasion of the Philippine island of Luzon, while in Burma, British, American, and Chinese forces pushed the Japanese toward the coast. The Central Pacific Theater of Operations was also preparing for the coming invasion of the Volcano-Bonin Islands, bombarding Iwo, Chichi, and Haha Jima and making photographic reconnaissance flights over those islands. In the Mediterranean, the 15th Army Group was preparing for its spring attack on the Gothic Line, the last German defensive position in Italy.

In the east, politics continued to affect events. Although an offensive by the Soviet Union's Red Army had been ready since early December, no attack had materialized. German propaganda viewed the situation as one where the Russians were pressuring their western allies to recognize the Polish Communist government based at Lublin, rather than the democratic exile government in London. In fact, the late winter thaw had caused Russian operations, which depended largely on heavy armor and mechanized equipment, to be postponed. Their equipment needed frozen roads and fields for their operations. British Prime Minister Winston Churchill inquired on 6 January of Soviet Premier Josef Stalin if a renewed Soviet offensive could be expected in January, as the western battle in the Ardennes was still severe. Stalin replied that as soon as the weather turned cold, or by the second half of January at the latest, the Red Army would launch its delayed offensive. It did begin on 12 January, when Marshal of the Soviet Union Ivan S. Konev's First Ukrainian Front attacked out of its Vistula River bridgehead at Baranow and struck out for the Oder River on Germany's eastern border.

CHAPTER 3
THE AMERICAN SOLDIERS

The XX Corps at the end of the first week in January 1945 consisted of three divisions and the 3d Cavalry Group. The 90th Infantry Division was awaiting relief by the 94th Infantry Division so that it could move north to assist the III Corps in the ongoing reduction of the German penetration. The 95th Infantry Division was holding the front line, still recuperating after its introduction to combat at the battle for Metz, where it had suffered severely. The 10th Armored Division in SHAEF reserve was similarly recuperating. The Ghost Corps was in a defensive posture, holding the line pending the outcome of the battles to its north.

On 7 January, Maj. Gen. Harry J. Malony, commanding general of the 94th Infantry Division, replaced Maj. Gen. James A. Van Fleet and his 90th Infantry Division in their section of the front line. The 90th moved north to III Corps, the 94th settled into its new positions facing the Siegfried Switchline. Earlier in November and December, the 90th and 95th Divisions, supported by the 10th Armored Division, had attacked into this fortified enemy stronghold and made some early gains. The prolonged battle for Metz had exhausted the infantry, and the attack had not progressed very far when the German counteroffensive had halted all offensive movement by XX Corps. The 10th Armored was pulled out and rushed north to delay the enemy thrusts and to assist the 101st Airborne Division in its epic defense of the town of Bastogne. The 90th and 95th Infantry Divisions had held the line under XX Corps while the Battle of the Bulge raged north of them. Resting and reorganizing as best they could under the circumstances, the two infantry divisions made no attacks against the Switchline. As a result the 94th Infantry Division found that the fortified defenses they faced had been little damaged by earlier attacks, and were by and large intact.

The arrival of the 94th Infantry Division within Third Army was viewed with less than enthusiasm. Several of the staff, knowing only that the division had arrived from the "rear," assumed without further inquiry that it was a new and "untried" unit that needed seasoning before it could be entrusted with a critical role in any major offensive.

Actually, the 94th had been in combat longer than its more trusted neighbor to the north, Maj. Gen. Harry L. Twaddle's 95th Division. The 94th had landed at Utah Beach in Normandy on 8 September 1944, and relieved the 6th Armored Division investing the German-held French ports of Lorient and Saint-Nazaire. For the next three months the soldiers of the 94th had fought to contain the enemy garrisons, while at the same time controlling the reorganizing French military forces in the area. At one point the division, including attached French forces, numbered nearly thirty thousand troops. Patrols were constantly sent out, and attacks up to battalion size were mounted and received. Several times during this period the division commander, General Malony, had appealed to Lt. Gen. William H. Simpson, who commanded Ninth Army, for a front-line combat assignment. Each time he was assured the division was scheduled for the earliest possible movement forward. Each time unexpected events caused delays.

When Malony and the 94th were beginning to despair of ever getting into the front lines, an unexpected event occurred. The German counteroffensive in the Ardennes raised a cry for all combat units to be rushed to the front to hold and defeat the enemy. Once again it appeared that the 94th would move forward. But SHAEF did not trust the French irregulars to hold the German coastal garrisons at bay without American support. So no call came to the 94th.

Finally, it was a German U-boat commander who presented the opportunity for the 94th to join Third Army. The need to rush all combat-ready units forward caused the 66th Infantry Division to move from England to France during the last week in December to reinforce the hard-pressed American forces. On Christmas Eve, however, a transport carrying a regiment of the 66th was torpedoed and sunk in the English Channel. The heavy loss of life and equipment rendered the 66th unfit for combat in the front lines, but it was still capable of handling the dormant German garrisons at Lorient and Saint-Nazaire. So the 66th relieved the 94th Infantry Division in Brittany on 29 December 1944, at just the time General Patton was looking for a replacement division for the 90th, which he needed elsewhere. The 94th was therefore ordered to report to the Ghost Corps.

The 94th was commanded throughout its combat service by General Malony, a New York native who had attended Yale University for one year before accepting an appointment to West Point. Graduating with the Class of 1912, he was commissioned in the infantry and assigned to the Panama Canal Zone. Transferring to the artillery in 1916, he was sent to France during World War I and served as officer in charge of aircraft armament. After the war he had the usual assignments, including prestigious ones such as attending the Command and General Staff School and service on the general staff. After teaching military science and tactics at the University of Oklahoma from 1931 to 1935, he graduated from the Army War College. Assigned to the War Plans Division in 1940, he was instrumental in preparing the Destroyers-for-Bases arrangement between the United States and Great Britain. After completing a number of high-visibility assignments, including working with President Roosevelt's close advisor Harry Hopkins, he was promoted to major general in June 1942 and assigned to activate and command the 94th Infantry Division in September the same year.

The progress of the 94th from orders handed to General Malony in June 1942 to the combat-ready force surrounding Lorient and Saint-Nazaire in December 1944 was in many ways typical of the way the U.S. Army went to war during World War II. Designated as an organized reserves division, the 94th was to be a brand-new unit. Activated on 15 September 1942, the division received a cadre of trained personnel from the 77th Infantry Division, which in turn had been cadred from the 8th Infantry Division. Some 172 experienced officers and 1,190 enlisted men combined with recent graduates from officer candidate schools and the Reserve Officers Training Corps to prepare the division to train new recruits from all parts of the nation. Originally stationed at Fort Custer, Michigan, the enlarged division needed more space for training and soon moved to

Camp Phillips near Salina, Kansas. Recruits arrived at the rate of a thousand per day for weeks, bringing the division to full strength. Beginning with basic training, the men progressed through individual and unit training, regimental exercises, and finally the divisional series of exercises. By August of 1943 it was pronounced ready to participate in field-army-size maneuvers. Assigned to the Second Army, the 94th moved to Tennessee and began to demonstrate its acquired military skills. These, however, were interrupted by the culling of some fifteen hundred men from its ranks for immediate shipment overseas as replacements. Many were sent to the Mediterranean Theater to replace losses suffered by American units in North Africa and Sicily. Despite this, the 94th was pronounced fully trained and ready for overseas shipment.

Upon completion of the Second Army's maneuvers, the division was ordered to Camp Forrest near Tullahoma, Tennessee. While awaiting further orders, the division again lost a hundred men per infantry battalion, or some nine hundred soldiers, to the 8th Infantry Division, which had been alerted for overseas movement. Finally, it moved in November to Camp McCain, Mississippi, where it trained the men received to replenish its losses. Training started again, from small unit maneuvers to full-scale tests of the individual regiments. These tests, designed to ascertain the skills of each infantry regiment, found that the three regiments were "Expert Infantrymen," with the 376th Infantry Regiment being awarded the first Expert Infantry Regiment designation, while the 94th as a whole won the distinction of the first Expert Infantry Division. Thoroughly trained and retrained, the men were relieved to learn on 5 May 1944 that the division had been alerted for overseas movement. Moving to New York, the 94th boarded the H.M.S. *Queen Elizabeth* and sailed to Glasgow, Scotland. Arriving on 12 August, they moved to Wiltshire in southern England. Assigned to Ninth U.S. Army, a follow-up force to the invasion already in progress, the division checked its equipment for readiness. Little time was available to enjoy the hospitality of the English people, however, for on 30 August the 94th was alerted for movement to France, departing England on 3 September.

During World War II, the American infantry divisions retained a configuration determined early on that such tactical units should be lean, with a minimum of units permanently attached so as to be mobile and thus easily controllable. After numerous tests and maneuvers, the infantry division of World War II consisted of three infantry regiments, each of three battalions. Three 105mm field-artillery battalions were included, each assigned to support an individual infantry regiment. A fourth artillery battalion, equipped with 155mm howitzers, was also a permanent part of the division and used for general support. It also contained a battalion each of combat engineers and medical-service support. A reconnaissance troop and quartermaster, signal, and ordnance companies were also integral parts, as well as a military-police platoon. In theory the need for additional support such as armor or tank-destroyer units would be met by a temporary attachment from corps or field-army assets. A separate tank and tank-destroyer battalion frequently became more or less permanently attached to each combat division.

The basic weapon of the American soldier in World War II was the M1 (Garand) rifle, a semiautomatic weapon capable of firing eight rounds rapidly, and reloaded by ammunition clips. Some soldiers still carried the Springfield Model 1903 bolt action rifle that had served so well in the First World War, but by 1945 these were relegated to sniping duties. A frequently encountered weapon was the M1 carbine. Developed from the decision to keep infantry units lean, which in turn required infantrymen to do double duty as drivers, mechanics, and signalmen, this semiautomatic rifle allowed these soldiers to carry a lighter but effective weapon into combat. Fed by magazines that contained fifteen rounds, by 1945 the carbine had become the second most issued shoulder weapon of the infantryman. Also used in considerable numbers were the Thompson submachine gun and the Browning automatic rifle (BAR).

Heavier weapons were also a part of the division's arsenal. Both light (air-cooled) and heavy (water-cooled) machine guns in common use were holdovers from the First World War era. They were of .30 caliber and manufactured by Browning. The light guns were in the weapons platoon of the infantry company with the 60mm mortar, and generally were attached to platoons or squads as required for a particular operation. The heavy guns were in the equipment carried in the weapons company along with the 81mm mortar. They were attached as necessary to companies. A still heavier weapon was the air-cooled .50-caliber machine gun, very few of which were ever at battalion level. These were used mainly for air defense, mounted on some trucks and tank turrets. Antitank weapons were the 57mm gun (at regimental level) and the shoulder-fired 2.36-inch rocket launcher, commonly called the "bazooka."

Although the 94th was typical of World War II U.S. infantry divisions through activation and training to combat, it was a division that suffered severely from unanticipated personnel levies to replace casualties in overseas divisions. During much of the war, the army ordered units like the 94th, which were in training, to provide replacements on short notice for overseas shipment. The 94th suffered greatly from this lack of foresight, and in total lost some 8,890 enlisted men between activation and embarkation from New York. Other losses occurred as the result of the army's desire to educate its more intellectually gifted soldiers in the Army Specialized Training Program (ASTP) in skills the army felt would be needed as the war progressed. Several divisions, including the 94th, lost trained men who applied and were accepted into the ASTP. General Malony remarked to an inspecting army ground-forces officer in July 1943, the time when the division was awaiting orders to move overseas, that "survey teams and fire-direction centers have had to be reorganized as many as five times" due to the loss of so many of his artillery specialists to the ASTP. In June 1944, only six weeks before shipping overseas, Malony reported to his superiors that "there was not a second lieutenant in his command who had been on duty with the division in maneuvers seven months before." Similarly, the division had lost 54 medical officers of its authorized strength of 52, (meaning even replacements had been taken), 32 of its authorized 27 engineer officers, and 16 of its authorized 13 chaplains. In addition, overall it had lost 873 of the officers assigned to it by the time it was ready to depart for England. Taken with the losses in enlisted personnel, the 94th Infantry Division that embarked at New York in August of 1944 was not the same division that had left Camp Phillips, Kansas, a year before.

Nor did the problem end there. The losses in trained personnel were serious enough for a unit whose existence depended on combat-ready personnel. Those individuals sent to the 94th Infantry Division to replace those stripped away were in many cases inferior to those they were replacing. General Malony reported this problem as follows: "The quality of the personnel we are getting is awful. Busted-down parachutists, guardhouse addicts from McClellan and Bragg and various other replacement training centers. Less than 50 percent are physically qualified." Officer replacements were similar. Many were not trained infantry officers, having come from disbanded antiaircraft or tank-destroyer units. Others who had infantry qualifications in their records hadn't served in that branch for years. A few units benefited from the army's decision in 1944 to disband the ASTP and send those men to infantry and armored units, and the 94th was so fortunate. Similarly, army air corps castoffs found their way into several combat divisions. The division's average age as it went overseas was 25.9 years, with the bulk of the enlisted men in the twenty to twenty-nine age group. Only 6 percent of the men had attended college, 25 percent had completed high school, and 20 percent had not begun high school. Two hundred and eighty-four were considered either illiterate or non–English speaking. There were 104 conscientious objectors assigned to the division, nearly all in the 319th Medical Battalion. Its men came from all states and some territories, but the largest contingents called New York, Pennsylvania, Missouri, Ohio, Illinois, or Wisconsin home. The division matched roughly the average Army General Classification Test scores for the entire army. Overall, the 94th Infantry Division was an average U.S. Infantry Division of World War II.

Finally, there was one factor that was not appreciated until the division arrived in the front lines. No tank battalion had ever been attached to the command. In Brittany, where the nature of the combat was fairly static, this absence caused no difficulties. It was assumed that the doctrine that armored units would be assigned as needed, would eventually be implemented.

Nevertheless, having already suffered personnel turbulence before ever getting overseas, combat losses in France, and without the normal attached armor, the 94th Infantry Division was now in the front lines facing the German main line of resistance at the base of the Saar-Moselle Triangle.

CHAPTER 4
THE TRIANGLE

The Saar-Moselle Triangle had been created by the flow of war. During the late fall and early winter of 1944–1945, Third Army had pushed across France into the border area with Germany. They had attacked and breached the Moselle River line of the German defenses at a number of places. To the south, Seventh Army under General Patch had also reached the Moselle River. Although both armies had cracked the Siegfried Line in this area, one significant exception remained. The Germans had managed to hold the east bank along the Moselle River in a triangle of land formed between the Saar and the Moselle rivers southwest of the important German city of Trier. This area was known to the Americans as the "Saar-Moselle Triangle."

The triangle began at the meeting point of the Saar and Moselle Rivers, then extended along a line running east-west, which generally followed the prewar border of Luxembourg. This section was just over sixteen miles long. Its base extended from the river to meet this leg and was barely thirteen miles in length. In the original prewar planning, this area was in front of the Siegfried Line, but to protect the important marshalling point of Trier, the Germans constructed an additional fortified line across the base of the triangle from Nennig in the west to Orscholz, as an extension of the Siegfried Line, just as strong and as well fortified, which the Germans called the Orscholz Oblique Switch. When the Third Army came up against it in November of 1944, they called it the Siegfried Switch.

The Switch consisted of a defensive position two miles in depth, protected by dragon's teeth and antitank ditches. The defenses themselves were pillboxes and concrete bunkers reinforced by field fortifications. In addition, the many small towns and villages within the zone were to be converted into strong points by the German defenders. These consisted mostly of concrete and stone buildings, which in many areas tripled the defenses available to the defending forces. The entire position was on high ground that formed the watershed of streams feeding the Saar and Moselle Rivers. An added bonus for the defenders was several dense woods scattered throughout the area. All the major roads in the area converged on the town of Saarburg, toward the center of the triangle on the west side of the Saar River.

The Ghost Corps had first approached the Saar-Moselle Triangle in November and December of 1944. Consisting at that time of the 5th and 90th Infantry Divisions, and the 7th Armored Division, the Corps was advancing on the fortifications of the city of Metz. Although supported by the XIX Tactical Air Command, it became bogged down in the struggle. Little more could be spared to reduce the defenses of the Orscholz Switch.

First to approach the triangle was the 3d Cavalry Group, moving on the flank of XX Corps until brought to an abrupt halt by the defenses of the Switchline. They found themselves facing the 416th Infantry Division, reinforced by the remnants of the 19th Volksgrenadier Division. These units had been pushed back by the American advance until they moved into the Switchline's prepared defenses. Here they reconstituted themselves and settled in to defend their homeland. Although only a part of the 416th was in the defense line at the time the 3d Cavalry approached, their response was sufficiently strong to bring a halt to American attempts to advance to the Saar itself. By 19 November, General Walker had ordered the cavalry to halt and await support.

The XX Corps was facing the experienced and most senior German commander on the western front, Karl Rudolf Gerd von Rundstedt, who was born in Aschersleben, near Halle, Prussia. Tracing its roots back to 1109, his was a family of tradition. Son of a major general in the Prussian army, Gerd entered the junior school for cadets at Oranienstein in 1888, when he was twelve years old. Graduating at sixteen, he joined the 83d Infantry Regiment as a junior officer in 1892. Most of his World War II contemporaries were still in diapers.

After serving in various regimental posts, he entered the War Academy in 1902 to undergo general-staff training. After graduating, he served for several years in a succession of staff posts. He moved to command for two years, serving as a company commander in an infantry regiment. Then he was back at staff duties when World War I broke out. He spent the war in various staff assignments from division to corps levels on both the eastern and western fronts. Selected for Germany's small army after the war, he was considered highly capable and rose rapidly through the officer ranks, so that by the time Hitler came to power in 1933 he commanded Army Group I in Berlin. Although believing that the army should not become involved in politics, he threw himself into the expansion that Hitler encouraged for the German military. By 1938, however, he had expressed his frank opinions too often for the good of his own career, and was retired as a colonel general, the first of four times his Führer would retire him in the next few years.

Colonel General von Rundstedt was recalled the following year to advise Hitler on the invasion of Poland. He willingly planned and led a major wing of that invasion. His success led to his transfer to the western front, where he was given command of Army Group A and assigned a key role in the invasion of France. Here again he succeeded, relying largely on capable subordinates selected and appointed with his consent or approval. For this latest success von Rundstedt was again promoted, this time to field marshal, and assigned a major role in the planned invasion of Britain, Operation Sea Lion.

When Sea Lion did not materialize, von Rundstedt was assigned to command Army Group South in the coming invasion of the Soviet Union, an operation he opposed from the moment he learned of it. Although he was successful in Russia, other armies accomplished more. Having few motorized units under command, and facing fierce Russian opposition, Army Group South lagged behind its countrymen to the north. Nevertheless the overall campaign was viewed as successful.

Next von Rundstedt was appointed commander in chief west and commander, Army Group B. In March of 1942, this quiet sector allowed the aging field marshal to enjoy the pleasures of conquest. He soon formed the opinion that the British and Americans could not be stopped at the beaches, and so spent little time concerning himself with those defenses. He preferred to defeat any invasion in the interior, away from the tremendous naval-gunfire support available from the large British and American navies. He had yet to learn of the overwhelming tactical air support developed by these nations.

By 1944 von Rundstedt had served fifty-two years in the army. He was tired and mentally worn down, so he left the details of the defense of France to his gifted subordinate Field Marshal Erwin Rommel. The loss of France resulted in another retirement for von Rundstedt, but he was soon called back to active duty after the failure of the July 1944 attempt on Hitler's life. In late 1944 he was presented with Hitler's plan for an offensive. After reviewing it he believed it had no chance of success and again, as he had in France, turned over operational control to his subordinates. Within a week of its start, von Rundstedt advised Hitler to call it off.

The failure of the Ardennes counteroffensive convinced von Rundstedt that the war was lost. His role for the balance of the war was minimal, and he retired for the fourth and final time on 9 March 1945.

Von Rundstedt's command in January of 1945 consisted of four Army Groups. The one facing Third Army was Army Group B, the strongest, and led by Germany's most successful leader in recent years, Field Marshal Walther Model. A noted defensive-warfare expert, Model had become known as "Hitler's fireman" for his frequent appointments to command desperate situations. Largely concerned with the continuing Battle of the Bulge, he split his southernmost sector with Colonel General Johannes Blaskowitz, commanding Army Group G. This placed the Saar-Moselle Triangle under the command of Blaskowitz's LXXXII Corps. Having no army-level command to place over the front lines, LXXXII Corps reported directly to Army Group G.

General der Infanterie Walther Hahm commanded LXXXII Corps. It contained the 416th Infantry Division, the 19th Volksgrenadier Division, and the 559th Volksgrenadier Division. Its sector ran approximately sixty kilometers along the Saar River, and encompassed the Saar-Moselle Triangle.

The 416th Division was originally formed from Wehrkreis—or military district—Ten. German divisions in the Second World War, particularly the infantry divisions, were formed from a particular area, which was then responsible for recruiting, drafting, inducting, and training the soldiers, as well as supplying trained replacements. They were also responsible for rebuilding and refitting units shattered by combat. Wehrkreis Ten was Hamburg and its vicinity. In 1940 this area was expanded to include a part of Denmark. Created in 1941 as a "special-purpose" divisional staff for the occupation of Denmark, the 416th Division was enlarged in the summer of 1942 into a full-fledged Infantry Division. At formation, it consisted largely of older men, with an average age of thirty-eight, and was nicknamed the "Whipped Cream Division" because many soldiers required special diets. After training and continued occupation duties, it was scheduled to participate in an invasion of islands in the Baltic Sea. The collapse of the western front canceled those plans, and the 416th Infantry Division was committed to action in France in October 1944. Before being dispatched west, it was "stripped" to provide cadres for newly forming *Volksgrenadier* divisions, as had the 94th Infantry Division. After losing this cadre, including twenty-eight company commanders, it proceeded west. There it met Third U.S. Army, who, after several initial engagements, pushed it into the defenses of the Saar-Moselle Triangle. The division commander, Lt. Gen. Kurt Pflieger, immediately established his troops in these ideal defensive positions to await the next move by the Americans.

The LXXXII Corps rated the 416th Infantry Division "conditionally fit for combat," considering it poorly trained with incomplete equipment. The average age was now estimated at between thirty-two and thirty-four years of age. The artillery regiment had a mixture of equipment, including French howitzers, which created ammunition problems. It was at full strength now, however, numbering some seven thousand men. In addition to the three infantry regiments, the 712th, 713th, and 714th, it had a full complement of divisional troops. Attached to the division at this time was a fortress machine-gun battalion of three companies and an additional fortress infantry battalion, which brought its total strength up to nearly ten thousand men. Similarly the 19th Volksgrenadier Division was also viewed as conditionally fit. It was about two-thirds of assigned strength and lacked many allocated officers and noncommissioned officers. The 559th Volksgrenadier Division, however, was considered "good for defense action."

The LXXXII Corps complained that the defenses it was assigned to man were based upon 1939 tables of organization, when each German infantry regiment had three battalions. Defense sectors were built with this in mind, but in 1945 those same regiments had but two battalions, making occupation of each sector more difficult. Additionally, orders from the army high command decreed that regimental and divisional headquarters be close to the combat zone, making communications more difficult. Barbed wire and land mines were also in short supply.

The Americans had little intelligence about the defenses of the Siegfried Switch positions when the Third Army first approached them. After the 3d Cavalry Group's initial repulse, Patton ordered Walker to send the 83d Infantry Division against the Triangle, but events elsewhere intervened, and Walker had only a part of the 10th Armored Division available. Combat Command A (CCA) of Maj. Gen. William H. H. Morris Jr.'s division moved against the Triangle first on 20 November, passing through the covering positions held by the 3d and 43d Reconnaissance Squadrons of the 3d Cavalry Group. Divided into four task forces, supported by four additional battalions of artillery in addition to those attached to the combat command, CCA found the going slow and difficult. One factor was the strong German artillery support fire. Due to poor intelligence about the defenses, the infantry had to locate each pillbox and bunker by dangerous search operations, exposing themselves to enemy fire from different directions. They adjusted artillery fire on each enemy position they found. Dragon's teeth in many places prevented friendly tanks from supporting the infantry, and the engineers could not get out to destroy the enemy positions because of the heavy enemy covering fire. One of the division's task forces could not even get past its line of departure, while the others made progress with heavy losses in men and equipment. After two bloody days, CCA had made only one opening beyond the dragon's teeth.

They had lost several tanks, and had nowhere gained an appreciable foothold in the German defenses.

General Walker knew that the 10th Armored was overextended. The battle for Metz was still in progress and General Patton had other parts of XX Corps attempting to outflank the Siegfried Line. Nevertheless, Walker attached one infantry regiment of the 90th Infantry Division to the 10th Armored to assist in its battle at the Switchline. This was the 358th Infantry Regiment, under the command of Col. Christian H. Clarke.

The 90th Infantry Division had had a checkered career thus far in the war. Activated on 25 March 1942 at Camp Barkeley, Texas, it was organized around a cadre from the 6th Infantry Division. In most respects, its history was similar to that of the 94th, although it suffered less from personnel stripping, furnishing only one major cadre for the 104th Infantry Division in September 1942. Departing the United States in March 1944, it landed in France on 8 June 1944, one of the very first follow-up D-Day forces. It quickly ran into trouble, proving itself unable to perform to expectations, nor equally with its sister divisions fighting alongside. At one point, serious consideration was given at army levels to disbanding the division altogether, and using its personnel as replacements for other units. But General Bradley decided to see what a change in command would do to improve its performance. The experiment was a success, for after several changes in command, it settled down and became one of the most combatworthy divisions in the European Theater of Operations. By the time of its participation in the Saar-Moselle battle, it was considered one of the best available divisions in the Third Army.

On 21 November the 358th Infantry Regiment was attached to CCA of the 10th Armored Division. Moving forward on trucks provided by XX Corps, its 3d Battalion unloaded at the outskirts of the Triangle, where the company commanders conducted a ground reconnaissance to determine the best approach to the enemy defenses. Originally, Col. Christian H. Clarke, commanding officer of the 358th, suggested a two-battalion attack with the objective of Berg, one of the major towns along the Switchline, but he was overruled by General Morris, who directed a one-battalion attack on the town of Tettingen and another single battalion attack on Berg. Tettingen was one of the anchors of the Siegfried Switchline, and it was believed that the direct approach was best. The 3d Battalion was selected to assault Tettingen, and the 2d Battalion under Lt. Col. Robert H. Shultz was directed against Berg.

Captain J. S. Spivey's 3d Battalion moved off at 10:00 A.M. on the twenty-third. Although they were forced to advance across "open and high ground" there was no enemy reaction. This was in large part due to a heavy fog that had unexpectedly blanketed the area. So successful was the advance that Captain Spivey was able to order up a bulldozer to bridge a major antitank ditch that had delayed the earlier advance. The bulldozer successfully bridged the gap without interference. Advancing into Campholz Woods, the battalion received the first fire from the enemy entrenched behind barbed wire. Control and coordination between units of the battalion were difficult, due to the thickness of the woods, enemy fire, and fog. Companies I and K, in the lead, crawled through the barbed wire and routed the enemy, taking eighty-four prisoners by the time they cleared the woods. The attack owed much of its success to 2d Lt. Glenn E. Rugh of I Company, who led a bayonet charge directly into enemy fire, clearing a trench and netting thirty of the prisoners. Captain Robert B. McHolland's Company K, nicknamed "Kraut Killers" by their commander, also had their hero that day, when Pfc. Harold R. McQuay charged alone against a machine-gun position and destroyed it. Lieutenant Rugh and Pfc. McQuay were each awarded the nation's second highest decoration for valor, the Distinguished Service Cross.

The 2d Battalion had less success. Although air support was unavailable because of weather conditions, the 2d Battalion was supported by the artillery of the 344th Field Artillery Battalion and armor from the 10th Armored Division. Problems arose quickly when the tanks became bogged down in the deep mud and those that were able to fire misdirected it against the 2d Battalion's advanced detachments. No appreciable advance was made on the twenty-fourth by the 2d Battalion.

The next day the 3d Battalion beat off a counterattack by some forty Germans, capturing eighteen. Directing Company K on Butzdorf and Company I on Tettingen, Captain Spivey renewed his attack. Captain McHolland of Company K ordered his men to run for the town of Butzdorf to minimize losses from the constant artillery and machine-gun fire. Most of the "Kraut Killers" made it into Butzdorf. Lieutenant Rugh's Company I, meanwhile, was delayed by numerous pillboxes and advanced only to the edge of Tettingen before dark. Throughout the night Lieutenant Rugh rotated his men through the shelter of the pillboxes they had seized to reduce sickness, already rampant in the battalion.

Although the 3d Battalion again had a successful day, the 2d continued to suffer setbacks. Stopped quickly by heavy machine-gun fire from a large bunker to their front, they took most of the day to reduce the position. Finally moving past the destroyed bunker, the 2d Battalion was again pinned by heavy fire coming from the town of Oberleuken. In order to assist the 2d Battalion and speed the attack, Colonel Clarke sent the 1st Battalion, under the command of Capt. Thomas Caldecott, into Oberleuken, where they battled on into the night.

The 3d Battalion, meanwhile, had Company K in the first three houses of Tettingen. Captain McHolland reorganized his command after the rush into the town, and then moved against the rest of the houses. Suddenly, they found themselves the objective of a German counterattack. Fighting in darkness, they were pushed back into the original three houses. After the Germans quickly surrounded the "Kraut Killers" with machine guns and flame throwers, making advance or escape impossible, the men of Company K fought on. They spotted a reinforcing company of Germans marching down the Tettingen road in a column of twos. Although their machine gun was inoperative, they attacked the German column with small-arms fire and grenades, causing them to seek cover and later withdraw. During this engagement, Captain McHolland was killed while breaking up an attack on his command post. His heroism was acknowledged by a Distinguished Service Cross awarded posthumously, but his loss affected morale in the 3d Battalion. The battle continued throughout the night, and the Germans destroyed one of the houses protecting the Americans using tank and bazooka fire. Survivors ran for the houses remaining under American control, but not all made it safely.

With dawn, Company I directed artillery fire onto Tettingen. Each house not held by Company K was shelled, and then, under cover of smoke from supporting arms, Company I charged through enemy artillery, tank, and small-arms fire to join the survivors of Company K in Tettingen. They found thirty-five survivors, who immediately joined with Company I to clear the rest of Tettingen. During the fight on the twenty-fifth, Lieutenant Rugh became a casualty, and by midday only Lieutenant Marron remained of Company I's officers. Captain Spivey sent in Company L to move through Tettingen and attack Butzdorf.

The attack on Butzdorf was more in line with the way attacks were usually conducted by American infantry at this stage of the war. Fighter-bomber support from XIX Tactical Command was available and prevented German reinforcements from reaching the defenders. Artillery support from both the 10th Armored and 90th Infantry Divisions was available, and tanks were provided by CCA. A platoon of Company L and two tanks "went clear through to Butzdorf." Here twenty-one Germans holding four Company K men prisoners surrendered to their prisoners, reversing the positions held moments ago. Captain Spivey quickly moved to spread out what remained of his battalion to cover the towns and the high ground surrounding them, until relieved by armored infantry of the 10th Armored Division. At dawn of the twenty-sixth, the 3d Battalion, 358th Infantry, was relieved and moved into reserve. In less than three days of battle, it had lost "at least" seven officers and 148 enlisted men, and earned three Distinguished Service Crosses. Their gallant conduct had earned them a reprieve, a promotion to major for Spivey, and caused the plans of generals Morris and Walker to be altered.

At the end of the twenty-fifth, Clarke had conferred with Morris, and they agreed that the 358th Infantry was in no shape to continue the attack. General Walker agreed with them, replacing the 358th Infantry on the twenty-sixth with units of CCA, 10th Armored Division. They had made a breach in the Siegfried Line, captured five hundred prisoners, and impressed the German defenders enough that they brought in reinforcements to augment the defenses of the Siegfried Switch. One of the last casualties of the 358th Infantry at the Saar-Moselle was the regiment's commander, Colonel Clarke, who contracted pneumonia and was hospitalized.

The Germans had reacted with alarm at the 358th's attempt to breach their defenses in the Orscholz Switch. On 24 November the German High Command in the west, known as Oberfehlshaber West, ordered reinforcements rushed to the Saar-Moselle sector. Generalfeldmarschall von Rundstedt saw the danger inherent in an attack toward Trier, and acted accordingly. The allies could not be allowed to get near Trier, for it was one of the major staging areas for the coming winter offensive. Von Rundstedt ordered artillery and armored reinforcements rushed to the 416th Infantry Division to assist in holding its positions.

Two supporting units were immediately available. The first was the 21st Panzer Division. Formed from Wehrkreis Three, the greater Berlin area, it first was organized as the 5th Light Division in 1940. Joining the famous German Afrika Corps, it fought in the battles for Egypt and Tobruk. In the summer of 1941 it received the 104th Panzer Grenadier Regiment from the 15th Panzer Division and was renamed the 21st Panzer Division. It fought in the remainder of the long North African campaigns, was seriously hurt in the battle of Second Alamein, and later turned and defeated the emerging American army at Kasserine Pass. Although the division surrendered at the time of the defeat of the Afrika Corps in Tunisia, a core of veterans was safely ferried back to Europe, where they formed the cadre for a new 21st Panzer Division, which was raised in Normandy in 1943. It was the only panzer division to counterattack the British landings on D-Day, and fought with distinction as it was pushed back into Germany. Commanded by Lt. Gen. Edgar Feuchtinger, it was considered a highly effective combat unit by both the Germans and the Allies, although its commander's reputation was poor.

The other available unit was the 404th Volks Artillery Corps. A new addition to the German order of battle, the Volks Artillery Corps was an effort by the Germans to make up for their inadequacy in artillery and motorized formations by concentrating artillery in one unit, and shifting that unit to threatened areas. The Volks artillery corps usually contained about seventy-six guns and howitzers, in various calibers, which could be moved comparatively quickly to threatened sectors. In addition, the Germans rushed the 719th Infantry Division forward on 10 December.

Advance units of the 21st Panzer Division had caused the difficulties for the 358th Infantry in its attack on Nennig and Butzdorf. The guns of the artillery corps assisted both the 21st Panzer and the 416th Infantry Divisions to hold their positions. With the withdrawal of the 358th Infantry, and its replacement by CCA of the 10th Armored, the Germans saw an opportunity for counterattack. The soldiers of CCA, stretched thin, gave up some of the hard won ground. Soon they, too, were relieved for action in the north, and the 3d Cavalry Group returned to hold the line. Stretched as thin as the armored combat command, but with less armor and artillery support, they soon lost nearly all the ground won in November. By 18 December, when the 10th Armored and 90th Infantry Divisions were being sent north to stop the German counteroffensive, the situation in the Orscholz Switchline was much the same as it had been on 19 November.

CHAPTER 5
FIRST BREACH

As the 94th Infantry Division arrived in XX Corps to replace the departing 90th Infantry Division, the attention of its army commander was elsewhere. General Patton was fully engrossed in the reduction of the "Bastogne operation," with three of his four corps engaged there. Only the Ghost Corps was not involved. But even with his other concerns, Patton was thinking about the employment of his under-strength reserve corps. Constantly concerned over his position within the Allied command, and recently enraged over the appointment of British Field Marshal Bernard Montgomery to command the majority of the Allied forces during the Bulge operation, he sought ways to enhance the reputation of American arms, particularly that of his Third Army. On 12 January 1945, just as his troops were about to join with the First U.S. Army and close the German Bulge penetration, he entrusted to his diary his interest in an attack by XX Corps "straight east through Saarlautern," which he believed would "be more crippling to Germany, as it would get the whole Saar Valley," a major industrial base.

General Malony had been ordered to report to Third Army head-quarters while his division started to move toward the front lines. Expecting to get his orders and promptly return to lead his division to its assigned area, Malony found he "made a bad estimate, for General Patton insisted that I spend the night at his headquarters. I had known him since his cadet days and was familiar with his colorful vocabulary and personality. Both were in evidence." General Patton, disturbed that "a visiting staff officer had left his army without visiting the front, and so without 'getting shot at,'" resulted in the outburst that greeted Malony.

Although neither General Walker nor General Malony was privy at this point to Patton's thoughts, both felt that they had to do something to contribute to the effort to defeat Germany. Sitting still in front of the enemy's fixed defenses was not what either had in mind. The 94th Infantry Division relieved the 90th Infantry Division at 9:00 A.M. on 7 January 1945, and almost immediately began receiving visitors from XX Corps headquarters, such as the corps artillery commander, the operations officer, and the corps surgeon, as well as SHAEF liaison officers. The last of the division's elements arrived at the front on 9 January, when the 302d Infantry Regiment reported back from attachment to the 28th Infantry Division. Satisfied with the situation, the XX Corps chief of staff passed on to Col. Earl C. Bercquist, the 94th's chief of staff, the "desire" of General Walker for the 94th to "prepare a plan for limited-objective attacks in battalion strength to shorten and straighten division front lines." Within hours General Malony, Colonel Bercquist, and Col. Harold H. McClune, commanding the 376th Regiment, were in conference, and by 10:00 P.M. that same day Bercquist issued the attack plan.

The plan assigned the 1st Battalion, 376th Infantry, to attack the village of Tettingen during the night of 13–14 January. Lieutenant Colonel Russell M. Minor's battalion had made limited attacks before in Brittany, but this was to be a full-scale assault against prepared defenses that had earlier turned back an armored combat command and an experienced infantry regiment. After Minor received his orders he proceeded to his command post for more detailed planning. The Germans held commanding positions in the thick forest of Campholz Wood, to the right of the battalion's attack axis. Directly between the battalion and its objective were a line of dragon's teeth, an antitank ditch, and extensive minefields. Pillboxes, bunkers, and field entrenchments covered the area.

The 376th Infantry had already patrolled the area extensively, learning that their uniforms, known as "olive drab," only made them more visible against the foot or more of snow then on the ground. So cold was the weather that Malony's aide, Capt. John C. Gehrig, froze one of his hands on the trip to the front. As had their comrades in the Battle of the Bulge, they appropriated sheets and linens from abandoned homes in the area and fashioned them into camouflage snowsuits. They had identified many, but not all, of both the enemy and friendly minefields in the area and approach routes. Although in place a scant six days, they were well prepared to attack.

Colonel Minor arranged for supporting fires from his attached platoons from the 607th Tank Destroyer and 81st Chemical Mortar battalions. Because Company B was manning the outpost line, Companies A and C would lead the attack, with B Company becoming the reserve when they passed its positions. The 3d Battalion, 376th Infantry, would take over the 1st Battalion's defensive positions as soon as they attacked. Minor's plans also included the defense of the town, once captured, so that "each squad and platoon leader worked out exact locations for his men and approximate locations for the automatic weapons."

The Americans were facing Major Becker's 1st Battalion, 713th Grenadier Regiment, 416th Infantry Division. The battalion numbered some five hundred men, reinforced with soldiers from a fortress battalion. Supported by a battery of 81mm mortars near Sinz, also available were 120mm mortars of the regiment's 13th Company and a battery of 88mm dual-purpose antiaircraft/antitank guns. Finally, division artillery 105mm and 150mm howitzers were available on call, in direct phone communication with observers in pillboxes scattered throughout the area. Although food and ammunition were low, the men were rested, warm, and relatively comfortable in the bunkers. Morale was not a problem.

At 6:00 A.M. on the morning of 14 January, General Malony and Brig. Gen. Henry B. Cheadle, assistant division commander, went forward to observe the division's first attack into the Saar-Moselle Triangle. Cheadle, a West Point graduate of the class of 1913, had seen combat before, serving at Veracruz, Mexico. Serving mainly with infantry units between the wars, he also had attended the Infantry School and the Command and General Staff School and served on the War Department's general staff. In 1941 he commanded the 16th Infantry Regiment of the 1st Division during the assault landing in French North Africa. Promoted to brigadier general in December 1942, he was assigned as the assistant division commander of the 26th Infantry Division. Subsequently transferred to the 94th Infantry Division, he had served in that same capacity during all the division's overseas service.

Cheadle observed the attack of Capt. Carl J. Shetler's Company A and Capt. Edwin F. Duckworth's Company C. Following a twenty-minute artillery preparation by the 919th Field Artillery Battalion, both companies attacked, with A on the right and C on the left. Opposed only by an occasional mortar or rifle shot, the men moved swiftly across the antitank ditch and into the town of Tettingen. With each company taking an assigned sector of the town, the troops went quickly through, grenading the buildings and then searching them for enemy soldiers. Twenty-three Germans were captured, and moved behind the lines along with some American casualties. At 8:12 A.M., less than an hour after the attack began, the 376th reported that they had taken their objective.

The planned defensive positions in and around Tettingen were occupied immediately by the 1st Battalion. In addition, one squad of Company A was sent beyond the town to see what the Germans had between Tettingen and Butzdorf, the next town. They found several skillfully camouflaged pillboxes and bunkers, including one they discovered by standing on it and hearing the Germans talking beneath them. Having neither the equipment nor the numbers to reduce these positions, the squad returned to report its findings.

Meanwhile, as Malony returned to division headquarters, Cheadle conferred with Colonel McClune and several of his staff. The attack had gone so well that they felt it should be exploited before the enemy could react. Consequently, they decided that the 1st Battalion should extend its attack to seize the town of Butzdorf. Receiving his new orders at 8:20 A.M., not ten minutes after successfully seizing Tettingen, Colonel Minor had his 919th Artillery Battalion liaison officer, Capt. Larry A. Blakely, order a ten-minute artillery preparation on Butzdorf, while he and his staff hurried forward to set up in Tettingen.

While all these preparations were going on, the Germans were reacting quickly, as they always did. Artillery fire from supporting units was now concentrating on Tettingen, causing movement between buildings to become hazardous. Soon the 88mm dual-purpose guns seemed to be sniping at individuals as they raced from one place to another. Casualties began to mount as Colonel Minor arrived in Tettingen under this increasing fire, and ordered Captain Shetler to prepare his Company A to attack at 10:00 A.M.

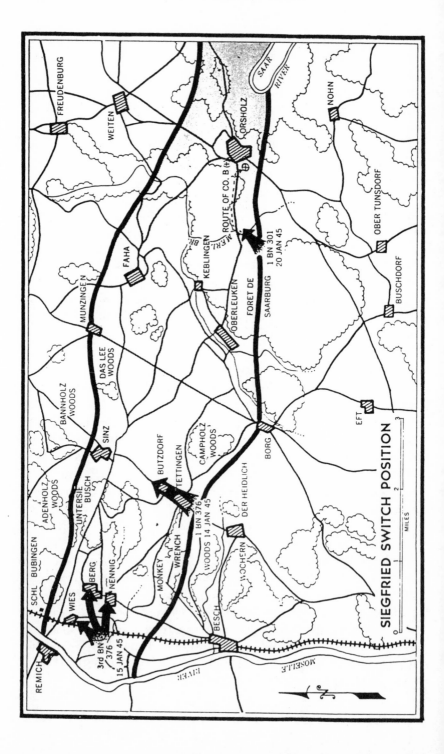

SIEGFRIED SWITCH POSITION

Company A was pulled from its defensive positions quickly and organized for an attack. When his patrol returned, Shetler became aware of the opposition he would face. Reporting this to Minor, he requested a postponement, which was denied, so A Company moved out to attack, being replaced in the defense position by a platoon of Company C.

The haste with which the attack was mounted delayed the actual departure a few minutes. While the leading platoons proceeded toward Butzdorf under relatively reduced small arms fire, thanks to friendly artillery fire, the command and support group of Company A was hit hard by enemy artillery fire. Captain Shetler went down, as did some fifteen of his men, while their leading platoons reached Butzdorf and began to clear it of enemy troops. Lieutenant David F. Stafford moved up to take command of Company A; within the hour Butzdorf had been secured.

While the Americans were busy preparing to defend their gains, the Germans sent out a counterattack force. Some fifty Germans were observed leaving Campholz Woods at about 1:00 P.M., and were mistakenly identified as prisoners captured by Company C. When Captain Blakely looked, however, he yelled, "Those aren't our guys, they're Krauts." Company A then began firing and calling once again for the support of the 919th Field Artillery. The counterattack was driven back, leaving ten enemy casualties in the snow. A second attempt a few minutes later was also easily turned back. Company B was now ordered forward from reserve to assist in the defense of both Tettingen and Butzdorf.

Defense positions would certainly be needed. The Germans had not expected Company A's attack, and certainly not to lose two towns in one morning. Fortunately for them, however, one of their best remaining units on the Western Front happened to be resting in the area. This was the 11th Panzer Division. Known as the "Ghost Division," it was formed from Wehrkreis Eight in Silesia out of the former 11th Motorized Infantry Brigade. First sent into combat in the Balkans in April 1941, it was credited with the capture of Belgrade. In Russia it fought at both Kiev and Moscow. The following year found it outside Stalingrad, where it suffered severe losses while attempting to relieve the Sixth Army. In 1943 it served at Rostov, holding open an escape route for the nearly surrounded Army Group A. That summer it took part in the massive tank battle at Kursk and was later surrounded in the Cherkassy pocket. Fighting its way free, it suffered such severe losses that it had to be rebuilt. Absorbing the remnants of the 123d Infantry Division, also destroyed in Russia, and adding the 273d Reserve Panzer Division to its cadre, it reformed in southern France. Its history of reappearing after reportedly being destroyed earned it the nickname of the "Ghost Division." When the Allies landed in southern France, it fought a delaying action against the Seventh Army until pulled from the line for the Ardennes counteroffensive. When that attack failed, the division, which had not been committed to battle, was withdrawn to Trier and then ordered to reserve positions to defend the Rhine. Under the command of Lt. Gen. Wend von Wietersheim, it was en route to its reserve position to prepare for a possible raid toward Metz when orders rerouted it to the Saar-Moselle Triangle. At full strength in men and equipment, although short on fuel for its vehicles, it was one of the best remaining assault divisions in the German order of battle. On 17 January von Wietersheim was ordered to stop the attack of XX Corps and regain the lost ground. So urgent were these orders that despite his protests he was allowed no time for reconnaissance, but ordered to immediately assume command in the sector and attack. Reinforced with the 714th Grenadier Regiment and 416th Replacement Battalion from the 416th Infantry Division, the Ghost Division was about to meet the Ghost Corps.

CHAPTER 6
MORE NIBBLING

General Malony had not been content to let the 1st Battalion, 376th Infantry, carry the load of attack alone. He had hoped to "be allowed to strike with all my division at once, but on 12 January I received orders from Corps to launch a series of limited objective attacks involving not more than one battalion." He protested this restriction, but was instructed to comply with the order. On the day that Colonel Minor's battalion attacked, orders went to both the 3d Battalion of the 376th Infantry and the 301st Infantry Regiment to prepare to attack sections of the German defenses. This was in accordance with Malony's plan, within the restrictions placed on him by corps for battalion-sized attacks. Thus, critical sectors of the enemy's line could be seized for future bases, breaching the line, while at the same time reducing enemy forces by using his own tactic of always counterattacking against him.

First to move was Lt. Col. Benjamin E. Thurston's 3d Battalion, 376th Infantry. Ordered to seize the three towns of Nennig, Berg, and Wies, which anchored the German line along the banks of the Moselle River, Colonel Thurston, before sunrise on 15 January, sent out Lt. Charles R. Palmer with a squad from the 319th Engineer Combat Battalion to clear mines. They cleared and marked an approach route over two miles long for the following infantry.

Thurston reclaimed companies I and L, which had been assigned as reserve for the 1st Battalion's attack on Tettingen. Augumented by the 4.2 mortars of Company A, 81st Chemical Mortar Battalion, and a platoon of the 774th Tank Destroyer Battalion, the attack force assembled. The men had heard that the attack on Tettingen had gone well, and they were confident. The news of the German counterattack on the 1st Battalion had not yet reached them when they crossed the line of departure.

Colonel Thurston assigned Capt. Julian M. Way's Company K to lead the attack, reinforced with a platoon of heavy machine guns and 81mm mortars from Company M. Captain William A. Brightman's Company L would follow. Company I would remain behind in reserve. Even before facing enemy fire, the battalion had difficulties. Temperature during the day hovered at eight degrees above zero, with more than six inches of snow and ice on the ground. The 319th Engineers had cleared and marked paths through the minefields, but they had not the time nor the manpower to bridge the numerous small streams in the area, so the troops had to march through them, sometimes up to their waists. Frostbite and trench-foot cases soon began to appear.

As the long and difficult approach march delayed the battalion, a request was made to continue supporting fires and to add smoke for concealment, as daybreak would reveal them to the enemy. These requests were granted, with the battalion crossing the line of departure some thirty minutes behind schedule. Problems continued to mount, however, as the smoke worked to confuse the Americans as well as to conceal them from the enemy. Company K was assigned to seize Nennig, and Company L was to move past Nennig and seize Wies. Confused by the smoke, several elements from Companies K and M, reinforced by a mortar section, missed Nennig and went into Wies. In addition, Captain Way found that he was approaching Nennig from the north rather than the west as intended. He then discovered Lt. Dwight M. Morse's platoon and several of his supporting attachments missing. Not knowing they had entered Wies, he could not afford the time to look for them. Moving up a replacement platoon, Way and the men of Company K "came into Nennig on the run, shouting at the top of their lungs and shooting everything in sight."

As had happened the day before in Tettingen, the German defenders were caught by surprise. Within twenty minutes, at a cost of three casualties, the company had secured the town, captured

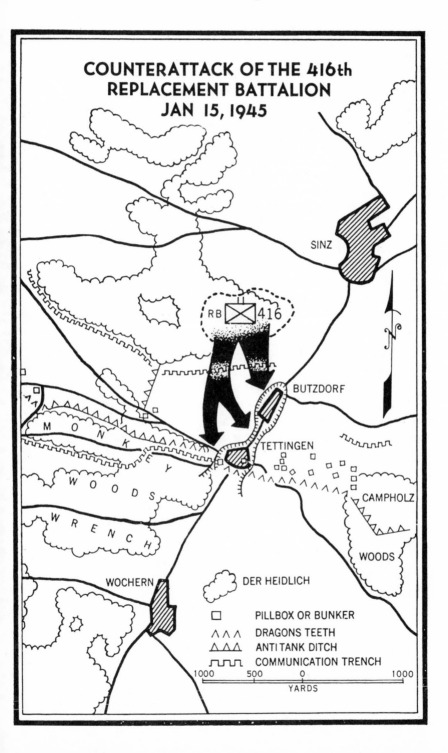

COUNTERATTACK OF THE 416th
REPLACEMENT BATTALION
JAN 15, 1945

SINZ

RB ⊠ 416

BUTZDORF

TETTINGEN

M O N K E Y

W O O D S

W R E N C H

CAMPHOLZ

WOODS

WOCHERN

DER HEIDLICH

☐   PILLBOX OR BUNKER

∧∧∧   DRAGONS TEETH

△△△   ANTI TANK DITCH

⊓⊔⊓   COMMUNICATION TRENCH

1000   500   0   1000
YARDS

twenty-three prisoners, and estimated a loss to the Germans of ninety-five casualties. The enemy survivors withdrew under rifle fire.

Meanwhile, Lieutenant Morse's reinforced platoon was having serious difficulties in Wies. The German defenders here resisted stubbornly and inflicted many casualties on the attackers, including Morse. Enemy machine guns positioned in buildings outside of town kept the Americans from securing their objective. Several men of the 2d Platoon attempted to silence these guns, but after moving out to the open hillside, they were pinned down by this fire, unable to advance or retreat. Attempts by the supporting mortar squad to use smoke to conceal the men's movements failed because of adverse winds. A mortar barrage similarly failed to lift the enemy fire.

Captain Brightman and the leading elements of Company I arrived and were told of the men trapped on the hillside. He sent Lt. William M. Goldensweig's platoon out to relieve the Company K men. This proved impossible, because the Germans knew that they had the men on the hillside trapped and were ready to defeat any rescue attempts. Goldensweig's platoon was driven back, while the enemy machine gunners continued to cause casualties among the trapped Americans.

Seeing no further attempts to rescue the men on the hillside, a German officer and medical aide man appeared under a Red Cross flag and offered the men a chance to surrender. The Germans promised that the wounded would be allowed to return to American lines, while the able-bodied would be kept as prisoners of war.

Having no alternative, the Americans agreed. The American medics took the wounded back to friendly lines, while the remaining men were marched away into captivity. Lieutenant Raymond G. Fox's platoon from Company I was ordered forward to reinforce Company K.

Although under constant harassing fire and probes by enemy patrols, Nennig was secured. Wies, too, was secured despite the continuing machine-gun fire from the enemy positions that had decimated the 2d Platoon of Company K. Finally, late in the afternoon, a platoon of Company L moved on Berg and secured that town as well. Although all three objectives had been secured, each remained under constant enemy fire from artillery, mortars, and machine guns.

As they had in Tettingen, the Germans soon counterattacked. Enemy artillery fire quickly sealed off all roads and known trails into Nennig, stopping resupply and reinforcements. Lieutenant Colonel Thurston led a forty-man resupply party over the same difficult track that the assault troops had used to get into the three towns, successfully resupplying the garrisons. Company K, even with Lieutenant Fox's platoon attached, could not garrison every house in Nennig. With the Germans infiltrating in the darkness Company K was forced to repeatedly clear the same houses. Captain Way and men of his company headquarters helped to clear vacant houses that the enemy patrols had occupied. Finally, just after darkness fell, Company I arrived in Nennig and took over part of the defenses.

In the early morning hours of 16 January the main enemy counterattack came. Supported by an estimated two artillery battalions, a company of German infantry attacked. They managed to get in among the defenders, and hand-to-hand fighting lasted for two hours. A machine gun of Lt. Dale E. Bowyer's platoon was lost to the enemy, and one rifle squad was temporarily captured, escaping later that day. A second supporting attack ran afoul of the platoon commanded by Lt. Thomas A. Daly, who had earlier gone on patrol over the ground in front of his position. The attack was stopped before it could do much damage, with a platoon of prisoners lost in the process.

After darkness fell, an unusual incident occurred in Nennig. Staff Sergeant Fred Grossi was on guard at a light machine-gun position in the town, when a column of Germans yelling slogans ran past his position. Aiming his machine gun, Grossi pulled the trigger only to find that it jammed after two rounds, so he fired his rifle, delaying the enemy attack until aid arrived. With daylight, he discovered fourteen dead Germans in front of his position, including a dozen officers. Sergeant Grossi was awarded the Distinguished Service Cross for his one-man stand.

Daylight also brought the final counterattack. Although most of two German platoons were repulsed by defensive machine-gun fire, one enemy gun crew set up near the battalion command post and fired on the Americans until Lieutenant Colonel Thurston killed the enemy gunners with an M1 rifle. Thurston also killed an enemy bazookaman who was stalking one of the battalion's supporting tank destroyers. After that, the enemy for the moment left the Americans in peace.

While interviewing prisoners captured in this battle, Thurston's troops discovered that they faced not the 416th Infantry Division, but the 256th Volksgrenadier Division. This division was formed in 1939 from Wehrkreis Four, and consisted of Saxons, Bavarians, and Sudeten Germans, and took part in the Dutch and Belgian campaigns in 1940. It was among the leading German divisions invading Russia in June of 1941, and spent the next three years on the Russian front. During this time in Russia, the division earned a reputation for being a reliable fighting unit at the Battle of Moscow in December 1941 and again at the Battle of Smolensk in 1943. The division was destroyed during the Russian summer offensive of July 1944, and its commander was killed during the fighting. With a cadre of veterans, the division was reformed in September 1944 as the 256th Volksgrenadier Infantry Division. The reconstituted division fought the British in Holland in October and the Americans in France in November, after which it had faced the Seventh Army in the Vosges. Commanded by Maj. Gen. Gerhard Franz, it had then been sent into the Saar-Moselle Triangle.

Despite the growing realization that the 94th Infantry Division was facing three enemy divisions, including first-class armor, the attacks continued. With one penetration begun along the Moselle River side of the triangle, and another toward the Saar River side, it was now time, General Malony decided, to join the two penetrations. He called upon Lt. Col. Olivius C. Martin's 2d Battalion, 376th Infantry, to accomplish this by attacking into the woods southwest of Tettingen. In addition to joining the two horns driven thus far into the Siegfried Line, it was hoped that clearing this area would relieve the constant pressure put on both penetrations from the woods.

The 2d Battalion's attack went off smoothly. By midday most of the area was secured, fifty-two prisoners were taken, and an ammunition dump and several machine guns were captured. Attempts to clear some outlying pillboxes were thwarted, however, when weapons, including machine guns, froze from the wet cold.

Clearly, 16 January had been the easiest day the division had since the attack began. It presented a good picture for six visiting officers of the 69th Infantry Division who had been sent up to observe operations before their unit entered battle. Unfortunately, it was the last good day for quite a while. The 11th Panzer Division was about to make its presence felt.

CHAPTER 7
GHOST VERSUS GHOST

The 11th Panzer Division was sent into the Saar-Moselle Triangle with express orders to restore the situation to what it had been prior to the first attack by XX Corps. On the evening of 14 January it assumed command of all units defending the Orscholz Oblique defense position. The units of the 416th Infantry Division in the area were to be relieved by the panzer grenadiers, once the operation had achieved its objectives. The three companies of the attached fortress machine-gun battalion were to remain to reinforce the panzers. A "shock troop operation" was planned to recapture Nennig. Panzer Grenadier Regiment 110 was directed to move on Butzdorf and Tettingen, while Panzer Grenadier Regiment 111 was to seize Wies and Nennig. The attack was scheduled for 15 January with concentrated artillery of both divisions and corps artillery supporting the attack. General von Wietersheim's objections about the lack of time for reconnaissance and his concern for his unprotected right flank along the Moselle delayed matters only briefly. While the counterattack force was getting into position to eject the Americans from their hard-won gains, the infantrymen of the 256th Volksgrenadier Division tried to make the Americans regret their success. Several attacks early on 17 January, mostly directed against Colonel Thurston's 2d Battalion, were unsuccessful, with severe losses to the Germans. They did succeed in establishing several machine-gun positions along supply routes for some of the forward American positions.

Lieutenant Raymond Fox's platoon of Company I was one of those whose resupply routes came under enemy fire. Late on the afternoon of the seventeenth two unidentifiable figures were observed crawling toward them, pushing a crate. Under close scrutiny, the two were allowed to approach the platoon's position, where it was learned that they were Lieutenant Colonel Thurston and his driver, T/5 Thomas M. Clausi. The box contained C rations, and Colonel Thurston carried a bandolier of rifle ammunition, which he gave to Lieutenant Fox. After instructing Lieutenant Fox to hold his position, the battalion commander returned to his more routine duties.

The remainder of the day was relatively quiet, although artillery and mortar fire continued to fall on the captured towns at the rate of two rounds per minute. Supply and communication remained a problem. Mail was received by many units, however, and enemy ground activity was light.

During the night the wind increased, and freezing rain soaked everything aboveground. Enemy patrols, covered by the miserable weather, became more active. Ominously, the sound of tanks and armored vehicles could be heard coming from behind the enemy lines. Surprisingly, the night of the eighteenth brought no unusual enemy activity. The Germans were as exhausted as the Americans.

The Germans had now placed the 11th Panzer Division where they wanted it. The Ghost Division had been in reserve during the Battle of the Bulge, then had the same mission during the second German counteroffensive in the Alsace region against the Seventh Army. As a result, it was rested and at nearly full strength in men and equipment. Colonel General Johannes Blaskowitz, commanding Army Group G opposite the Third and Seventh Armies, had decided to have the division make a spoiling attack out of the Saar-Moselle Triangle to delay any attack coming from the allies in his area. The axis of this planned attack ran through the towns of Butzdorf and Tettingen.

General Malony's attack and seizure of these two towns had spoiled the attack plans of Colonel General Blaskowitz, but it did provide General der Infanterie Walther Hahm's LXXXII Corps a ready reserve to repulse the Americans. Consequently, Blaskowitz ordered General Hahm to have the Ghost Division attack the Ghost Corps. The sounds of armored vehicles moving forward was confirmed the following day by American observation planes, who observed and reported German armor crossing the Saar into the Triangle. Malony alerted his division, so the time was available to install antitank defenses effectively by the 376th Infantry. Before dawn on the seventeenth a patrol from Company A returned with two prisoners who were quite willing to reveal that they were part of the Ghost Division.

Soon after the prisoners had been interviewed, dawn broke with a storm of artillery fire of twenty minutes' duration from German lines on Butzdorf, Tettingen, and Wochern. What was left of the towns was shattered. The relief soldiers felt at the end of the barrage was quickly dissipated by the sound of tank engines filling the air. Almost immediately, a strong column of men and armored vehicles appeared to the north and east of Tettingen and Butzdorf, their objectives.

The First Battalion, 110th Grenadier Regiment, supported by the 10th (Engineer) Company in half-tracks and elements of the 714th Infantry Regiment, stormed toward Company A of the 1st Battalion in Butzdorf. Accompanying them were four self-propelled 75mm guns of the 21st Antitank Battalion and "several" Mark IV tanks of the 7th Company of the 15th Panzer Regiment. Led by a self-propelled gun, they attempted to enter the town, but the leading vehicle hit a mine only recently laid by the 319th Combat Engineers as a part of the antitank preparations, and was unable to move. Two following half-tracks attempted to go around the stalled assault gun, only to fall prey to Company A's bazooka teams. Although all the armor had been kept at arm's length, several German soldiers managed to occupy two houses on the outskirts of the town.

Meanwhile the balance of the enemy force attacked Tettingen. Defended by Company C, Tettingen was equally prepared for an armored attack. Again, the leading German vehicle was disabled by a mine, and a second was destroyed by bazooka fire. A tank was disabled by Pvt. Thomas H. Goggins and his bazooka, but this tank continued to fire its weapons despite being unable to move. Other tanks and half-tracks managed to get into Tettingen, however, because of defective bazooka rockets that failed to explode upon hitting their targets. Nevertheless, using their organic weapons, the men of Company C managed to destroy most of the infantry carried into Tettingen by the half-tracks, but they could do little about the tanks.

Despite some early successes, the Germans had exhausted their assault power by midmorning, and the armor withdrew to reorganize. Companies A and C of Lieutenant Colonel Minor's 1st Battalion quickly counterattacked and by 11:00 had regained all the buildings lost to the initial attack.

General Cheadle observed the attack, and reported back to division headquarters "that tank attack of about fifteen tanks had been met and that five tanks had been knocked out." He also reported that he believed the front-line troops had sufficient antitank means to hold their positions.

General von Wietersheim was not finished, however. After reorganizing his attack force, he launched the next attack at 11:30. This time the tanks kept their distance from the town and shelled it at point-blank range. Company A took to the cellars, leaving one man in each house as an observer to warn of the approach of enemy infantry. Division artillery kept up a steady protective fire, and Lieutenant Colonel Minor, 1st Battalion commander, kept the regimental cannon company busy with direct support of Company A. He also attempted to get tank destroyers forward to force the enemy armor to withdraw, or better, to destroy it. Neither was possible because enemy snipers were active, and the unprotected crews of the tank destroyers were easy targets. This made it difficult to get into firing positions.

General Cheadle was still in the area, and he quickly put in a call to General Malony for help. Malony immediately ordered a battalion of the 302d Infantry attached to the 376th and a light tank company of the 3d Cavalry Group to move to Tettingen. A few minutes later, Malony was called by General Walker, who had heard from General Patton that the 94th Infantry Division was "in full retreat," but that the army commander had been joking. In a more serious vein, however, Walker complimented Malony on his division's performance so far and indicated that plans were in the works to require him to take the entire Saar-Moselle Triangle in the near future.

General Malony had his hands full with the ongoing struggle, so he could spare little time for future plans. He found that "It was impossible to reinforce them there [Tettingen-Butzdorf] or even to evacuate the wounded by day." Efforts to assist the embattled battalion were fruitless. "Nine of our tank destroyers were playing hide-and-seek with the tanks. They couldn't help Butzdorf very much, but our lone company hung on determinedly." He also noted that "our ineffective 57mm antitank guns were overrun." Before that event, however, a squad under Sgt. Charles Foxgrover managed to use its gun to destroy a tank shelling the battalion command post. The crew was immediately knocked out by counterbattery mortar fire that also damaged the weapon.

After several hours of long-distance sniping by the tanks, the enemy decided the time had come to take their objectives. In midafternoon the three battalions of the 110th Panzergrenadier Regiment, supported by the 2d Panzer Company of the 15th Panzer Regiment, attacked into Butzdorf. Division artillery and the automatic weapons fire of Company A decimated the ranks of the German infantry, but the survivors still came. Assault after assault was pushed out of town, each attack costing both sides heavy casualties. The Americans matched the Germans in determination. In one instance, three mail clerks of Company D volunteered to bring supplies up to Company A. Corporals Bernie H. Heck, Earl N. Vulgamore, and Pfc. Virgil E. Hamilton filled a jeep with food and ammunition, and proceeded from Tettingen into Butzdorf. Before they could enter Butzdorf, however, they spotted four enemy tanks. Hiding the jeep behind a building, they rummaged through their cargo and found a bazooka and ammunition. Although none of the men had had any experience with the weapon, they managed to put it together and load it. Then Hamilton carefully aimed it at the nearest enemy tank, about forty yards away, and let it fly. The round hit the tank squarely, destroying it. The enemy platoon leader, surprised by the sudden appearance of opposition where there had been none a moment before, opened his tank's top hatch to look around, just as Hamilton and his team fired their second rocket. This time they had aimed a trifle too high, but amazingly the rocket ricocheted off the raised hatch cover directly into the second tank, destroying it as well. The team needed five rockets to demolish the third enemy tank while the Germans desperately searched for their attackers. The crew of the fourth and last tank preferred discretion to valor, and quickly withdrew, but the mail-clerk bazooka team caught it at a range of 150 yards and also killed it.

The battle continued on into the late afternoon. Company A and the Company D men attached to it continued to fight off the tanks and infantry with every weapon at hand. So intense was the fighting that ammunition, especially antitank ammunition, began to run out. Lieutenant Stafford grew increasingly concerned as the day wore on. Without antitank ammunition, with only one heavy machine gun left in operation, and with his radio beginning to fade, he and the men of Company A were in an increasingly untenable position. The Germans occupied a few buildings at one end of Butzdorf, and they showed no signs of slowing down in their attack. Adding to his worries, he had thirty wounded men sheltering in his command post, plus several prisoners.

General Cheadle continued to monitor the action. He reported to General Malony that the Germans had between twelve and eighteen tanks, "coming in from all sides of Butzdorf." This prompted Maloney to authorize the abandonment of Butzdorf. He reported to XX Corps that the division had "got knocked off Butzdorf" and that Company A had been overrun by eighteen tanks supported by infantry. After reporting, he went to the front to see things for himself.

While Malony was on his way up front, Cheadle placed the reinforcing battalion of the 302d Infantry in position, and when Malony arrived, they decided that the light tank company of the 3d Cavalry Group was of no help and ordered it to return to its parent unit. Malony also realized that his men still held Butzdorf and so advised XX Corps.

While Butzdorf blazed with battle, Tettingen simmered. The arrival of the 302d Infantry Battalion enabled the 2d Battalion of the 376th to move forward to relieve elements of the 1st Battalion in Tettingen. Company F, led by Lieutenant Colonel Martin, soon arrived and proceeded to clear out Tettingen along with Company C. With the town proper cleared of snipers, the tank destroyers could now move into protected positions where they fired upon enemy armored vehicles outside the town. Firing from Tettingen, the tank destroyers also fired upon and hit several of the enemy armored vehicles on the fringes of Butzdorf.

General Malony, after observing his troops in action for some time, decided that Butzdorf should be abandoned, because it could not be supplied or reinforced without serious losses. It had served the purpose for which the division had attacked, causing the Germans to commit their reserves, and thus depleting those reserves. General Malony ordered the 376th to evacuate Butzdorf.

In Butzdorf, Lieutenant Stafford had arrived at the same conclusion. His condition had not improved any and night was coming, which gave additional advantages to the attacker. He decided to withdraw before he was overwhelmed.

He called for supporting fires on his radio, which now could only send but not receive messages. The 919th Field Artillery responded, supported by the 284th Field Artillery Battalion, and artillery began falling as the survivors of Companies A and D withdrew, carrying their wounded on doors pulled from wrecked houses. After a harrowing march through a pitch-dark night, pelted by sleet and rain, the troops from Butzdorf succeeded in withdrawing successfully, bringing their prisoners with them. The next day the entire battalion moved to a rear reserve position.

Meanwhile, General Malony returned to division headquarters convinced that his men were wasting their time in battalion-sized attacks. He contacted General Walker and asked for permission to "exploit what he had gained." Walker hesitated, but said that he would approach General Patton for permission to increase the size of the XX Corps attacks in the Triangle, and also try to get assistance for the 94th. Ironically, a few minutes later the XX Corps chief of staff phoned Colonel Bercquist to complain that the division was expending more than its allotted share of ammunition. Colonel Bercquist replied that the ammunition had been expended in repelling five enemy counterattacks, but that they would be more careful in the future. The division was also notified that it had been taken off the "secret" list, and that its presence in the front lines could now be reported in the press.

Late in the evening Walker called Malony to tell him that he had spoken with Patton and had received preliminary permission to increase the size of the division's attacks in the Triangle. Pending final approval from Third Army, Walker authorized Malony to "shoot the works." And shortly before midnight, division headquarters was visited by Brig. Gen. Charles R. Colson, commanding Combat Command A of the 8th Armored Division. The help requested by General Walker had arrived.

CHAPTER 8
TORNADO ARRIVES

The appearance of General Colson was a bright spot for the 94th Infantry Division. Colson and his staff heralded the arrival in XX Corps sector of the 8th Armored Division. Both corps and division personnel welcomed heartily the American armor in force in the sector, as one of the major problems during their attacks had been the lack of armor.

Although the XX Corps had tank destroyers and artillery, the scarcity of tanks made the attacks of the 94th division more costly. Although at this point in the war many U.S. infantry divisions had one or more tank battalions attached to it, the 94th did not. Probably this was because most of the armor resources of Third Army were concentrated in the Battle of the Bulge.

Tanks provided close support of attacking infantry who were assaulting concrete defensive positions. The standard tank was known as the "Sherman." Officially the M4A1 through M4A4 medium tank, it carried a crew of five and was armed with a 75mm or 76mm main gun and .30-caliber light machine guns. A .50-caliber machine gun was mounted in the turret. Powered by a gasoline engine, it was highly inflammable, but more mechanically reliable than the German tanks. Neither its armor nor firepower equaled that of the current German tanks, but when used in the infantry close support role, it was highly successful. The standard tank destroyer was the Gun Motor Carriage M10, armed with the 76.2mm main gun. No machine guns were standard, although it was common for a .50-caliber machine gun to be mounted on its turret. With a crew of five and using the same basic hull and engine as the Sherman, it was often used to support infantry attacks in the absence of tanks or artillery. Tank destroyers had open, unprotected turrets and thus were unable to provide close support when under direct fire. This had occurred at Butzdorf, when sniper fire kept them from advancing against the attacking German armor. But now, on 18 January, American tanks moved into the Saar-Moselle Triangle.

The 8th Armored Division was activated on 1 April 1942, from cadres drawn from the 2d Cavalry Brigade and the 4th and 5th Armored Divisions. Early in its career it was designated as a training unit, selected to train and prepare men for other armored units leaving for combat. During the course of its training it provided cadres for the 10th, 11th, 12th, 13th, 14th, and 20th Armored Divisions. Just as its men were despairing of getting overseas, orders were received to move to the New York port of embarkation.

Shortly before those embarkation orders arrived, the division received a new commander, Maj. Gen. John Matthew Devine, who was to lead it overseas and throughout combat. General Devine was born in Providence, Rhode Island, on 18 June 1895, and graduated from West Point with the class of 1917. Commissioned in the field artillery, he served overseas in World War I with the 6th Infantry Division. After the war he attended Yale University and received a master of science degree in communications engineering. Between the wars he attended the Field Artillery School and was an instructor at West Point. He next was a student at the Command and General Staff School and then taught military science and tactics at Yale. With the outbreak of the war he was assigned to the 1st Armored Division as a staff officer. Subsequently he served as the intelligence officer of I Armored Corps at the Desert Training Center and was assigned as a combat team commander in the 6th Armored Division. He was promoted to artillery commander of the 90th Infantry Division and served with that unit in Normandy, where he transferred to the 7th Armored Division and fought in the battles for Metz as a part of XX Corps. In September, as part of the army's program to distribute combat-experienced officers among new units, he was ordered back to the United States to bring the 8th Armored Division to Europe.

Because of remaining concerns that dictated a strong reserve be kept ready to handle any counteroffensive, SHAEF ordered the 8th Armored Division into combat, but only one combat command at a time. The balance of the division was to be retained in Third Army reserve, and could not be committed without SHAEF's approval. Code-named Tornado, the division was not attached to XX Corps, only to Third Army.

General Colson commanded Combat Command A of the 8th Armored Division. Although infantry divisions had three infantry regiments as tactical units, armored divisions had three combat commands made up of interchangeable units drawn from the major units of the division. Armored divisions had three tank battalions and three armored infantry battalions, which, with artillery support from the division's three self-propelled armored field artillery battalions, made up the striking forces of the division.

General Devine on 18 January met with Brig. Gen. William A. Collier, chief of staff of XX Corps, and received his orders to provide "elms (sic) of 8 Armored Division for combat training by Third Army in support of operations of 94th Division." There were strict restrictions on the use of the reserve, that only one combat command at a time could be used, and no replacement combat command could leave the reserve area until the forward combat command had returned. All in all, these restrictions limited severely the use of the only armor available to the XX Corps, but some armor was better than none at all.

Generals Devine and Colson had decided which units of the division would make up Combat Command A's first combat force. Colson then coordinated with General Malony on the use of his command. As a result, Colson appeared just when the frustrations of attacking fortified positions without armored support were beginning to tell on Generals Walker and Malony.

General Malony had given much thought to the way he should continue his division's mission. Although he earlier had asked permission to use more than one battalion at a time, he changed his mind and told Walker that he now felt it best to continue with single-battalion attacks until the situation changed. Walker left it up to Malony, saying, "It is your show and I am going to leave it to you." Walker did give final approval for the 94th Infantry Division to use up to a regiment at a time, reinforced by a combat command of the 8th Armored.

Later on 19 January, General Devine arrived at Malony's head-quarters and together they decided how best to use Combat Command A. Malony planned to combine the combat command with his own 302d Infantry Regiment and envelop the enemy line between Berg and Sinz. Arrangements were made to begin the attack as soon as Combat Command A could arrive at the front, 21 or 22 January.

Malony "was not too impressed with the idea of giving this unit battle indoctrination in one of the most strongly fortified areas in the theater and under such weather conditions." He knew that in the Triangle, "the roads were so slippery that tanks could climb gentle grades only with considerable difficulty and cross-country traffic was out." Yet he believed that they could help, because "the 11th Panzers were using their tanks and I could certainly use mine."

Meanwhile, the infantrymen of the 94th Division had not been idle. The 302d Infantry, previously held in XX Corps reserve, was released to the division on 18 January, replaced by the 8th Armored Division's CCA. Early on 20 January, the 302d relieved the battered 376th Infantry, which went into reserve. The 302d immediately went to work to eliminate the remaining enemy defenses left within their perimeter. Several pillboxes had been left by the 376th, which had neither the time nor the resources to eliminate them. First to try these pillboxes was the 1st Battalion, 302d Infantry, commanded by Lt. Col. Silas W. Hosea. He sent Capt. Altus L. Woods Jr.'s Company B against the five pillboxes that still dominated the only supply road into Nennig. Generals Malony and Cheadle feared that another German counterattack was certain to come against Nennig and so it was vital that this supply route be available when the attack came.

Captain Woods's men, supported by a single tank destroyer, succeeded in taking one pillbox and capturing a dozen prisoners. The tank destroyer exhausted its ammunition as well as the explosives necessary for destroying concrete installations. Attempts to resupply Company B were unsuccessful, so the attack was called off for the day. The following day Company B returned to the attack, this time reinforced by Company A, a heavy machine-gun section, two platoons of Company B of the 319th Engineer Combat Battalion, and several tank destroyers of the 607th Tank Destroyer Battalion using M36 Gun Motor Carriages armed with 90mm main guns. Most of

Company A's troops were used as resupply parties, ensuring a steady flow of supplies to the attacking platoons of Company B. After six hours of intensive combat under artillery bombardment and small arms fire, the remaining pillboxes were seized and 108 prisoners were taken. Once the area had been comparatively secured, the engineers loaded the pillboxes with explosives and destroyed them.

While the engineers went about their work, Companies A and B entered an unnamed nearby woods, which on the map looked to some like a monkey wrench, so was named accordingly. No serious resistance was encountered, and the infantry withdrew to the town of Besch in accordance with earlier plans. The following morning Company B returned to Monkey Wrench Woods to take up defensive positions there. They were met with an avalanche of rifle and machine-gun fire from enemy troops who had infiltrated back into the ruins of the destroyed pillboxes. Company B was caught in the open and suffered heavy casualties. Ordered to withdraw, they returned to Besch while A Company moved to attack the enemy force. It was not until the following day, however, that the two companies cleared the woods and established defensive positions on the northern fringe.

The division's next regiment, the 301st Infantry, commanded by Col. Roy N. Hagerty, was given the town of Orscholz, a key anchor of the Siegfried Switchline, as its objective. This was the town for which the line had been named originally. Orscholz was on a hill some four hundred feet high, surrounded by an arc of pillboxes that ran for more than a quarter of a mile. The Saar River flowed close by, and the surrounding countryside was heavily wooded and marked by steep cliffs near the river. Open fields south and east of Orscholz, which were between the Americans and their objective, were the only approach route for the men of the 301st's 1st Battalion, selected to make the initial attack. Orscholz was a naturally defensible position enhanced by German ingenuity.

The capture of Orscholz was the other prong of General Malony's plan to envelop the Triangle from each end. One penetration at Nennig had already been accomplished. Now it was time to enter the Triangle defenses from the Saar River side. Lieutenant Colonel George F. Miller selected Companies A and B to make the attack, with Company C in reserve. Captain Herman C. Straub's Company B would lead the attack, guided by Sgt. Ernest W. Halle of the regiment's intelligence and reconnaissance platoon. Reinforced by Lt. Robert W. Jonscher's 1st Platoon of Company D (Heavy Weapons), Company B moved off in the pitch darkness of a snowstorm on midnight of 19 January.

As had happened before in the hostile terrain and weather, the long approach march depleted the strength of the troops and delayed their departure. So heavy was the storm that the two assault companies lost contact with each other, causing the attack to be delayed further until contact was restored. Finally, nearly ninety minutes later, Capt. Charles B. Colgan's Company A advanced toward a line of houses believed to be camouflaged pillboxes. Hardly had they crossed the dragon's teeth than "the stillness was broken by a series of loud explosions." Company A had walked into a thickly laid minefield. Attempts at mine clearing by the attached teams of Company A, 319th Engineers, were negated by the heavy snowfall. Hidden under the snow and ice "was a field of Shu (sic) mines, S mines, and a tangle of barbed wire." Company A was stopped in its tracks.

Company B, meanwhile, advanced alongside Company A. They had missed the minefield and against no opposition quickly came to the initial objective, the road between Orscholz and Oberleuken. Moving off to the right along the road, the reinforced company moved directly on the battalion objective, Orscholz. After overcoming a few German automatic weapons positions and capturing some prisoners, Straub placed his men in the woods overlooking Orscholz, to wait for the rest of the battalion to catch up.

Colonel Miller and the other troops tried to move forward. To follow Company B's route they had advanced halfway up an exposed slope when they were attacked by numerous enemy automatic weapons skillfully camouflaged and hidden further by the snowfall. The survivors of Company A managed to provide covering fire that enabled the battalion to withdraw down the slope, but advance along this route was now impossible. The enemy knew they were there, and the element of surprise that had enabled Company B to get through no longer existed. Calls went out to the supporting 301st Field Artillery Battalion to blast a hole so the battalion could advance.

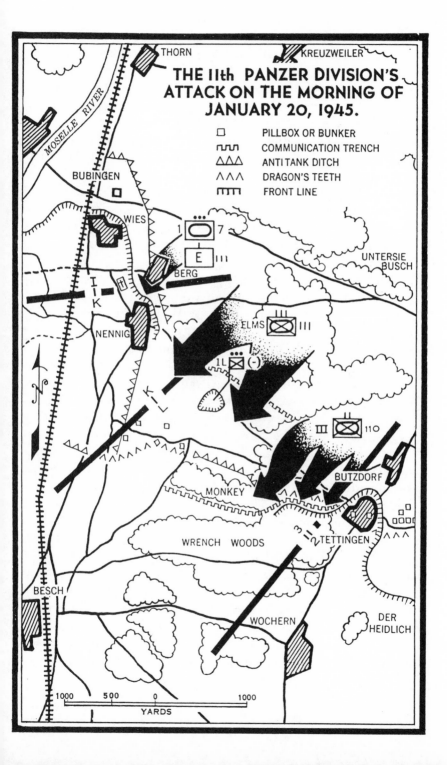

THORN KREUZWEILER

THE 11th PANZER DIVISION'S
ATTACK ON THE MORNING OF
JANUARY 20, 1945.

□ PILLBOX OR BUNKER
ᴖᴖᴖ COMMUNICATION TRENCH
△△△ ANTI TANK DITCH
∧∧∧ DRAGON'S TEETH
ᴨᴨᴨ FRONT LINE

MOSELLE RIVER

BUBINGEN

WIES

1 [ ] 7

E III

BERG

UNTERSIE
BUSCH

I
K

NENNIG

ELMS III

1L (-)

K

III 110

BUTZDORF

MONKEY

WRENCH WOODS

TETTINGEN

BESCH

WOCHERN

DER
HEIDLICH

1000 500 0 1000
YARDS

While General Cheadle was reporting to General Malony that things had gone well so far in the 301st Infantry's attack, things were just beginning to fall apart. After the barrage by the 301st Field Artillery Battalion, Company A again moved out onto the deadly slope, only to face the same intensive enemy fire. Every weapon available to the battalion was used without results. Finally, German artillery fire began to fall among the attacking Americans. Colonel Miller came forward to see what could be done to get his battalion moving. Concerned over the plight of Company B as well as his exposed men on the open slope, he moved into enemy artillery range and was cut down by a burst of fire and was killed almost immediately. Within an hour of reporting to General Malony that the 301st was making progress, Cheadle reported the death of Colonel Miller to the division commander.

The heavy losses suffered in Company A, the separation of Company B, and the loss of the battalion commander served to disorganize the 1st Battalion. Major Arthur W. Hodges, the battalion executive officer, came forward and assumed command. He withdrew the remnants of the battalion into the woods and began to rally the unit. Company I was attached from the 3d Battalion and a new attack was launched midafternoon. Despite effective fire from the 301st Field Artillery, the enemy was still covering the slope. Companies C, I, and the remnants of A pushed forward despite the enemy fire. As they moved they encountered obstructions left by the Germans that delayed movement and made the soldiers easier targets. Although the battalion advanced farther than previously, once again they encountered a hidden minefield and all progress stopped. "One of the companies had sixty casualties from antipersonnel mines in a matter of minutes, when attempting to remove the obstructions."

Colonel Hagerty sent his regimental executive officer, Lt. Col. Donald C. Hardin, who had previously commanded the 1st Battalion, forward to retake command and get the assault moving once again. He moved the battalion farther to the left and launched another assault. Once again mines, booby traps, and enemy artillery fire stopped the attack in its tracks. Company B was on its own.

General Malony had concentrated on the 302d Infantry's attack near Nennig on the nineteenth. It wasn't until early on the morning of 20 January that he called General Cheadle at the regimental headquarters of the 301st and learned of the situation in the 1st Battalion. Cheadle reported that the situation was "very bad."

Indeed, things could not be worse. Company B was trapped well behind enemy lines, its parent battalion was incapable of relieving or reinforcing it. There was also no way to resupply the isolated men. Weather prevented air drops and the enemy kept ground supply impossible. Late on the twentieth Captain Straub's reinforced company was discovered by the Germans and came under increasing fire. Moving the soldiers to positions for all-around defense, Straub had the forward observers from the 301st Field Artillery keep the unit surrounded by friendly artillery fire. As day turned into night, no solution to the situation presented itself. Patrols time and again failed to find a way through enemy defenses. Even using tanks of Company A, 748th Tank Battalion, at last assigned to the division, no progress could be made until the infantry could breach the antitank ditch. Finally Colonel Hardin phoned Colonel Hagerty and advised him that there was simply no way to reach his isolated troops. Reluctantly, the 1st Battalion was granted permission to withdraw.

Withdrawal was difficult at Orscholz because the 1st Battalion had made some progress into the enemy defenses so its units were intertwined with the Germans. One soldier had fought throughout the day in the cold, wet snow only to be wounded in the last hours of daylight by artillery fire. Treated by a medical aid man, he was placed in a captured bunker with others before they moved back. There were no beds in the bunker, so the wounded had to lie on the floor in an inch or more of cold water. Nevertheless, it was "warmer than out in the trenches." After he'd spent the night there the man's buddies came back to try to carry him to American lines. His buddies had been cut off, but had convinced Polish defectors from the German army to pretend to have captured them and escort them to friendly lines. A passing American officer ordered them to leave the soldier behind, however, believing that the chances for success were poor enough without trying to carry wounded with them. Later that afternoon "came the most frightening experience of all." From the open door of the bunker the soldier observed German troops approaching. There were several German aid men, wearing Red

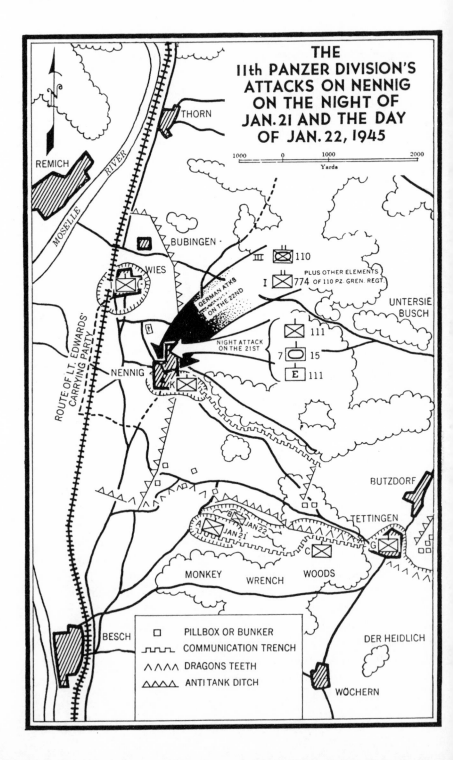

THE
11th PANZER DIVISION'S
ATTACKS ON NENNIG
ON THE NIGHT OF
JAN. 21 AND THE DAY
OF JAN. 22, 1945

Crosses but carrying machine guns, coming toward the bunker. He passed out, to recover later as a prisoner of war tended by these same German medics.

Colonel Hagerty still had Company B cut off behind enemy lines. "Throughout the night of the twentieth–twenty-first, the German artillery relentlessly pounded the troops in the woods. The enemy shells crashed into the treetops and burst, in deadly showers of shell fragments. By the time a count could be taken of the strength of a unit, additional casualties rendered the total incorrect. The reinforced company was gradually being whittled away." Hagerty spoke with Lt. Col. Samuel L. Morrow of the 301st Field Artillery to arrange a smokescreen to cover a withdrawal of the trapped Americans. Attempts to contact Captain Straub during the night of the twenty-first failed due to the need to preserve radio batteries. Straub had kept his radio in a bunker to prevent the batteries from freezing, and it wasn't until the morning of the twenty-second that he spoke with Hagerty. Ordered to "attack to the rear," Straub declined. He reported to the colonel that "his men were practically out of ammunition and one man had already frozen to death." Every time his men moved, they drew heavy enemy fire. Any movement would risk entry into hidden minefields. Straub determined to surrender his command to save their lives.

But with the arrival of the promised smoke, Straub "passed the word down the trench that battalion had called on the artillery and mortars for smoke shells to try to give us a chance to get out of the woods back to our lines." Using German prisoners captured earlier to confuse the enemy, "Captain Straub led the way." Stepping over their own dead and wounded, the men went down the trench and moved into the open. Enemy fire increased and they broke up into smaller groups of soldiers trying to escape and survive. One group successfully left the trench under direct machine-gun and artillery fire to the temporary safety of a pillbox, where they "found the frozen bodies of several of our men who had died during the night and six or eight badly wounded men lying on the cold concrete floor not knowing what was going on outside." Looking in all directions, the group discovered Germans everywhere. There was no way out. The bunker was a trap, and when the men learned that Lieutenant Jonscher had been killed in the trench, the fight went out of them. A few minutes later a strange silence descended over what had been a furious battlefield. The survivors of Company B, with elements of Companies A and D, attached engineers, and artillery observers, surrendered. Initial concerns by the men; that because their captors were from the 11th Panzer Division, the Germans would repeat the atrocities of the Malmédy massacre; proved unfounded. Later reports indicated that ten officers and 230 men, including Captain Straub, went into German captivity.

The remnants of the 1st Battalion, 301st Infantry, were withdrawn from the front line. The 2d Battalion assumed the front-line positions. Major Hodge was confirmed as the new battalion commander and Maj. William E. MacBride was assigned as the new executive officer. Lieutenant Joseph E. Cancilla was appointed as the new commander of Company B and ordered to create a new company.

General Malony met with the survivors of the 1st Battalion to encourage them and to find out how things had gone wrong. He determined that no further effort would be made against Orscholz until fighting in other sectors had been resolved. For although matters at Orscholz had gone badly, the 302d Infantry Regiment also had a vicious fight in progress at Nennig.

CHAPTER 9
COUNTERATTACK

General Malony's plan to create two breaches in the enemy's line and then join them into one major breach had been frustrated by the defeat of the 1st Battalion, 301st Infantry, at Orscholz. But the Americans still held the shoulders of the penetration at Nennig. This entry into the Orscholz Switchline had to be kept, so with the 376th Infantry Regiment being exhausted, Malony ordered the 302d Infantry to relieve them and to maintain control of the town of Nennig. Colonel Earle A. Johnson, who had entered the army in 1917 with the Oklahoma National Guard, ordered the 3d Battalion under Lt. Col. Otto B. Cloudt to move forward to relieve the 3d Battalion, 376th.

Colonel Cloudt, his staff, and his company commanders moved forward for a briefing and received their first information from the enemy when they were unable to take their jeep more than halfway along the only road into Nennig. Enemy mortar and machine-gun fire prevented any vehicles from entering the town. Cloudt and his officers had to walk and crawl into town. After being briefed by Lieutenant Colonel Thurston, Cloudt ordered Capt. Allan R. Williams's Company I into the towns of Wies and Berg. Lieutenant Carl W. Seeby's Company K would defend Nennig itself, with an attached platoon from Capt. John N. Smith's Company L. Captain Smith's company, less the platoon led by Lt. John R. Travers attached to Company L, was to outpost the open ground between Nennig and a woods that overlooked the area. Captain Francis M. Hurst's heavy-weapons Company M was to have its mortar platoon under Lt. Douglas LaRue Smith provide covering fire from the Luxembourg side of the river while the two machine-gun platoons were supporting the assault companies.

During the late afternoon and evening of 19 January, the 3d Battalion, 302d, completed the relief of the 3d Battalion, 376th Infantry. As Captain Smith was relieving Captain Bowden of Company B, he was asked how long he expected to remain in the positions they had just exchanged. Captain Smith responded, "About seven days," to which Bowden said, "Somebody may be up here in seven days from now, but it won't be you."

Bowden knew what he was talking about. Within hours of assuming their new positions, Company L was under attack by roving patrols of varying size. By daylight, TSgt. Frank A. O'Hara's platoon had been driven out of the woods and back into Nennig. An attempt to regain their positions found the Germans ready for them, and they were repulsed by enemy fire. Sergeant O'Hara's platoon linked up with Lt. Henry J. Fink's 2d Platoon in a position east of Nennig. Company L's other platoon under Lt. John R. Travers, occupying the positions formerly held by Lieutenant Fox of Colonel Thurston's battalion, soon realized that the enemy was attempting to surround its position. The wooden bunker Captain Smith was using as a command post also came under direct fire, and the company's first sergeant was killed.

All this enemy activity forecast a major counterattack. It came at dawn with a heavy artillery barrage followed by a full-scale attack by infantry and armor from the 11th Panzer Division.

The suddenness of the attack was blunted somewhat by artillery fire directed by Lt. William Burke, a forward observer from Lt. Col. Harold S. Whiteley's 356th Field Artillery Battalion. His fires delayed but did not stop the panzer grenadiers, who pushed Company L back. By afternoon Captain Smith could only find forty men left to command, and had no knowledge of what had happened to the rest of his company.

Lieutenant Travers's platoon was still in position, but out of touch with anyone, and well aware that they had been bypassed by the enemy attack. There was neither radio nor telephone communication with any other American unit. Travers took two volunteers and moved toward Besch in the hope of contacting someone from his battalion who could aid his trapped platoon. Evading enemy groups and minefields, they managed to reach the road running between Nennig and Tettingen. Here they ran into the regimental executive officer, Lt. Col. John W. Gaddis. Gaddis took the men to both battalion and regimental command posts, where Travers pleaded for help to extract his trapped platoon. None was available, as he discovered, because the entire regimental front was under a full-scale counterattack.

During the time Lieutenant Colonel Cloudt's battalion was moving into position, the 2d Battalion of the 302d Infantry commanded by Lt. Col. Frank P. Norman was relieving the 1st Battalion, 376th, holding Tettingen and Berg. They, too, were attacked at the same time as Colonel Cloudt's men. Captain James W. Griffin's Company G in Tettingen was attacked from three sides, and only after three furious hours was the attack beaten off. While the fighting raged in Tettingen, the 1st Battalion, 302d Infantry, was ordered into Monkey Wrench Woods to clear some remaining enemy positions. Leaving Capt. Norbert C. Marek's Company C behind as regimental reserve, the 1st Battalion moved out.

Captain Marek and his platoon leaders moved forward to Company L headquarters to learn from Captain Smith what they could of the situation. While they were there, Marek was advised that his company was now attached to the 2d Battalion, as was Company L. Marek was ordered to assist Captain Smith to restore his positions.

After ordering his troops forward, Marek began to plan an attack with Captain Smith. As the troops advanced through the remnants of Company L, Company C was hit by a fierce artillery barrage, followed by automatic-weapons fire from concealed pillboxes and rocket fire from several directions. Casualties quickly mounted, and leaders began falling. In one of the Company C platoons, the lieutenant was killed and the platoon sergeant was missing in a matter of minutes, so fast in fact that the platoon guide, SSgt. Francis J. Kelly, did not know he was in command for several critical moments. Captain Marek went forward to get this platoon reorganized and helped to clear out some remaining enemy positions in the woods. By nightfall many, but not all, of these had been recaptured. During the night the enemy kept up a constant barrage of artillery and rocket fire on the exposed Americans. Wounded from the day's fighting were joined by wounded from the enemy barrage. Technician 3d grade John F. Riskey, a medical aidman attached to Company L, worked tirelessly all day and night to succor the wounded. Disregarding his personal safety, he ignored direct automatic-weapons fire, moved into enemy artillery barrages, and stayed behind with wounded men who could not be moved when the company pulled back to reorganize. His coat was shredded by enemy fire, but his efforts saved many men. He survived to wear the Distinguished Service Cross he earned that day.

Losses continued throughout the night in the two companies. In addition to losses from enemy fire, trench foot and frozen feet produced fifteen casualties during the night. In trenches whose bottoms were covered with water, they were unable to light fires, or to dry their feet. The resulting injuries would continue to plague the men of the 94th Division during their entire time in the Saar-Moselle Triangle. When Colonel Norman came up to inspect Company L during the night, he discovered that in addition to the casualties from enemy fire and frostbite, Captain Smith had several men whose hands were beginning to freeze. After these had been evacuated, there were only eighteen men left in Company L. Norman ordered Smith and his survivors into reserve in Wochern. They had lasted less than two full days instead of the seven Smith had predicted to Captain Bowden.

Captain Marek and his men remained in position, and were soon joined by a patrol from Company A, uniting them however tenuously with the main line of resistance. There was still no word on Company L's missing platoon. It was assumed that they had been captured, but more would be heard from these men, now commanded by TSgt. Arnold A. Petry.

The German counterattack was also aimed at the major American penetration of the Switchline, the towns of Nennig, Berg, and Wies. The 3d Battalion, 302d Infantry, held these towns, and was now without the services of its own Company L, replaced by an already depleted Company C of the 1st Battalion. German infantry aboard and alongside tanks attempted to storm into Nennig early in the afternoon of 20 January. Coming after an already busy morning, the attackers gained a brief hold of a small part of the town, but were quickly ejected. The panzer grenadiers of the Ghost Division were not finished and returned with additional armor just as darkness fell. Using illumination from mortars, the Germans charged into town, supported by four tanks. Artillery and small arms fire from the defenders decimated the attacking ranks, although once again a small number managed to occupy briefly a few of the outlying houses. This time the Germans needed to rest and think about their next move, so the balance of the night and the next day were "quiet."

The definition of *quiet* in the Saar-Moselle Triangle was relative. Artillery, rocket, and mortar fire fell at regular intervals on the American front-line positions. The cold continued to be intense and made the defensive positions especially uncomfortable. The American infantry lived in holes dug in muddy ground, usually with water up to their ankles. The use of blankets taken from dead or captured Germans to line the holes did little to make conditions more bearable. While under fire or during hours of darkness a man could only relieve himself inside the same hole, further aggravating the miserable conditions.

Private First Class Robert K. Adair recorded how the infantryman suffered from the weather conditions as well as the enemy. "During this time the temperature ranged from as low as zero one night to as high as forty degrees during the day. At times we faced rain and wet snow in our face from the north." Adair, a member of Company I, 376th Infantry, and a native of Wisconsin, knew better than most how to protect himself from the elements. "I gathered pine boughs and filled the bottom of my six feet or so of trench with the boughs and stood and slept insulated a bit from the ice and frozen earth." He was also careful about his feet, the basic transportation of the infantryman. "I carried extra socks stuffed under my shirt, and regularly I took off my shoes, took off the three—later more—pair of socks, and replaced the innermost layer with a warm dry set from my chest store." Not all were as careful or had the opportunities related by Private Adair, and weather casualties began to mount alarmingly.

The quiet at Nennig was not destined to last. After dark the Germans returned in force once again. A furious barrage thundered into the three towns, and after a while the part of the barrage covering

Nennig was moved to cover Besch and Wies. Again, German infantry and tanks came down the hill toward Nennig. Aided by the guns of the 356th Field Artillery, the 3d Battalion of the 302d Infantry once again set about the business of repulsing an enemy armored attack. Other artillery battalions were called upon to assist, but despite every effort the Germans fought their way into the main part of the town of Nennig. One tank reached the town center and knocked out an antitank gun position as well as two machine guns. By midnight, the northern half of Nennig was in German hands. A call went out to Lt. Henry J. Fink, whose platoon was holding an open field position on Nennig's flank. Given fifteen men and orders to clear northern Nennig, Fink managed to clear a portion of the captured sector, but reported that he would need fresh troops to finish his assignment. There was no reserve available, so the survivors of Company K could only hold their new positions. By daylight, there were at least three enemy tanks in the German-controlled portion of Nennig, and an early morning counterattack by Company K could not advance very far. By midafternoon Colonel Cloudt was reporting to division head-quarters that "he was getting hell from all sides," and that the town had been hit by a tremendous explosion that he thought might have been some sort of rocket. He reported further that he could hold his positions. As the day waned, the men of Company K withdrew to a more defensible position about halfway through Nennig, along a stream that ran through the town.

Although Nennig was the center of the German attack, they paid considerable attention to Berg as well. Held by Lt. William J. Do-herty's 2d Platoon of Company I reinforced by a section of heavy machine guns from Capt. Francis M. Hurst's Company M, the town was attacked throughout the day by tanks and panzer grenadiers. The Americans were attacked at point-blank range by armor that blasted holes in the houses they occupied. This was to open the way for more fire and help the accompanying German infantry. Despite this, the soldiers managed to hold their positions, using their bazookas and the occasionally available artillery fire to keep the enemy at bay. The platoon had some men in a castle outside of Berg, known as Schloss Berg. The Germans concentrated their fire against this position, and by nightfall they had seized the castle and the two squads and heavy machine guns defending it. One American gun was later turned against its former owners.

Back in Nennig, Lieutenant Seeby and the remnants of Company K were having difficulty holding on to the half of the town in their sector. German infantry continued to infiltrate and attempts to recover lost ground were fruitless. Early on the morning of the twenty-second, General Malony called XX Corps to tell Brigadier General Collier that "we are having a helluva time holding Nennig this morning" and asked what use he could make of the 8th Armored Division's elements in his immediate area. Told they were available for two days, Malony ordered General Colson's combat command forward.

While the 8th Armored moved up, Company K held on to its toe-hold in Nennig. Its 1st Platoon under Lieutenant Carpenter was surrounded but fighting and refusing surrender demands in the German-held portion of Nennig. The line along the stream was being held. But reoccupying Nennig was beyond Company K's ability. Some help came from the Army Air Force when eighteen B-24's bombed the towns of Büren and Kreuzweiler, where it was believed some of the enemy's artillery was located.

General Colson came forward to look over the terrain, which he declared unsuitable for armor. He decided to divide his command into two task forces. The first he placed under the command of Lt. Col. Arthur D. Poinier, a highly respected officer who commanded the 7th Armored Infantry Battalion. Designated as Task Force Poinier, the unit was attached to the 302d Infantry Regiment with orders to seize and hold Nennig. Consisting of the 7th Armored Infantry Battalion, Company C of the 18th Tank Battalion, and a detachment of Troop A, 88th Cavalry Reconnaissance Squadron, Task Force Poinier moved forward to seize Nennig.

Captain Joseph Finley's Company A of the 7th Armored Infantry was ordered to assist Company K in retaking the northern portion of Nennig. Supported by the assault gun platoon of the 7th Armored Infantry, the attack pushed off against strong resistance. The main street of Nennig was "a fire-swept lane" when the attack jumped off but slow progress was made until several additional houses in the town had been recaptured. In one the heavy machine gun lost by

Company M, 302d Infantry, in Schloss Berg the day before was re-captured.

There was no lull as night fell on the twenty-second. Company A moved into the recaptured positions in Nennig and prepared for defense. The German counterattack that night, however, succeeded once again in pushing the Americans back to the area of the stream line where they had started that morning. Like Company K, Company A also left behind some of its members when a patrol of the command that had reached the church was trapped inside by a Mark IV tank and forced to hide all night behind the altar.

General Malony kept XX Corps informed of the difficulties, telling General Collier "that things were red hot" and that Nennig "has been a knock-down-drag-out affair all day." Malony also advised the XX Corps of the results of the disaster that had hit the 1st Battalion, 301st Infantry. The battalion, which had numbered nearly one thousand men before the attack, had only nineteen officers and 415 enlisted men remaining.

The fighting had taken its toll on the enemy as well. The battle for Nennig on the twenty-second spelled the end for the 3d Battalion of the 110th Panzergrenadier Regiment, which was so decimated that it was disbanded and its survivors distributed among the other battalions of the regiment.

While the struggle for Nennig continued, the 1st Battalion of the 302d was ordered to clear up the remaining pillboxes that had held up the advance of Companies L and C on Nennig's flank. Captain Marek's men moved forward late on the morning of 23 January to be "met with a heavy barrage of rockets and artillery, in addition to intense automatic weapons fire." Despite this intense fire, MSgt. Nicholas Oresko, a platoon leader in Company C, moved forward while his men were pinned to the ground. Realizing that his platoon was helpless against the enemy bunkers, he worked his way to one enemy bunker under direct small arms fire. Using grenades, he disabled the machine gun, then rushed the occupants of the pillbox and killed them with his rifle. As he turned from this position, another machine gun opened fire on him and critically wounded him in the hip. He refused medical treatment and led his platoon against this other position. Once again his men were pinned down, but Oresko continued on alone and repeated his earlier one-man assault with grenades and rifle fire, eliminating the second critical position. By this time although weak from the loss of blood, Sergeant Oresko refused evacuation and continued to lead his platoon until the objective had been accomplished, before reporting unaided for medical treatment. Credited with a dozen enemy casualties and two concrete pillboxes, this native of Bayonne, New Jersey, who had just celebrated his twenty-eighth birthday on 18 January, survived to wear his nation's highest decoration, the Medal of Honor.

Another soldier of Captain Marek's company was also instrumental in helping to seize the company's objective. Private James F. Cousineau charged several enemy pillboxes with only his rifle and grenades. After destroying the enemy positions and eliminating a dozen enemy troops, he helped wounded men moving back for aid. While doing this, he and another soldier were surrounded by enemy troops who demanded their surrender. Instead, Cousineau fought his way out, bringing his companion and additional wounded with him to safety. He survived and was awarded the Distinguished Service Cross. Yet, despite the bravery of men like Sergeant Oresko and Private Cousineau, the Germans still held positions overlooking Nennig.

Fighting continued for possession of Nennig. More enemy armor was committed to the action, along with the 1st Battalion, 714th Infantry Regiment. Staff Sergeant George W. Potticary's squad of Company A, 7th Armored Infantry, encountered these reinforcements while in an attack mode and was nearly wiped out when a Mark IV tank fired into the room where they had taken shelter to regroup. In addition to enemy reinforcements, Task Force Poinier had to contend with a "blinding snowstorm and bitter cold." In order to bring sufficient strength to counter the enemy reinforcements, division sent the 2d Battalion, 376th Infantry, back into Nennig. Attacking at 7:30 A.M., Colonel Martin's battalion led with Company E in the assault. Lieutenant Gus E. Wilkins's 1st Platoon moved into Nennig, while the others moved on Berg. Initial progress was good, with three houses and twenty-seven prisoners taken, when suddenly the platoon was confronted by three Mark IV tanks. The advance stopped, with the danger of another retreat. Lieutenant Wilkins's platoon sergeant, TSgt. Nathaniel Isaacman, and Pvt. John F. Pietrzah decided that they would confront the enemy armor from above. Racing to the roof of the nearest building, they emerged above the enemy tanks but were under machine-gun fire from the enemy in nearby Berg. Private Pietrzah opened fire on the leading tank with his bazooka, and with his second round destroyed it. Turning his attention to the last enemy tank, Pietrzah improved his performance, knocking out his tank with one round. Trapped in the middle of its two destroyed comrades, the middle tank was knocked out by a rifle grenade fired by Pvt. Albert J. Beardsley. As they attempted to escape, the enemy crews were cut down by rifle fire.

While Company E of the 376th was moving through Nennig, Company K of the 302d and Company A of the 7th Armored Infantry were also pushing ahead. Their attack moved forward steadily, and by midday they had secured "about 80% or 85% of Nennig," but enemy tanks along the outskirts of the town prevented further advance. The afternoon was a series of attempts by both infantry battalions and the armored task force to clear Nennig and Berg. The enemy held firm, but their losses continued to mount, causing the 1st and 2d Battalions of the 111th Panzergrenadiers to be moved forward to reinforce the survivors of the German garrisons of both towns. The 1st Battalion launched a counterattack late in the day, which was unsuccessful. By day's end both the 110th and 111th Panzergrenadier Regiments were down to 50 percent of the personnel they had brought into the Saar-Moselle Triangle.

As darkness fell over the carnage, Lieutenant Colonel Cloudt and Lieutenant Fink crawled forward under enemy fire to communicate with Lieutenant Carpenter and his trapped platoon. Unable to reach them, they did manage to shout encouragement, promising relief as soon as possible. The platoon, who had held the position despite direct fire from an enemy tank at point-blank range earlier in the day, settled down for the night.

After dark, Colonel Poinier sent out Lt. James P. A. Carr's platoon of the 88th Cavalry Reconnaissance Squadron to protect Company A of the 53d Armored Engineer Battalion as they attempted to breach in three places the antitank ditch that had so often frustrated American efforts to get armored support to the infantry. Tomorrow would be the Americans' turn to attack in force.

CHAPTER 10
FORTY-EIGHT HOURS

General Malony was anxious to get the most use possible out of the forty-eight hours he was allowed to have Combat Command A of the 8th Armored Division under his command. Accordingly, he proposed an attack in conjunction with the armor and his own infantry to clear once and for all the Nennig-Berg-Wies area. His plan included an attack by the combined force and then a strong defense against any enemy counterattack. Division headquarters believed that the entire plan to reduce the Saar-Moselle Triangle by XX Corps "depends on what Martin and Cloudt do." To aid the 376th Infantry at Nennig, Malony also planned an attack on the towns of Sinz and Butzdorf by a combined infantry and armor force as both a diversion and an attempt to exploit any weakness in the enemy's defenses that might develop as a result of the Nennig attack. He hoped that the capture of Sinz would lead to the securing of the high ground immediately north of the town, and put his division completely through the Switchline defenses.

CCA of the 8th Armored had spent an "unpleasant" first night under combat conditions. Constant barrages by German multiple barrel mortars, known to the Americans as "screaming meemies," and sounds of enemy armor moving in the darkness combined to make a sleepless night for these soldiers. Enemy observation was so accurate that someone remarked that enemy observers were "right in the battalion perimeter."

During the night before the attack, preparations were being made with dispatch. Concerned that he could lose the services of CCA before any appreciable hole had been made in the enemy's defenses,

Malony was determined to get it into action at once. General Cheadle, along with General Colson, went to Colonel Martin's battalion
to see if things could be improved to help CCA make an armored attack. Cheadle ordered Colonel Martin to have his battalion attack before dawn to prepare the way for the armor. Martin explained to the
generals that "his men were exhausted and that the battalion was so
far under strength that it could not possibly accomplish the task." He
added that if ordered he would attack, but that he believed a fresh
battalion had a much better chance of success.

Martin's suggestion was discussed and approved by Cheadle and
Colson. Referred to General Malony, a change was approved and put
into effect. The 7th Armored Infantry Battalion would make the initial attack. Early in the morning, Generals Malony and Devine came
to Nennig to observe Combat Command A's attack.

Colonel Poinier's men moved out at dawn with Companies A and
B attacking and Company C in reserve. Greeted by intense enemy
fire, the attacking line made it to the antitank ditch, which had been
successfully breached during darkness by Capt. James J. Gettings's
Company A of the 53d Armored Engineer Battalion. Having been
in the lines only one day, the infantrymen of the 8th Armored had
not acquired the camouflage clothing necessary in the snowy area
and stood out as clear targets to the enemy in their olive drab uniforms.

In addition to the usual artillery and mortar fire, enemy sniper
and automatic weapons fire began to cause severe casualties. Company C of the 18th Tank Battalion supported the attack and gradually the Americans made progress. Casualties were heavy, especially
among leaders. The commander of Company C, 18th Tank Battalion, and most of his platoon commanders fell, and the battalion operations officer took command briefly, only to be killed shortly
thereafter. Lieutenant Colonel Poinier was wounded by mortar fire,
and his replacement, Maj. Richard Moushegian, executive officer of
the 7th Armored Infantry, also was wounded. All senior officers of
the battalion having fallen, Capt. Harry Craddock, battalion intelligence officer, took command.

Just as had the men of the 94th Infantry Division, the men of Combat Command A learned how to overcome seemingly impregnable

defenses. A bazooka team consisting of Pfc. Joseph L. Bisch and Wilfred L. Murray Jr. crawled behind the German defenses under small arms fire and employed their weapon against the enemy positions. Unable to pry open the wooden ammunition box with their frozen hands, they used their teeth to do it. Then they knocked out one of the pillboxes holding up the advance and took fifteen prisoners.

Generals Devine and Colson were up front throughout the attack. They observed their men's reactions to battle and encouraged them to push forward. Colson's brigadier general's star was knocked from his helmet by an artillery fragment during the attack. The men of the combat command responded to their leaders' presence and, although suffering severe casualties, moved forward into the German defenses. Captain Grover B. Herman's Company B, supported by the tanks of 3d Platoon, Company C, 18th Tank Battalion, bypassed the enemy strongpoint at Schloss Berg and managed to seize the high ground behind the enemy. Attacking the last enemy position, Captain Herman was killed, and 2d Lt. Arthur J. Fisher, the sole officer left in the company, led the final assault. By day's end privates were leading squads and in some cases platoons. Most platoons were now led by sergeants.

Despite these heavy losses, the 7th Armored Infantry, supported by the 18th Tank Battalion, cleared Berg by midday. Only the enemy strongpoint at the castle remained. For days the 94th Infantry Division had poured artillery fire on this position, without noticeable results. Now the artillery of CCA tried, and again no noticeable results could be seen. General Colson ordered Lt. Andrew T. Boggs's 3d Platoon, Company C, 18th Tank Battalion, supported by Lt. John D. Stinson's Tank Assault Gun Platoon, to move forward and fire directly on the castle.

The 105mm guns of the assault gun platoon, aided by fire from the 398th Armored Field Artillery Battalion, caused the fire from the castle to slacken. Company B, 7th Armored Infantry, advanced to the antitank ditch surrounding the building, where they quickly found themselves trapped by automatic weapons fire. Like the men of the infantry division before them, they were now pinned down in ice water up to their waists, and soon lost men to frostbite and trench foot. The company was forced to withdraw.

Despite this temporary setback, the constant artillery and direct fire began to tell on the German troops. Late in the afternoon, Lt. Peter F. Godwin's platoon of Troop A, 88th Cavalry Reconnaissance Squadron, managed to storm the castle and take thirty-three prisoners, the survivors of the enemy force. Once inside they learned why it had been held so stubbornly. As one American described it, "The luxuries enjoyed by the enemy in the Schloss—food, liquor, and even heated rooms—were beyond belief." For men who had existed for days on "C rations so thoroughly frozen that only the biscuits and candy were edible," this was almost unbelievable.

With the capture of Berg and its castle, the task force had accomplished its objectives. It counted five destroyed Mark IV tanks, seventy-two prisoners, and uncounted enemy dead. To accomplish this, the task force had lost three M-4 tanks and four half-tracks. Personnel casualties had been heavy, especially among its leaders. There remained the task of resupply and evacuation of wounded. As always in the Saar-Moselle Triangle, this was easier said than done. Lieutenant Sidney Grau, the battalion surgeon, set up his aid station in a building as the attack started. Later that day he was asked by the 8th Armored Division's surgeon why he was using a ruined building in danger of collapse as an aid station. Lieutenant Grau explained that the building had been in good condition when he had set up, and since then he had been too busy to move. Corporal Robert A. Shapiro of headquarters company, 7th Armored Infantry, was driving wounded to the rear for treatment, using his half-track. On one trip he was blown completely out of it, yet got back in and continued to transport wounded men to safety.

The morning had been a difficult one for General Malony. He received several calls from XX Corps asking about progress, and explained that things were going slowly. General Walker told Malony that he was not satisfied with progress and that he was taking all restrictions off use of both the 94th Infantry Division's resources and those of the attached units as well. Before Malony could act upon Walker's message the news came that Berg had fallen and the castle had been taken.

Walker's concerns reflected the Third Army commander's. General Patton was having a bad week. Third Army had been ordered to send reinforcements to Sixth Army Group to help them reduce the Colmar pocket. Patton sent the 101st Airborne Division, which had recently been relieved from its epic defense of Bastogne. The 10th Armored was also sent to Sixth Army Group. Patton feared that he would lose more troops unless he could show a clear breakthrough somewhere on his front. Although all his corps were attacking, none yet showed a clear indication of penetrating the German defenses. In XX Corps, the 95th Infantry Division was being replaced by the 26th Division. The 95th was being sent to Ninth Army while the 26th was in the XX Corps area to rest and regroup after fighting in the Ardennes. Losing full-strength units and having them replaced with combat-weary formations did not sit well with General Patton, who saw it as a part of the general conspiracy to keep him out of the forefront of a victorious campaign. His anger grew daily and would soon be vented on General Malony and the men of the 94th Infantry Division.

Meanwhile, Malony continued to do his best with the resources at hand. In addition to the use of the armor of the 8th Armored Division, he was gratified to learn of the arrival of shoepacs for his infantry. Because the front-line soldier lived in the cold, wet, snow-and-ice conditions for days or weeks at a time, many casualties had resulted from frostbite and trench foot. The arrival of shoepacs would help alleviate this problem.

The taking of Berg on the twenty-fifth had cleared things for the attack on Sinz. Although originally designed as a possible diversion, the success at Berg released additional troops for the Sinz attack. This now became the prime division objective, because if successful it would herald a clear breakthrough. The assault battalions were to be the 2d Battalion of the 302d Infantry, and the 3d Battalion of the 376th Infantry, under the overall command of Col. Harold H. Mc-Clune, commander of the 376th Infantry. The initial objective of the attack was the wooded ridge overlooking Sinz.

The 3d Battalion's attack was led by 2d Lt. Dale E. Bowyer's 3d Platoon of Company I. As they approached the line of departure there were several explosions and Lieutenant Bowyer fell, seriously wounded by a mine blast. Men of his platoon rushed to his aid, only to fall victim to other mines. Lieutenant Bowyer (awarded the Distinguished Service Cross), although he'd had his feet blown off by the explosions, refused medical treatment, and, together with the platoon leader of the 2d Platoon, Lieutenant Joseph Klutsh, also wounded, organized the attacking-force survivors and directed the evacuation of the other wounded. Both officers then refused aid and crawled back on their own to the aid station some four hundred yards to the rear.

Enemy artillery fire began to fall on the attacking troops, and efforts at mine detecting failed because the minefield consisted of plastic and wooden "shu" (sic) mines. Although enemy machine-gun fire was stopped by accurate counterfire from the battalion mortars, the attack remained stalled at the line of departure.

The attack of the 2d Battalion, 302d, was not affected by the minefield encountered by the 376th. Both assault companies moved forward, and although Company F lost several men at the edge of the minefield, the advance did not halt and the initial objective of the woods was reached by Colonel Norman's battalion, which dug in waiting for further orders.

In order to replace the stalled 3d Battalion, 376th, Colonel McClune ordered his reserve battalion, Colonel Minor's 1st Battalion, 376th Infantry, to follow the route of Norman's men to secure the right flank of the attack. Although under artillery fire, Colonel Minor's men moved forward without delay.

While awaiting the arrival of the 1st Battalion, Colonel Norman's battalion had observed tanks approaching. As CCA of the 8th Armored was to assist in this attack, Norman inquired of General Cheadle if these were American tanks. Cheadle informed him that there were none in the vicinity. Friendly artillery fire was directed promptly at this enemy armor, and the now accompanying infantry. The counterattack was repulsed by the artillery fire and by Capt. James W. Griffin of Company G, who rallied his men and directed his bazooka teams against the attacking vehicles. After the enemy had been repulsed, German artillery fire was directed against the battalion, which dug in as best it could for protection from the deadly tree bursts.

Colonel Minor's 1st Battalion made contact with the men of Colonel Norman's battalion and coordinated a defensive line together. While Companies B and C were on the line, Company A, commanded by Capt. Chester B. Dadisman, remained in reserve in Monkey Wrench Woods. Captain Dadisman ordered Sgt. Joseph Sanniec to take a patrol to the rear and establish a safe route for resupply and evacuation. While on this mission Sanniec's patrol also checked the Nennig-Tettingen road for mines. As they moved along the road, they noticed several men to the north in American uniforms. Calling out to the strangers, they learned that they had found the lost platoon of Company L.

When Lieutenant Travers had left his platoon in the defensive positions surrounded by the enemy, to get help before the counterattack of the 11th Panzer Division overwhelmed his men, he had no idea of what had occurred after his departure. Platoon Sergeant Arnold A. Petry had taken command. Only six years immigrated from Germany, where he had been a member of the Hitler Youth, Sergeant Petry found the food supply to be his first problem on taking command. There was only one can of C rations for the entire platoon. Between artillery barrages, the Americans searched the equipment of German dead within their position and found a slice of black bread, a bag of biscuits, and a can of meat. One of the soldiers remembered leaving a can of C rations back in the former position and SSgt. Victor J. Carnaghi crawled back to locate the food. Unfortunately, after a hazardous trip under enemy fire, Carnaghi discovered the food was out of reach at the bottom of a foxhole covered completely by a tree felled by artillery fire.

By day's end the troops knew that Lieutenant Travers was not returning, so for the next two days they stayed in position, rotating guard and awaiting relief. Disappointed as they were, no thought of surrender was discussed. After three days trapped behind enemy lines they decided that because no help was coming, they should break out to reach friendly lines. Led by scouts Pfc. John A. Dresser and James F. Meneses, they looked all through the third night for a route out, without success. The food was gone and the cold was causing constant suffering. Patrols were sent out to find a route home, but none met with any success. Thirst became a critical problem, but eating snow was not a viable alternative. Instead, the men filled their helmets with snow and sat on them until it thawed enough to provide some drinking water. There was also a small brook running near their position, which they used occasionally until Sergeant Sanniec discovered them. Miraculously only one man was killed during the ordeal. Having lasted for seven days in Company L's former position, they had redeemed Captain Smith's prophecy to Captain Bowden a week earlier.

Combat Command A was still attempting to move forward. Company A of the 53d Armored Engineer Battalion, supported again by Troop A of the 88th Reconnaissance Squadron, moved forward to bridge two known antitank ditches that lay to the front. Mines were a constant hazard, but the engineers managed to clear the first ditch and a path for the armor following. The attacking force this time was Task Force Goodrich. After being led across the antitank ditch by the 7th Armored Infantry Battalion, Capt. Odin Brendengen's Company A of the 18th Tank Battalion attacked toward Sinz, only to learn that they could not pass over a second antitank ditch. They were forced to halt under heavy mortar and artillery fire, as was the accompanying infantry of the 2d Battalion, 302d Infantry. After repelling a brief armor counterattack, the men and equipment of Task Force Goodrich were withdrawn into Nennig while the 302d held the front lines.

During the night, the engineers erected a treadway bridge over the second ditch, and on the morning of the twenty-seventh Capt. Russell D. Miller's Company B of the 18th led the attack toward Sinz. Approaching the bridge, Miller discovered that the enemy had moved an antitank gun into position and was able to prevent any armor from crossing. Looking for another route not covered by enemy fire, Russell moved his tanks to the left, uncovering an ambush consisting of fifteen enemy tanks concealed in the woods. Obviously, the Germans had known of the engineers' work and set up an ambush to attack the force they knew would follow.

Having been advised that there was no enemy armor in the area, the tankers, although surprised, recovered quickly, producing a tank-versus-tank battle. The novice Americans gave a good account of themselves, knocking out four Mark IV tanks, the antitank gun that had held them up at the ditch, and an antiaircraft gun also used against them. By early afternoon Company B was running out of ammunition and gasoline. Advising the task force commander, Captain

Miller was told that Company A would pass through and continue the attack.

Company A pushed to the ridge overlooking Sinz, where the armor of Task Force Goodrich could fire directly into the town to support the 302d Infantry's attack. By late afternoon, Company A had also exhausted its ammunition and fuel, so Capt. Paul R. Halderson's Company D was passed through to continue the attack. Led by 1st Lt. James P. Bolinger, Company D moved into Sinz itself. Within moments after destroying a Mark IV, Lieutenant Bolinger's tank was knocked out by a *Panzerfaust,* so he transferred to another tank to continue the attack. By darkness the combined armor-infantry force had cleared most of the town, but the task force had six tanks destroyed and four disabled. Having accomplished most of their mission, they called the 7th Armored Infantry Battalion forward to join with the 1st Battalion, 302d Infantry, in clearing the rest of the area. But before operations could begin on 28 January, the task force commander, Colonel Goodrich, was ordered to cease all operations and withdraw to join the rest of the 8th Armored Division. The Tornado Division was being sent out of Third Army's area.

While the men of CCA were fighting their way into Sinz, the infantries of the 302d and 376th were operating alongside them. The 1st Battalion, 376th, had begun to move toward Sinz when they were hit by a part of the same armor-infantry attack that struck Task Force Goodrich. After repelling that attack, Minor's battalion was relieved by Lieutenant Colonel Thurston's 3d Battalion. Although the 1st Battalion had been halted by the enemy counterattack, the adjoining battalion, Colonel Norman's 2d Battalion of the 302d, attacked as scheduled. Within minutes Norman was a casualty, so the executive officer, Maj. Harold V. Maixner, took command. The attack continued and the unit moved into Sinz. As they approached, the men of Company G were fired upon by one of Task Force Goodrich's tanks, who mistook them for enemy troops. Several casualties were inflicted before Sgt. Edward P. Regan jumped on the tank and clarified the situation. Moving farther into town, Company G was pinned down by sniper fire coming from a barn. Private James Guerrier fired his light machine gun from the hip, using tracer ammunition that set the barn on fire. Exhausting his own ammunition, Guerrier picked up ammunition from a nearby tank and killed the snipers as they ran from the burning barn.

By the end of the day, Major Maixner had two companies in Sinz, but the combined strength of Companies E and G numbered less than one full-strength company. His reserve, Company F, had only sixty effective fighters left. Maixner advised Colonel McClune, who ordered him to rest and refit. Reinforcements in the shape of eighty men drawn from the 376th Antitank Company, armed as riflemen, were attached to Major Maixner's battalion. Plans were being made to attack again the following morning in conjunction with the 7th Armored Infantry Battalion to secure Sinz once and for all. But before dawn, word came that the 8th Armored Division was being withdrawn and all attacks should cease.

General Malony tried with everything at his disposal to make the final break in the German line. He had asked the chief of staff of the 8th Armored if it was possible to commit more armor to the attack but was told that weather and terrain precluded this. Malony turned to his neighbors across the Moselle River, the 2d Cavalry Group. This unit was a part of Third Army's XII Corps and was charged with maintaining contact between the two corps. They held positions across the Moselle and were able on occasion to get across the river behind the German defenses. On 26 January they tried to outflank the enemy facing the 94th but were quickly pushed back to their own side of the river. General Walker then appeared at division headquarters on the afternoon of the twenty-sixth, again demanding progress. It was a few hours after Walker left that his chief of staff called to advise Malony that the twenty-seventh of January was the last day that XX Corps could use the 8th Armored Division.

Similar messages came in all day long on 27 January. By nightfall Malony knew that the 8th Armored Division was leaving that night and that there would be no replacement. As it had been for weeks, the 94th would again have to carry the offensive alone. Knowing that his men had no hope of holding against an armored counterattack, Malony reluctantly called upon Colonel McClune to withdraw from Sinz. Having cleared his decision with General Walker, who authorized him to "change the line as he saw fit," Malony ordered McClune's remnants to withdraw to the high ground overlooking Sinz.

Withdrawing from Sinz was as difficult as getting into the town had been. Company B of the 7th Armored Infantry had remained behind in Sinz to secure some of the task force's disabled armored vehicles until they could be towed back for repairs. They spent the morning of the twenty-eighth with the 302d Infantry engaged in fending off a counterattack. By the time the attack was beaten off, they had spent most of an extra day in battle. Overall, CCA of the 8th Armored Division, which had contributed greatly to the reduction of the German defenses, had lost twenty-three men killed in action, and 268 wounded. Most casualties were incurred by the 7th Armored Infantry Battalion in only two days of combat. By nightfall of the twenty-eighth, CCA and the rest of the 8th Armored Division had left the 94th's zone of combat and prepared to move to a new assignment in the Ninth Army's area.

As the final disappointment to a promising few days, General Walker contacted General Malony and ordered him to rest and reorganize his division, while continuing to launch small attacks "by a battalion at a time pecking off little spaces." It appeared that the division was back where it had started weeks before.

CHAPTER 11
HOLDING THE LINE

XX Corps had been battering against the Saar-Moselle Triangle defenses for more than two weeks without a breakthrough. The loss of its only armored unit, Combat Command A of the 8th Armored Division, put a halt to further efforts. For the time being the corps would hold its positions, improve them as best it could, and await further orders. The 95th Infantry Division, which had been under orders to move and therefore took no part in operations, left to join Ninth Army in the north, and was replaced by the exhausted 26th Infantry Division.

The 26th was drawn from the Massachusetts National Guard. Known as the "Yankee Division," it had a distinguished record in the First World War. Called into federal service in January of 1941 as a "square," or four-regiment, division, it lost two of its regiments to other divisions, while acquiring a draftee regiment as a replacement, making it a standard triangular-type division. This turbulence of integral units was undoubtedly the result of concern expressed from losses suffered by individual communities when the units recruited from one local area suffered excessive casualties. Filled in with draftees, the division completed its training and departed the United States on 20 August 1944.

The division landed in Normandy on 7 September 1944 and was assigned defensive duties until October, when it was assigned to the Third Army's XII Corps and joined the offensive that carried it across France. Then the "Yankee Division" attacked the German-occupied Maginot Line defenses until early December, when it was pulled out of the line and sent to Metz to rest and regroup. After barely ten days' rest, it was called back to the front to participate in the defeat of the German counteroffensive in the Ardennes. Throughout December and January, Patton's "cold weather boys" fought in the Ardennes, recovering the critical towns of Wiltz and Clerf. Exhausted, at the end of January the division was sent to XX Corps to rest and refit. On 28 January it relieved the 95th Infantry Division and moved in beside the 94th Infantry Division.

The 26th Infantry Division was commanded throughout its combat career by Maj. Gen. Willard S. Paul. Born 28 February 1894, he enlisted in the Colorado National Guard as a private during the Mexican border crisis of 1916. Commissioned a second lieutenant in the regular army on 5 June 1917, he was assigned to the 11th Division and went to France in October 1918 with its advance detachment. Arriving too late to see combat, Paul returned to the United States and had several staff appointments until he attended the Infantry School, graduating in June 1921. During a tour teaching military science and tactics at Johns Hopkins University, he earned a bachelor of science degree there.

After assignments with infantry units, he returned to the Infantry School, Fort Benning, Georgia, and attended the advanced course. Graduating in June 1930, he remained as an instructor. Later, he graduated from the Command and General Staff School and again taught tactics, this time at Culver Military Academy in Indiana. Graduating from the Army War College in 1937, he was then assigned to a number of staff appointments in Washington, DC. After the war broke out, he commanded the Seventh Service Command in Missouri, and later activated the 75th Infantry Division. In August 1943 he was assigned to command the 26th Infantry Division, a post he held until June of 1945.

As January drew to a close, most allied forces around the world were in a preparatory stance, waiting to move against Axis forces. In the northernmost group of armies on the continent, the 21st Army Group, composed of British, Canadians, and Americans, were preparing to clear the Ruhr River sector as a prelude to a Rhine crossing. The 12th Army Group under General Bradley was still clearing the remnants of the Ardennes counteroffensive and looking toward entering Germany. South of Third Army, General Devers's 6th Army

Group was clearing the remnants of the German counteroffensive in that area and also preparing to enter Germany. The Colmar pocket still concerned Devers and his men, but additional American units were now being sent to assist the French facing that German enclave west of the Rhine.

In Italy, the 15th Army Group was reorganizing its Fifth U.S. and Eighth British Armies to begin the final campaign in that theater. In the Pacific, the Navy and Marines were about to assault Iwo Jima, while in the Philippines the Sixth Army continued to clear Luzon. On the eastern front, Russian forces entered Germany, seized several major towns in East Prussia, and established a siege of the fortress city of Königsberg. Once this bastion fell, the Russian advance would continue.

The Ghost Corps was no exception to this waiting phenomenon. The loss of the 8th Armored and the 95th Infantry Divisions had made the seizure of the Saar-Moselle Triangle remote with the resources at hand. The 94th Division was the only combat-ready force available to it at the end of January 1945. The 26th Infantry Division was exhausted and integrating replacements, while the 3d Cavalry Group was underequipped to make any real progress. Alone, the 94th could not carry on the advance.

Waiting was not something that General Patton accepted willingly. Convinced that the time to strike was now, despite fatigue and understrength units, he could not convince any of his superiors of the validity of his thinking. Frustrated by Generals Eisenhower and Bradley, Patton strove to use his own resources to fulfill his ideas. Together with Maj. Gen. Manton S. Eddy, commander of the XII Corps, he planned an attack east toward the city of Trier and into the German Palatinate. Eddy agreed to attack on the sixth of February, but Patton insisted on attacking on the fourth. The attack was never executed, however, because of orders from the 12th Army Group to halt offensive action and that no armored support would be provided to the planned XII Corps attack.

These orders came on top of 12th Army Group's refusal to return one of Patton's favorite divisions, the 35th Infantry, to Third Army. Yet another blow came when he learned that Third Army would not attack into the Palatinate, but would move north to support First Army. Seventh Army was designated to attack into the Palatinate.

As he often did when frustrated or angry, Patton went out to visit his troops. On 30 January he began his round of visits by going to Bastogne to visit with Maj. Gen. Troy H. Middleton and his VIII Corps. Moving south, he visited several of his divisions in each of the corps, and on 1 February was in the XX Corps zone. He had by this time learned of the indefinite postponement of General Eddy's attack, so what was left of his good humor had deserted him. It was at this juncture that General Walker called General Malony and ordered him to get "as many senior officers and unit commanders down to noncoms of each company that could be assembled without too much trouble" at the division's reserve position in the town of Veckring by 2:30 P.M.

Arriving a few minutes early at division headquarters, Patton, accompanied by Walker, announced to Malony and his assembled staff "that 94th was only Div in Army whose nonbattle casualties exceeded its battle casualties." Patton, Walker, and Malony with their staffs then went to Veckring, where Patton repeated his statements to the assembled officers and men of the 94th. Patton included the number of prisoners lost by the division in his complaint. What the troops did not know was that after threatening General Malony with relief, he then turned as he was leaving and remarked to Malony, "You're doing fine otherwise—but Goddammit, do something about those slackers." What neither Patton nor Malony was aware of was that Patton's figures were wrong.

The men of the 94th Infantry Division who knew of General Patton's visit found it "interesting." One squad leader present "found Patton impressive—after his first few sentences. It was kind of startling to hear this famous general, a big strong man, about six feet two inches tall, carrying fancy revolvers, speak in a high, squeaky voice." Feeling that while at home the general's speech may have sounded silly, the background of bursting artillery made it seem real. "He complimented us first, telling us we had done a good job, then he lit into us, telling us that in the last week we had lost more men in nonbattle casualties (trench foot) and had had more men captured than any division in the 3d Army and that was not acceptable."

Considering that most of the men in the division had only just received adequate winter footwear, a responsibility of Third Army Headquarters, Patton's comments were as much a criticism of his own staff as that of the infantrymen he addressed.

Patton returned to his headquarters and more frustration. Called to a meeting at 12th Army Group, he learned that his worst fears had come to pass. General Eisenhower had ordered that 21st Army Group, under Field Marshal Montgomery, would be given priority on supplies and equipment in order to launch a massive assault to and across the Rhine in northern Germany. Patton did manage, however, to obtain permission to continue with his ongoing attacks until Montgomery's attack was launched, which was expected on or about 10 February.

Returning to his headquarters, Patton began to look for a breakthrough anywhere on his front, knowing that neither General Eisenhower nor Bradley would stop an ongoing successful attack into the German homeland. His two best opportunities appeared to be in General Eddy's XII Corps zone, near to the German city of Trier, gateway to the Palatinate, and in General Walker's XX Corps zone, provided it could be accompanied with armor to create a clear breakthrough in the Saar-Moselle region.

At the front in the Orscholz Switchline, the 94th, still stinging from the lash of General Patton's outburst, paused to regroup and refit. Its battalions were mixed together, with regimental unity lost due to the needs of combat. It was the most understrength infantry division in Third Army due to its recent losses, and it needed an opportunity to receive and integrate its new replacements. To accomplish this, General Malony ordered the battalions returned to their parent regiments. The 301st Infantry was to reorganize holding the right of the division's line, while the 302d Infantry would do the same on the left. The 376th Infantry would go into reserve. By nightfall of 1 February these plans were well along. But barely had the 376th Infantry arrived in the reserve area when orders from General Walker arrived for the resumption of limited-objective attacks not to exceed one regiment in strength.

Things were also difficult for the defenders of the Triangle. The elite 11th Panzer Division was forced to draft replacements from hospitals in order to keep enough men in line for defense. One such replacement was captured by Company I of the 376th Infantry. He informed his interrogators that those selected for the division spoke of being assigned to *"Der himmelfahrt Kommando"* or "The command ascending to heaven." The German commanders had also noted the arrival of "elements, at least, of a new armored division," a reference to CCA of the 8th Armored. They decried the lack of sufficient tanks to stop the American attacks, as well as a growing weakness in their armored infantry units. While citing the paucity of fuel to properly support their infantry with armor, they also blamed the weather for not being sufficiently cold to freeze over the rivers, which would allow the heavier divisional tanks to cross and enter the battle. Patrols had crossed the Moselle, much like American patrols from the XII Corps's 2d Cavalry Group, and ascertained that there were no strong American forces present, thereby allowing the defenders to concentrate their resources against XX Corps.

CHAPTER 12
RECONNAISSANCE
IN FORCE

While XX Corps was awaiting additional troops or different instructions, the infantry continued to eat away at the Siegfried Switchline. Both the weather and insufficient armor in support made all such attacks dangerous and costly. Nonbattle casualties continued to occur due to the high water table, about four inches below the surface, and the continuing poor weather conditions: "light and intermittent drizzles with a rising temperature that reached 32° above zero." Not only did the weather increase casualties, but it prevented yet another supporting arm, the air corps, from coming to the assistance of the struggling infantrymen.

Not that efforts weren't made to get the army air force into the battle. XIX Tactical Air Command was quite willing to lend its support to the infantry. In order to make sure that the pilots of the support aircraft could readily identify both Allied and enemy positions, it sent forward to the infantry several pilots to see firsthand, and at ground level, the characteristics of the terrain. "This was just after the big thaw and the melting snow had left mud everywhere—especially on us," noted Sgt. Robert K. Adair of Company I, 376th Infantry. "The pilots picking their way along the muddy path past our positions found it hard to believe that anyone could live in such circumstances. We were amused when they asked if we went back to town at night, and I'm not sure they believed us when we said no."

To continue to reduce enemy defenses in the Saar-Moselle Triangle, and yet remain within SHAEF and Third Army instructions not to commit to a major attack, XX Corps began what is recorded as a "reconnaissance in force," to cover the ongoing attacks into the Triangle.

The first of these involved the reconstituted 1st Battalion, 301st Infantry, which had been decimated during the battle for Orscholz. Lieutenant Harrison H. Walker's Company A, which had lost half its strength at Orscholz, led the attack on the castle known as Schloss Bübingen. This fortified building stood just to the north of the village of Wies and had harassed all American efforts in the area of Nennig and Berg. Suspicions that it was being used as an enemy observation post and an assembly point for German counterattacks caused it to be placed on the list of targets for the authorized limited-objective attacks.

Every effort was made to ensure that the attack was successful and that the battalion regained its confidence. The XX Corps artillery brought forward one self-propelled 155mm gun from the 558th Field Artillery Battalion to place direct and devastating fire on the building. Under the fire of this gun, Company A attacked. Two platoons rushed toward the building as the artillery crew shifted their fire to adjoining enemy positions, permitting the infantry to get under the protection of the castle walls. Lieutenant Walker led his men toward the front door of the castle, only to be wounded and see his men repulsed. Five of the men with the lieutenant did manage to find a way into the castle, only to be bottled up inside by the enemy. The remaining platoon, under TSgt. George Montgomery, saw the attempt and decided to enter the castle by blowing a way in through the walls. Finding that the equipment they carried was inadequate, they sent for the engineers.

Sergeant Joseph C. Castanzo of Company A, 319th Engineer Combat Battalion, brought forward and placed the ordered explosives. Working under direct enemy fire, it took nearly four hours to site and fire the demolitions. The explosion had the desired effect, dazing the defenders and opening a way into the castle. Staff Sergeant Harry T. Schmidt and Pfcs. B. D. Tarbel and Afton B. Bullard charged through the opening with a flamethrower and Browning automatic rifle, swiftly eliminating all opposition. Several enemy soldiers were killed, including the radio operator observing for the artillery. Forty-two prisoners were taken. Later, the company cleared the surrounding buildings and settled in to defend their positions. A German counterattack late that day was easily repulsed. The 1st Battalion, 301st Infantry, was again an effective force.

Next on the list of limited objectives was Campholz Woods. This heavily wooded ridge had served repeatedly as the launching point for German counterattacks and provided observation on the supply routes into the villages held by the 94th. This enabled the German artillery and mortars to accurately disrupt attempts at reinforcement or resupply. In addition some of the towns they could observe had been designated as divisional rest areas. Several structures had been established as "hash houses" to permit the men an opportunity to get dry shoes and socks, hot food, and coffee. Comfortable mattresses were set up in cellars for the men to rest and relax. The intent was to reduce the number of nonbattle casualties. Conditions would improve if the enemy could no longer harass this one bright spot in the infantryman's existence.

Company C of the 302d Infantry drew the assignment of clearing Campholz Woods. Moving out at 4:00 A.M. on 1 February, the company initially encountered only sporadic resistance, capturing intact an entire German artillery observation party. As the company moved deeper into the woods its major opposition was from enemy minefields, which claimed several victims. After they reached a communication trench and paused to reorganize, the enemy reacted. Rockets, artillery, and mortar fire began to fall with intensity on the woods. Unable to advance farther, the company held its positions throughout the afternoon. During the night, Company B moved forward and assumed responsibility for half of the line.

The following day the two companies resumed the attack. Company B made good progress against the entrenched enemy, capturing several pillboxes and prisoners. Company C, suffering more from enemy minefields, similarly moved forward and captured seventy-five prisoners whom they used to transport American wounded to the rear. As darkness fell once again, Company A moved forward and relieved Company B. Although a major portion of the woods had been cleared, the Germans, from the 11th Panzer Division, did not move back. Instead they clung closely to the American forward positions, making evacuation of the wounded difficult. Only the courage of aidmen such as T/3 John Asmussen saved many wounded. Moving through known minefields, Asmussen gathered wounded soldiers into a bunker, ignoring the fact that one of the men attempting to assist him was killed at his side by a mine, where he treated the wounded by candlelight. So close were the panzer grenadiers that they were able to throw grenades through the door of the bunker from their own concealed positions. Finally, aided by a mortar barrage and the assistance of Capt. (Chaplain) Edward H. Harrison, T-3 Asmussen managed to move the wounded to safety.

Getting supplies in was as difficult as getting the wounded out. Enemy observation continued to be excellent; all routes of resupply were closely watched, often shelled, and always made dangerous. The supply officer of the 1st Battalion, 302d Infantry, Lt. Joseph P. Concannon, wouldn't let that stop him from supplying his men in the woods. Going to the 465th Antiaircraft Artillery Battalion, he borrowed several half-tracks to carry supplies forward. These vehicles, very lightly armored, were no protection against the shelling, but using speed and luck, Lieutenant Concannon and his assistant, Sgt. Robert H. Fluch, managed to keep supplies flowing to the infantry.

For the next two days, 3 and 4 February, the 1st Battalion mopped up in the area of the woods they had seized. Several bunkers and entrenchments had been bypassed or left on the fringes of the American perimeter, and these were now reduced individually. In one instance, on the morning of 3 February, 1st Lt. Carl J. Baumgaertner took four men forward to attack an enemy bunker that threatened the battalion's flank. Moving in darkness and fog, they at first couldn't find their objective, but help came from the enemy when they heard German voices. Throwing in a hand grenade, Baumgaertner announced in fluent German to the enemy soldiers that the position was surrounded and that if they did not immediately surrender, a flamethrower would be used against them. Thirteen Germans promptly surrendered their entrenched position to five Americans who had no flamethrower. Not all such attempts were successful. The following day Baumgaertner made two attempts to reduce an enemy observation bunker that had been directing harassing fire on the American positions. Both were unsuccessful, even with artillery and mortar support.

After four days of fighting in the Campholz Woods, the 1st Battalion was relieved by the 2d Battalion. Just prior to the relief, Company C made a full-scale attack on the observation bunker, supported by the full assets of the 301st Field Artillery Battalion. When they ran into newly laid minefields, the attack was once again repulsed. This stubborn position now became the problem of Major Maixner's 2d Battalion.

Although there were some positions left untaken, the work of the 1st Battalion had pleased division headquarters. General Cheadle, who had been observing the attacks, reported that the battalion "was getting along all right." Later the same day, shortly before the battalion was to be relieved, he advised General Malony that the battalion had "accomplished its mission successfully as of 1500. Approx 100 prisoners, approx 55 casualties."

The 2d Battalion had not had an opportunity to rest or receive replacements. After leaving Sinz it had marched across the division's front to return to its parent regiment. During the march, several men were lost to shelling while others succumbed to the crippling trench foot from the Sinz battle. Even while supposedly in reserve, the battalion had unsuccessfully attempted to seize two pillboxes in its area, near Orscholz. Despite its condition the battalion relieved its sister battalion in Campholz Woods during the night of 5–6 February. Company E held the secured western half of the woods, while Company G, numbering only forty-five effectives, were on the eastern half.

During the next few days, benefiting from an attack being conducted by the division in the Sinz-Bannholz Woods area, the 2d Battalion seized a number of enemy pillboxes in and around Campholz Woods. Finally, only the observation-post bunker remained in enemy hands. This, however, was the critical position and had to be taken. Major Maixner ordered Company G to make the attempt. Led by Lt. Ralph E. Ginsburg and SSgt. Arthur Ernst, Company G, which now numbered only thirty-four men, was reinforced for this attack by the battalion's ammunition and pioneer platoon serving as infantry. Engineers from the 319th Engineer Combat Battalion were added to provide demolition and flamethrower support.

While the battalion commander, Maj. Harold V. Maixner, was coordinating supporting fires with Lt. Douglas A. Barrow, commanding the mortar platoon of Company H, a plan was prepared at Barrow's suggestion that a barrage be placed on the pillbox, then a brief halt to the barrage, followed by another heavy mortar barrage. Barrow had observed that the Germans took cover during the barrage, then rushed to their defensive positions the moment it lifted. He hoped to catch them in the open with an unexpected second barrage. For once, things went according to plan. The Germans were caught unaware and Company G seized the observation bunker against minor resistance. Although only four prisoners were taken, the Americans had removed a major thorn in their side. "From the bunker, the men looked toward Tettingen and Campholz in amazement. Both town and woods lay below them completely visible. The accuracy and intensity of the enemy artillery fire were then understandable."

General Malony notified General Walker of the seizure of Campholz Woods. Walker both congratulated Malony and instructed him to "congratulate your people down there for me too." Malony also learned that he had been awarded the Bronze Star for meritorious service during the last two weeks of January. Despite this good news, Malony remained frustrated at the lack of a clear break in the enemy's defenses. Earlier, on 3 February, he had called a conference of all his staff and regimental commanders to discuss the plan for future operations. The result of this meeting was Field Order Number 10.

While the 94th continued to hack away at the Siegfried Switchline, the 26th Division settled into its new positions. The 328th Infantry Regiment secured the right flank of XX Corps, and the 104th Infantry, reinforced by the 3d Battalion, 328th Infantry, held the rest of the front including the Saarlautern bridgehead across the Saar River. This small bridgehead had been inherited from the 95th Infantry Division and was Third Army's only existing bridgehead across that river. Holding the 101st Infantry in reserve, the division rested and reequipped as best it could. As additional support the division had the 5th Ranger Battalion attached.

Meanwhile, the supreme allied commander, General Eisenhower, was busying himself with broader matters. Writing to General Marshall on 9 February, he concerned himself with the matter of promotions for his leading generals and current operations. He expressed concern that while the U.S. Navy had many five- and four-star admirals, the army, much larger in size, was not, in Eisenhower's opinion, equally represented; so he pushed for promotions for Generals Bradley and Spaatz, his air commander. Eisenhower further explained that he had temporarily slowed his attacks in the Ardennes to concentrate on closing the Rhine in preparation for the final assault into Germany proper. He believed that Field Marshal Montgomery's attack had started well and that the long-festering Colmar pocket had been finally eliminated. Other issues were the improvement of the replacement centers that had recently been criticized for poor treatment of American soldiers, the project to retrain rear-area troops as infantrymen to alleviate the replacement shortage; and the possible use of black volunteers to be assigned in segregated units to combat forces. Finally, he offered General Marshall a list of "thirty to forty outstanding general officers arranged roughly in accordance with my ideas of the value of the services they have rendered in this war." Nowhere is there any mention of an attack to seize the area of Trier, nor an advance to the Palatinate by Patton's Third Army. Indeed Patton is mentioned only in passing as having already tried successfully to use segregated black combat platoons. Clearly, the efforts of General Malony's men, and the XX Corps in general, were not a pressing concern of General Eisenhower, were he even aware of them.

General George C. Marshall (wearing raincoat), senior American Army commander, in the field speaking to the troops. (National Archives)

General Patton meets with his corps commanders late in 1944. The officer standing to the right, front, is Gen. Walton M. Walker, commanding the Ghost Corps. (Courtesy Dwight D. Eisenhower Library)

Three high ranking officers of the 94th Infantry Division confer near Nennig, Germany. From left to right: Brig. Gen. Henry B. Cheadle, Maj. Gen. Harry J. Maloney, division commander, and Col. Roy N. Hagerty. (National Archives)

Generalfeldmarschall Gerd Von Rundstedt, commanding Oberbefahlshaber West, the senior German field commander facing the Allies on the western front. (National Archives)

Lieutenant General Jacob L. Devers, commanding Sixth U.S. Army Group. (Photos from the National Archives)

Generaloberst (Colonel General) Johannes Blaskowitz, commanding Army Group G.

Lieutenant General Alexander M. (Sandy) Patch, commanding Seventh U.S. Army.

Medal of Honor recipient MSgt. Nicholas B. Oresko, 94th Infantry Division.

Major General Walton Walker, Commanding XX Corps, Major General Morris, Commanding 10th Armored Division, confer with Lieutenant General Patton, commanding Third U.S. Army. (National Archives)

German dead are removed from Nennig, Germany, by men of the 302d Infantry, 94th Infantry Division. (National Archives)

Three men of Company D take cover in a ruined building, Nennig, Germany. (National Archives)

Troops of the 302d Infantry, 94th Division, follow white tape marking safe route through mined woods near Borg, Germany. (National Archives)

Troops of the 94th Infantry Division, Third Army, cleaning out snipers in Beurig, Germany. (National Archives)

Men of the 390th AAA Battalion, 26th Infantry Division, stand guard by their multiple .50 caliber machine guns near Saarlautern, Germany, 15 February 1945. (U.S. Army photo)

A platoon leader fires his M-1 rifle from a burning building which had been hit by mortar fire, Saarlautern, Germany, 16 February 1945. (U.S. Army photo)

Sentries from the 104th Infantry, 26th Infantry Division halt a jeep at a check-point near the Saar River Bridge, 18 February 1945. (U.S. Army photo)

Engineers of the 319th Engineer Combat Battalion, 94th Infantry Division, crossing footbridge over the Saar near Faber, Germany to build a ramp for the division's heavier vehicles. (National Archives)

Troops of the 10th Armored Division dig in to support the crossing of the Saar River near Saarburg, Germany, by the 376th Infantry Regiment. (National Archives)

German prisoners captured in Irsch, Germany, by the 61st Armored Infantry Battalion, 10th Armored Division, are marched to a tank roadblock for safekeeping, 22 February 1945. (U. S. Army photo)

Riflemen of Company B, 54th Armored Infantry Battalion and 90th Cavalry Reconnaissance Troop, guard the road to Saarburg in the early morning fog common to the area, 22 February 1945. (U.S. Army photo)

A half-track of the 10th Armored Division crosses a pontoon bridge over the Saar River in the 94th Infantry Division's Taben bridgehead, 25 February 1945. (U.S. Army photo)

Combat Command "B" of the 10th Armored Division moves through newly captured Irsch, Germany, 26 February 1945. (U.S. Army photo)

Artillerymen of the 10th Armored Division dig gun positions near Trier, Germany, 27 February 1945. (U.S. Army photo)

Major General Willard S. Paul, commanding General of the 26th Infantry Division, looks over map of his units' positions before leaving for the front, 1 March 1945. (U. S. Army photo)

Troops of Company C, 301st Infantry Regiment, march down a road near Sinz, Germany, to stop an armored counterattack. (National Archives)

Men and tanks of the 10th Armored Division advance cautiously across the bridge spanning the Moselle River which they had just captured at Trier, 5 March 1945. (U.S. Army photo)

CHAPTER 13
FIELD ORDER NUMBER 10

General Malony held a meeting with his staff and regimental commanders on 3 February as the result of his continuing frustration with the limited-objective attacks he had been held to by army and corps orders. Determined to produce a clear break in the enemy defenses in the Siegfried Switchline, he discussed with his commanders how best to accomplish this within the limits of a regimental attack, the largest authorized by General Walker. The defeat at Sinz still rankled with division headquarters, especially as it had come so close to success. It was decided that the regimental attack would be directed at Sinz and the adjacent Bannholz Woods. If this attack succeeded, another regimental attack would be mounted to seize Münzingen Ridge and the town of the same name. Combined with an attack on the town of Oberleuken, this would break once and for all the enemy defenses protecting the Saar-Moselle Triangle. The plan was issued as Field Order Number 10. The 301st Infantry was assigned the attack on Sinz-Bannholz, the 376th to the Münzingen Ridge attack, and the 302d Infantry to take Oberleuken. The starting date for this coordinated effort was to be 7 February.

General Walker came to the division headquarters on 5 February to review the plan contained in Field Order Number 10. Pleased with the plan, Walker approved it. Within hours of receiving Walker's approval, however, Malony was on the phone with General Collier, XX Corps chief of staff, complaining that he had just learned that the 704th Tank Destroyer Battalion had been ordered to leave the division on 8 February. The loss of this battalion would leave the division with only one tank-destroyer battalion, the 774th, severely impacting the success expected of Field Order Number 10. Collier called back to say that the 704th was being ordered out at General Patton's direction, but that the order could be delayed until the "ninth or tenth," which would give the division time at least to get its attack started. Although the 748th Tank Battalion had been ordered to the 94th Infantry Division, only a part of it had arrived, and every piece of armor was needed if the attack on Sinz was to succeed.

Preparatory work for the upcoming attack began immediately. Lieutenant Colonel Noel H. Ellis, the division's engineering officer, went over the ground and prepared to construct a supply road. Colonel Hagerty's 301st Infantry used the days preceding their attack to study the terrain and enemy defenses between them and their objective, Sinz. Lieutenant Colonel James M. Caviness's 919th Field Artillery Battalion plotted targets in Sinz itself, while the 356th Field Artillery Battalion planned to cover the approaches to the town. The 390th Field Artillery Battalion, a XX Corps unit, would use its delay-action artillery shells on Bannholz Woods itself. Company B of the 81st Chemical Mortar Battalion would deliver a smoke screen in front of Bannholz Woods before the attack, then move it as the attack progressed to continue protecting the assault forces. By 6 February, all was in readiness.

The attack of the 301st against Sinz went off as scheduled. Moving forward in the same cold, wet, and muddy conditions, the men of Lt. Col. Dohs's 2d Battalion managed to get into Sinz and began reducing the enemy house by house. German resistance was fierce and their artillery concentrations caused severe casualties among Company G's weapons platoon when they crossed their line of departure. Moving forward, the Americans were fortunate because a sudden thaw had melted the snow over a newly laid minefield, enabling them to see the now exposed mines and avoid them. Lieutenant Knox L. Scales's company moved from house to house in Sinz, using all available weapons to capture one after the other. German resistance continued to be intense and Lt. Sylvester Beyer, forward observer for the 356th Artillery, was forced to place artillery fire on each house in turn, while observing each fire from the house next door. Although dangerous, the procedure worked well enough to obtain for the Americans a secure hold on the southern portion of Sinz.

Meanwhile, Capt. Charles H. Sinclair's Company F moved past Sinz toward Bannholz Woods. Moving into the woods, Lt. Henry J. Smythe, another forward observer from the 356th Field Artillery, called back and asked that the preparatory barrage be lifted to allow Company F to enter the woods. The reply was that the 356th was not firing on Bannholz Woods. The fire was from the enemy guns, as the Germans had realized that the American attack must include the woods to be successful and planned their preventive fires accordingly. Nevertheless Company F moved into the woods.

Once inside, visibility dropped drastically. The smoke from the 81st Chemical Mortar Battalion began to drift back into the woods and this, combined with the dense trees, prevented the Americans from seeing very far. As a result, the 3d Platoon stumbled into two enemy tanks. A bazooka team consisting of Pfcs. Curtis C. Darnell and Ernest Atencio confronted the tanks and scored two hits, which did little to deter the enemy, now alerted to the presence of the 3d Platoon. Return fire wounded Atencio, and his place was immediately taken by Pfc. Stanley Bock. As the team was firing its third round, the enemy gunners scored a direct hit on the tree behind which the team sheltered. Both rounds hit together. The tree shattered, spraying wooden splinters into the bazooka team, incapacitating them. The tank, hit yet again, continued to fire at the platoon. With nothing left to deter enemy armor, the platoon withdrew. A report went back to division headquarters that tanks had been encountered in Bannholz Woods. General Cheadle immediately ordered tank destroyers sent up to the battalion.

The weapons platoon had begun to dig itself in at the edge of the woods. Meanwhile, the 2d Platoon, advancing alongside the 3d Platoon, also encountered tanks. The platoon called for artillery support, but all available artillery was being directed on Sinz, and none was available for Company F. Then, in midmorning, Captain Sinclair's men began to see German infantry move to support the tanks of the 4th Panzer Company. This force united and began to move forward to clear the woods. Unable to get close enough to use their bazookas due to the presence of the panzer grenadiers, the men of Company F had no defense against a counterattack. Lieutenant Smythe could not accurately direct artillery fire on the tanks as they began to mix within the lines of Company F. Captain Sinclair called Lieutenant Colonel Dohs, advised him of the situation, and received permission to withdraw.

As always in the Triangle, withdrawal was as difficult as attack. The machine gunners at the edge of the woods did not get the order to withdraw and neither did most of the 2d Platoon. These two groups remained in defensive positions at the edge of the woods, ignorant of the withdrawal. Under the command of Lt. John G. Trueis of the weapons platoon, who had already been wounded, these men soon saw the enemy tanks and infantry approaching their position. Without knowing the whereabouts of the rest of their company, these men prepared for a last-ditch defense. Fortunately, the enemy did not enter the woods and did not notice the Americans. The rest of Company F had retired safely to the woods outside of Sinz and reported that there were no living Americans in Bannholz Woods. The resulting artillery barrage pounded the woods, somehow missing the twenty-one Americans dug in at the edge. Unable to withdraw, these men had to wait until nightfall before attempting any escape. In the meantime they had to endure friendly fire.

Colonel Dohs had ordered up the battalion's antitank guns as soon as he learned of Company F's encounter. Moving his command post into Sinz, still bitterly contested, he also ordered up his reserve company, Capt. Walter J. Stockstad's Company E. This unit was ordered to assist Company G in clearing Sinz. Although about half the one hundred buildings had been taken, the attack was still bitterly opposed. Casualties in Company G had been heavy, so they could no longer cover the entire area of the attack. The remainder of the day was exhausted in clearing Sinz, using both companies. By late afternoon Sinz belonged to the 301st Infantry, which sent over two hundred Germans back to the division's prisoner-of-war enclosures. Nightfall also brought an end to the trials of the remnants of Company F in Bannholz Woods. Under cover of darkness, they filtered through enemy positions and managed successfully to reach the rest of their comrades.

The following morning Lieutenant Colonel Dohs used the attached Company L to clear the area immediately around Sinz of enemy pillboxes. Moving out to the slopes of Münzingen Ridge, the company successfully seized several enemy positions, and by midday prepared defensive positions to hold their gains. While they were digging, enemy tanks, which had approached within two hundred yards before being discovered, opened fire. Two machine-gun positions were destroyed and several casualties incurred before American artillery fire drove off the panzers. Casualties from the attack on the pillboxes and the tank attack were removed under cover of smoke. Company L dug deeper into the hillside under continuing enemy fire observed from Münzingen Ridge. Tank destroyers from the 704th came forward as ordered by General Cheadle to relieve the pressure on Sinz but found themselves outranged and outgunned by the enemy armor. The men of the 704th later recorded these battles as "some of its hardest battles under the worst conditions encountered in its entire history. Dragon's teeth, pillboxes, minefields, artillery fire, and tanks, combined with the natural obstacles of rain, snow, and ice, made almost inconceivable odds. . . ." The town and its only supply road remained under direct enemy observation and fire.

Colonel Dohs still had to take Bannholz Woods. Given the depleted condition of his battalion he decided to send four groups of twenty-five men each into the woods to locate the enemy positions, particularly those of their tanks, and to lead the tank destroyers up there to engage them. Four groups formed from Companies E and G and the battalion's Reconnaissance Platoon moved out early in the morning of 9 February and entered the woods. None of the groups could really muster twenty-five men, and as men became lost in the darkness, numbers declined. By the time the group led by Sgt. Harry K. Poynter entered the woods, he had only ten men left. Nevertheless they located several enemy tanks and dug in while men were sent back to bring up the tank destroyers. Six came up to join the infantry in the woods. With dawn, the Germans began to notice and fire upon each group.

The 704th Tank Destroyer Battalion was commanded by Lt. Col. James W. Bidwell and had been assigned to the division on 7 January when it had arrived in the Saar-Moselle Triangle. It was an experienced unit that had originated as Battery D, 22d Field Artillery Battalion, 4th Armored Division. The battalion was equipped with the Gun Motor Carriage M18 "Hellcat." This tank destroyer was capable of speeds approaching 50 mph but was very lightly armored and armed with a 76mm main gun. The battalion had trained and fought with the 4th Armored Division, one of the premier such divisions of the war, until the Battle of the Bulge, when it was detached and used alongside several different infantry units. Having already fought its way across France in the forefront of American armored thrusts, it had now "moved out on a mission that will always bring back haunting memories—the brawl in the Saar-Moselle Triangle." Even while moving forward to support the attack of the infantrymen, the battalion had suffered losses. Mines had disabled one of the M18 "Hellcat" tank destroyers as well as the recovery vehicle that had moved forward to retrieve it. Its battalion headquarters, located in the town of Halstroff, was the target of a huge German railway gun, estimated by the Americans as 340mm. The battalion reconnaissance officer had gone forward to plan routes of advance and come back a few moments later, a mine casualty. The tank destroyers often felt that they were individually followed by enemy artillery pieces trying to knock them out. When Company C was dispatched back to the 4th Armored Division on 7 February, those remaining behind in the Triangle felt these men had gotten "a break."

As the German attack in the woods gained momentum, Sergeant Poynter tried to call for artillery support and to report his position. Radio troubles quickly developed, and as he attempted to fix the radio, enemy artillery fire began to fall on his position. The first platoon, Company B, 704th Tank Destroyers, came up in response to Sergeant Poynter's call. The company commander, who didn't accompany the platoon, "was furious that we were being led by an infantry sergeant in the attack," recalled T/4 Harry E. Traynor, a driver on one of the M18's. An enemy round landed on one of the two tank destroyers with him, wounding one crewman. The sergeant commanding the vehicle ordered two of his crew to return with the wounded man to Sinz while he joined the other tank destroyer, leaving his unattended. Within moments a panzer grenadier managed to occupy the abandoned tank destroyer. As Sergeant Poynter was continuing to repair his radio, it was shot from his hands by this daring infiltrator. Before any action could be taken, the tank-destroyer sergeant shouted that enemy tanks were trying to surround the position and ordered his remaining vehicle to withdraw into Sinz. Five of Sergeant Poynter's men jumped on the tank destroyer and took off with it. Left with only four men, there was little Sergeant Poynter could do. Leading his men out of the woods, he and the little group reached safety without further incident.

The other three groups fared no better. One, after reporting itself in position, was never heard from again. A second came under direct attack by enemy armor, who fired their cannons into each individual infantryman's foxhole. Those very few who survived ran for their lives. The fourth group fought against yet another tank attack, and was cut down trying to withdraw. When the vehicles of Company B, 704th Tank Destroyer Battalion, passed three enemy tanks that they had been told had been knocked out by the infantry, they left themselves critically exposed. "Our tank, called Blondie, lurched forward and we soon came abreast of the two Tigers. They seemed dead enough at the time. We then almost took one across our turret from a [German] bazooka team. We sent them to glory. Suddenly a Panther tank came upon us, but one shot with our armor-piercing shell and we got him." After they passed, the enemy vehicles came to life and fired on the tank destroyers from the rear. Two were destroyed by this surprise attack in exchange for one enemy tank knocked out. A third was destroyed by a direct mortar hit in its unprotected turret. Technician Fourth Class Traynor recalls, "Suddenly it looked like the whole damn German army of panzers was coming at us." Deciding it was time to withdraw, the destroyermen found that their batteries had failed. Before they could do anything, they were hit in the engine compartment by one of the bypassed tanks. Abandoning their damaged Hellcats, they walked back to friendly lines.

By midday on 9 February there were no Americans in Bannholz Woods. Of the six tank destroyers that had entered the woods with the men of the 301st Infantry, only the one that had escaped with Sergeant Poynter's men survived. Twenty prisoners were taken by the men of the 11th Panzer Division.

Yet a major change had resulted from the battle. The German command finally heeded the complaints of Generalleutnant Wend von Wietersheim, claiming that his assault quality division was being wasted in defensive battles and slowly destroyed in the process. In mid-January the 416th Infantry Division had also been placed under von Wietersheim's command. The newcomers found that the garrison was "seriously battered, confused with one another, and hardly fit for further resistance." This condition, the result of the initial attacks of the 94th Infantry Division, had forced the use of the 11th Panzer Division. Having failed to eject the Americans from their early gains, it now tried only to hold the Orscholz Switchline.

Von Wietersheim did not want the job. He protested repeatedly that an armored division of the quality of his "Ghost Division" would be wasted in such conditions. Nevertheless, "in spite of all protests the attack was ordered" by his higher headquarters. Difficult road conditions delayed the first intended counterattack, and most of a tank regiment was unable to cross the Saar River "for want of fuel," and therefore remained outside the battle zone. Their first attacks on Butzdorf and Tettingen had run into exactly the same difficult conditions as had faced the Americans. The German support vehicles "ran into a German antitank ditch covered with snow and had considerable losses on account of the stoppage thus caused."

Still opposed to a defensive attack, von Wietersheim proposed instead an attack against XX Corps starting from Oberleuken and Orscholz. This proposal was rejected as his division had not been assigned that sector. Although outraged by the orders he was receiving, he continued his attacks and counterattacks as ordered, which often frustrated the gains of the 94th Infantry Division in their own attacks. Unknown to the Americans, however, these attacks, particularly those of 19 and 20 January, caused "heavy losses" to the attacking Germans. Even the temporary recapture of the northern part of Nennig on 21 January was bought at the price of losses described as "serious." Von Wietersheim noted the arrival of CCA of the 8th Armored Division during the battles for Nennig, although the new division's exact identity was not immediately known. The lull around 1 February was followed from the German point of view by continued attacks that "seriously weakened" the panzer division's armored infantry units, which in some cases had to be consolidated. Fuel shortages continued to plague the "Ghost Division" throughout the battle. The ice over the rivers was not strong enough to hold tanks, and so presented obstacles to the German attacks as well. American artillery was "ever more oppressive." By 5 February von Wietersheim was reporting that the strength of his 111th Panzergrenadier Regiment was down to a total of "just over fifty men, although, according to instructions from above, the drivers of motor vehicles were already being used."

Von Wietersheim could take no more. On or about 5 February he reported himself sick, "since his constant protests were never given a hearing" and sent one of his staff officers to Berlin to see the Inspector of Tank Troops "in order to ask him to persuade the higher headquarters to see that the division was assigned a mission appropriate to its branch of service." Apparently the staff officer was convincing, as shortly afterward new orders were handed down concerning the employment of the 11th Panzer Division.

Orders were received replacing them with the 256th Volksgrenadier Division. The 15th Panzer Regiment would remain behind until the new division settled in, or forty-eight hours, whichever came first. Then they, too, would withdraw into reserve. Although the relief was delayed because of the same conditions of weather and terrain that continued to plague the Americans, the 11th Panzer Division was out of the Saar-Moselle Triangle by the fifteenth of February. The "Ghost Corps," and particularly the 94th Infantry Division supported in part by the 8th Armored Division, had beaten the reinforced "Ghost Division."

The Americans knew the battle was telling on the Germans, and General Malony was interested to learn from prisoner-of-war interrogations that many of the captured enemy soldiers were "tickled to death to surrender." However, concern arose at this time when it was discovered that the massive artillery fires used to support the attacks had depleted the ammunition stocks of the divisional artillery to dangerous levels. Malony called on XX Corps to replenish the dwindling stocks. Although they were reluctant at first, a loan was eventually agreed upon. Colonel Bercquist also ordered Lieutenant Colonel Bidwell of the 704th Tank Destroyer Battalion up to Sinz to confer with Colonel Hagerty on how best to use his equipment in Bannholz Woods after the failure earlier in the day.

In retrospect 8 February had been a good day for General Malony. In addition to the seizure of Sinz, he had received a phone call from General Walker, who was almost embarrassing in his praise of both Malony and his division. Telling Malony that he was doing a "grand job" and "fine work," Walker went on to say that the division was "doing just what the high command wants." When told that the division had identified elements of another enemy division facing them, Walker replied, "Well, if you're holding three divisions, you're doing more than your share."

To top off the good news coming from higher headquarters, Walker called back an hour later and asked Malony if he "could use 8th Armored Division were it available." He replied that if his attack continued successfully, he could certainly use armored support, and that his answer was yes. In fact, the only annoyance came late in the afternoon when the corps chief of staff visited division headquarters to complain about the division's ammunition expenditure. General Malony's response was not recorded.

Taking advantage of the good feelings at Corps, Malony called General Walker early on the ninth to ask if it were possible to have the 5th Ranger Battalion attached so that he could relieve one of his battalions for a forthcoming attack in accordance with Field Order Number 10, as the 5th Ranger Battalion was attached to the 26th Division alongside the 94th, and it could easily sideslip into the 94th's zone. After some hesitation, Walker agreed, provided the rangers were not used offensively. Shortly thereafter Colonel Hagerty reported to General Malony that his regiment was exhausted, and that any more attempts by his men to take Bannholz Woods were doomed to failure. Malony now turned to the 376th Infantry to complete the first phase of Field Order Number 10.

Colonel Harold H. McClune, learning that he was now responsible for taking Bannholz Woods, looked over the situation and immediately requested that army air force units "drop a couple drums of high powered gas with a fuse in them and burn" Bannholz Woods. Unfortunately the weather, as it had nearly every day in this battle, prevented close air support, but the wet ground would probably have negated any efforts to burn out the woods. The burden of breaking the Orscholz Switchline remained where it had always been, on the shoulders of the infantry.

CHAPTER 14
DEADLY WOODS

The defeat of the 301st Infantry in Bannholz Woods was due to two factors. First was the lack of any adequate armor, as no tanks had been available to support the attack. Second was the exhaustion in the depleted ranks of the 301st Infantry. Having been in combat for three weeks, attacking most of that time, the men who had survived were spent. There had been only a small number of replacements available, resulting in more and more fatigue among those who remained. One soldier who reported to Company F of the regiment was Donald E. Mulry, a twenty-year-old fresh from the United States. He would recall decades later that all the members of his replacement draft were agreed that the last place they wanted to be assigned was Third Army. Its reputation, especially that of its commander, did not encourage them to seek assignment there.

Other replacements were men returning from hospitals. These were often barely recovered from previous wounds or illness. Indeed, the entire division was suffering from fatigue. The 356th Field Artillery, having fired nearly seven thousand rounds of 105mm ammunition in less than three days, needed rest and time to restore its howitzers. Yet there was no other unit available to replace the 94th Division. The battle had to be fought to a conclusion.

One of the returning veterans was Pfc. Leon C. Standifer. After having been wounded while on patrol in Brittany, he had spent two months in a hospital in France before being certified fit to return to duty. Standifer was one of the men who had joined the division when the ASTP program was disbanded, and he had taken quickly to the camaraderie of a front-line infantry company. During combat in Brittany he had served as the first scout for a platoon of Company K, 301st Infantry. He had witnessed intense personal combat, and one of his closest friends had won a posthumous Distinguished Service Cross in one of the company's first actions.

Standifer's return to his company was marked at first by a realization of the weather. At the reception center he drew two pairs of long underwear, larger-size pants to accommodate the extra clothes, larger socks, and larger boots. He noted that the rear-area supply sergeant wore the new shoepacs, but was told that he would get a pair once he reported back to the 94th Infantry Division. Rather than awaiting transfer through channels he simply left the reception center without permission and hitchhiked a ride back to his division, a clear indication of the state of morale in the 94th. He returned to find Company K decimated, with more than 70 percent casualties, including many of the friends he had last seen alive in Brittany. The company's strongest unit was its first platoon, which boasted twelve men. Standifer found he was the only scout left in the entire company.

The weather again hit Standifer and he requested his shoepacs, only to learn that they were not available. Somehow they had never made it up to the combat troops, although the rear-area personnel seemed to have a plentiful supply. He resorted to the classic infantry routine of obtaining an old blanket and cutting it into strips to pack his boots and also to make a heavy muffler for his neck. Toilet paper and dry socks were stored under his helmet liner. A wool knit cap and gloves with a slit cut into the trigger finger completed his winter ensemble.

Despite the conditions under which the infantry fought, the battle went on. Once again General Malony called upon Lieutenant Colonel Martin's 2d Battalion, 376th Infantry, to come forward. In the original plan contained in Field Order Number 10, the entire 376th Infantry was to be held in reserve to take the last of the major objectives of the division, Münzingen Ridge, and the towns of Münzingen and Faha. Seizing them would signal a clear and decisive breakthrough of the enemy's defenses in the Saar-Moselle Triangle. Faced with the exhaustion of the 301st, Malony modified the plan, hoping Lieutenant Colonel Martin and his battalion could seize Bannholz Woods, leaving the rest of the 376th Infantry available for the attacks on Münzingen Ridge.

The 2d Battalion prepared for its attack on Bannholz Woods on the evening of 9 February. A reconnaissance party that included leaders from assault Companies F and G moved forward to observe the terrain and enemy positions. This group was constantly harassed by German artillery and mortar fire, which wounded the executive officer and communications sergeant of Company F. Results were disappointing. Lieutenant George Desmaris, commanding the weapons platoon of Company F, reported to his company commander, Capt. George P. Whitman, "We couldn't see a thing. We couldn't see a Goddamn thing!"

Nevertheless the attack had to go forward. Colonel Martin, knowing that tanks from the 11th Panzer Division were still present in strength in the woods, although being relieved, attached bazooka teams from the regimental antitank company to the assault units. Captains Larry Blakely and William C. Jones of the 919th Field Artillery Battalion were assigned to provide covering fire and preparatory barrages.

Captain John D. Heath's Company G moved out in the darkness of the morning of 10 February, followed after a brief delay by Company F. Both companies moved into the western edge of Bannholz Woods, opposed only by enemy small arms fire from German outposts. Once they were in the woods, enemy fire increased and visibility declined quickly. Within minutes the Americans had been separated into several groups out of touch with one another. Enemy tanks were soon encountered and the bazooka teams moved into action. One team scored several hits on two panzers without results. Finally the enemy armor withdrew on its own, still undamaged. Enemy mortar fire then fell on the bazooka team, killing one man and wounding another. The failure of the bazooka teams to destroy the tanks left the infantry in a precarious position. Their only defense against the enemy armor was now artillery.

Captain Blakely and his radioman, Cpl. Adolph Singer, had entered the woods and joined the infantry of Company G. Spotting two enemy tanks outside the woods firing into Bannholz, Captain Blakely directed the fire of the 919th Field Artillery on them. Despite accurate shelling with high-explosive ammunition, the enemy tanks were undamaged. Moving constantly, they became elusive targets for the artillery while at the same time knocking out the remaining bazooka teams who dared to face them. It soon became apparent that the enemy tanks had been equipped with "bazooka plate," which deflected the explosive power of the Americans' antitank weapon.

Despite the disorganization and accurate enemy fire, Captain Whitman and some of his men of Company F proceeded through the woods and had nearly reached the eastern edge when they encountered dug-in German troops. These Germans, armed with captured American M1's and Browning automatic rifles, overpowered Captain Whitman's small group. The Americans had no option except to withdraw deeper into the woods. While trying to locate the rest of his company, Captain Whitman was wounded by mortar fire. Nevertheless, he managed to locate another of his platoons and sent that unit forward to assist the troops closest to the edge of the woods. As this reinforcement arrived, a German tank appeared and forced the Americans back. There were barely forty men left in Company F.

Back at division headquarters, the chief of staff called upon the 301st Infantry to assist as best they could the 376th Infantry's attack. Colonel Bercquist was advised that the 301st was sending forward everything it had available, including flamethrowers, which it was hoped would destroy or at least intimidate the enemy armor. Lieutenant Colonel Martin had meanwhile been observing the attack of his battalion. He quickly saw that there was German armor throughout the area. In addition to what his men were reporting in Bannholz Woods itself, he personally observed three enemy tanks in Geisbusch Woods, a smaller forest flanking Bannholz, close enough to provide protection for the tanks while they fired on the Americans in Bannholz Woods. In midmorning a tank destroyer from the 704th Battalion managed to score a hit on one of the enemy tanks, but it quickly moved to a protected position and continued firing. Communications between battalion headquarters and the men in Bannholz Woods broke down, and every attempt to restore communications met with bloody failure. Only the wounded returning from the woods could provide any information, which as the day went on, became worse and worse.

The steady flow of wounded from Bannholz Woods concerned Lt. Percy Heidelberger, the 2d Battalion's medical officer. Proceeding into the open between the woods and Sinz, he waved his helmet with the Red Cross toward the German lines. Attracting the attention of one of the enemy tanks, he was addressed by an officer of the 11th Panzer Division, who agreed to let him proceed into the woods provided he agreed to treat German as well as American wounded. Heidelberger agreed and went to work in the woods. Although at times under fire from both sides, he managed to save several American and German wounded. When he eventually left the woods with his charges, the enemy tank commander expressed his satisfaction.

Back in the woods things were stalemated. The Americans were now dug in, but the enemy tanks shelled them at will. Tree bursts continued to cause casualties. On the other hand, American artillery kept the tanks at bay, but could not destroy them, as they moved regularly. The battle within the woods became a brawl. Group organization was lost as communications failed and each group struggled for survival. The enemy soon realized that the "bazooka skirts" protected them from the American antitank weapons and they moved closer to the dug-in infantrymen. Only the continuing calls of Captain Blakely, now calling in fire from his own 919th Field Artillery, the 284th Field Artillery, and the 390th Field Artillery, kept them at bay. The sole success the artillery had other than keeping the tanks at arm's length was the damaging of two panzers by use of white phosphorus ammunition, which set them afire but did not destroy them. The tank destroyers of the 704th Battalion continued to assist, but conditions were against them, and while they scored an occasional hit, they could not halt the enemy attack. Then, to complete the day, it began to rain.

This served to make conditions for the Americans more intolerable than ever. The American tank destroyers could not maneuver in the mud, making them less effective. Wounded were harder to evacuate in the rain, and resupply was made even more difficult. By midafternoon Captains Heath and Whitman were jointly calling for permission to withdraw. Enemy tanks were now within twenty-five yards of the American foxhole line and sniping with their cannon at individual infantrymen. The only communication was over Captain Blakely's artillery radio. The bazookas were useless against the enemy armor, no matter how gallant their operators. Lieutenant Colonel Martin ordered the beleaguered troops to hold on, as he was bringing up reinforcements. At four in the afternoon he moved forward, leading Company E toward Bannholz Woods.

It was too late. Captain Whitman, who had been wounded nearly seven hours ago, finally agreed to go to the rear for help and medical attention. Leaving Captain Heath in command of the remnants of both companies, he moved to the rear to guide the reinforcements forward. While Lieutenant Colonel Martin and Captain Whitman were approaching each other, the Germans launched a full counterattack. Using five tanks and 150 infantry, the Germans overran Company G's positions, and Company F soon followed. Before Martin and Company E could enter Bannholz Woods, they met the survivors of Companies G and F withdrawing. Bannholz Woods once again belonged to the 11th Panzer Division.

It was now the 376th Infantry's turn to lick its wounds. Of the 124 men who had entered Bannholz Woods with Company G, only seventy-eight remained. Company F was down to one officer and about fifty men. The division's "best battalion" had been decimated. The remaining battalions of the 376th came forward and relieved the 2d Battalion. The division needed a few days of rest.

While the 376th was licking its wounds, other events were in motion that would make all their suffering productive. On the division's flank, the 5th Ranger Battalion reported for duty to Colonel Johnson's 302d Infantry. Ordered to relieve the 1st and 3d Battalions, the Rangers, under the command of Lt. Col. Richard P. Sullivan, immediately began patrols to harass the enemy and give the impression of greater strength. Both relieved battalions moved to reserve positions to rest and absorb replacements. Even while supposedly resting, the 302d was tasked to reduce some especially troublesome pillboxes left in the Campholz Woods area, which they did successfully over the next few days.

General Malony visited the 376th Infantry on the morning of 11 February and then conferred with General Cheadle, Brig. Gen. Louis J. Fortier, division artillery commander, and Colonel Bercquist to plan a renewed attack on Bannholz Woods. Malony wanted a complete critique of the failed attack to pinpoint its errors and to correct them. Over the next two days several conferences were held at division headquarters with all commanders of divisional units. Details of the next attack were planned and errors of past attacks were reviewed. Coordination between attacking and supporting units was stressed. Of particular concern was the coordination between the infantry and the tank destroyers, which seemed to break down regularly. Malony also decried the panic and rumors that always abounded in such situations, as well as air-support difficulties and the ongoing trench-foot crisis.

General Malony, determined to make the next attack the successful one, placed major operations within the division on hold while all preparations were being made. This did not pass unnoticed at corps headquarters, and on 13 February General Walker complained to General Malony that the division "hadn't had anything happen in about three days." Malony replied that he was preparing for a new approach and that the division was not idle.

General Walker's anxiety was not merely one commander prodding another. It appeared to him that the 94th Division was close to a clear breakthrough into the rear of the German defenses. He had already contacted General Patton with a request for armor. Although the 8th Armored Division had left XX Corps, Walker noted that the 10th Armored Division was in his area, resting and resupplying. General Patton, always eager to attack, quickly approached General Eisenhower for permission to use the armor in an attack into the Triangle. General Eisenhower, still under pressure to maintain a strong reserve, only agreed to release the 10th Armored Division to Patton if and when the infantry achieved a breakthrough. That left the burden on the shoulders of the infantrymen of the 94th Division.

Meanwhile General Malony continued to prepare for the next big attack. Again on the fourteenth he called a meeting of his major commanders and invited them to "take down their hair and air their troubles" so as to improve coordination. With Generals Cheadle and Fortier in attendance, the regimental commanders, staff officers, and representatives from the 704th Tank Destroyer Battalion, 774th Tank Destroyer Battalion, and 748th Tank Battalion, part of which was now attached to the division, met for two hours to get to understand each other's problems.

Although Malony may have suspected it, his meetings to iron out difficulties in coordination could not have been better timed. General Walker arrived at the division command post on 15 February to review the situation with Malony and Bercquist. Walker stressed the need for a clear breakthrough, and agreed that the Münzingen Ridge capture planned by General Malony would suffice to convince General Eisenhower that the corps was through the main enemy defenses. After Walker left, Malony called his staff together to advise them that the division's mission had been changed. Explaining that "the mission of the Div now is to secure the Mensingen [sic] Ridge and the high ground to the N of Oberleuken," Malony closed the meeting by stressing that "I am planning to hit w/everything the Div got."

In order to ensure success this time, Colonel Bercquist contacted the XX Corps chief of staff to request the attachment of a tank battalion. Apparently feeling this request was not being adequately received at corps, General Malony also contacted General Walker directly, making the same request. The 778th Tank Battalion, less Company B, was attached to the division but could not reach the area before 16 March. In responding to this request, Walker said to Malony, "All right, shoot the works.

CHAPTER 15
SHOOT THE WORKS

General Walker's order releasing the full power of the division to General Malony was more than welcome. For nearly a month it had battered itself against the defenses of the Orscholz Switchline with one hand tied behind its back. Unable to bring its full resources to bear against the enemy, the division had expended itself a battalion at a time against an attack-grade armored division supported by two infantry divisions entrenched in concrete defenses. That any progress was made was a compliment to the skill and daring of the division's infantry, engineers, and artillerymen.

General Walker's order to use the full strength of the division in the next attack resulted in Field Order Number 11. Issued 16 February, it called for all three regiments to attack together on the morning of 19 February. The 301st Infantry was to make the main effort against Münzingen Ridge and the towns of Münzingen and Faha, the ultimate goals of the earlier Field Order Number 10. The 302d Infantry was to attack out of Campholz Woods and seize Orscholz, settling scores with the enemy troops there. Finally, the 376th Infantry was to seize Bannholz Woods, then move east to support the attack on Münzingen Ridge by seizing der Länge Woods. The 376th was also responsible for protecting the division's flank as it moved forward.

Careful plans for artillery support and preparation were made between General Fortier and Brig. Gen. Julius E. Slack, who commanded the XX Corps Artillery. For ten hours before the attack the corps artillery battalions would fire on known and suspected enemy routes of supply and communication. While the corps artillery worked the enemy rear areas, the division artillery would fire on the enemy's front-line defenses up to a depth of five thousand yards from the front line. The cannon companies of the 301st and 302d Infantry regiments were to add their fires to the division artillery fire plan. The 774th Tank Destroyer Battalion was also assigned to a fire support role.

Reconnaissance was stressed. Each unit was ordered to send more than the usual patrols out to be sure that they knew what to expect when they attacked. These patrols were quite successful, one patrol even penetrating to the final objective on Münzingen Ridge and plotting the enemy positions in the area. Another patrol, under Sgt. Frederick J. Ramondini of the 301st's intelligence and reconnaissance platoon, penetrated into the town of Münzingen and found enemy tanks hidden among the buildings.

As they had before the first attack into the Triangle, each unit of the division carefully plotted its route of attack, enemy defenses, and supporting fires. Again as had been done during the attack on Tettingen, defenses were plotted once objectives had been seized. Nothing was left to chance. This time the 94th was determined to finish off the Siegfried Switchline.

General Malony kept General Walker apprised of his plans and progress. On 16 February, as Field Order Number 11 was being prepared, Malony told him that he had a plan to use the entire division "after a reasonable time to get set." With this in mind, Walker called back the next afternoon to advise Malony that there were plans at corps to use the 10th Armored Division in conjunction with the attack of the 94th. They also discussed the details of Field Order Number 11 once again. Walker had his corps staff draw up XX Corps Field Order Number 16, the attack to clear the Saar-Moselle Triangle, which included all corps-assigned units in the attack, based upon the 94th Division's Field Order Number 11.

XX Corps ordered the 10th Armored Division to assemble at the town of Perl, on the left flank of the corps and along the Moselle River. Two combat commands were to be in readiness for a call to push into the Triangle once the 94th Division had achieved a clear breakthrough. General Walker sent several plans to the 10th Division that were to be issued as field orders, depending on which way events developed. These could be put into immediate action by a simple code calling for plan A, B, or C. The 10th Division, resting in a rear area, had to rush to recover many of its personnel from the delights of Paris and assemble its units behind the 94th Infantry Division by the scheduled date of 20 February.

The 10th Armored Division was still commanded by Maj. Gen. William Henry Harrison Morris Jr., and had been activated at Fort Benning, Georgia, on 15 July 1942. Cadred from the 8th Armored Division, the division had processed through the usual training and maneuver assignments until it departed the United States 13 September 1944. After entering France, the division was sent to the XX Corps for its first combat assignment during the battles for the fortress city of Metz. It was during this operation that elements of the division entered the Saar-Moselle Triangle for the first time in support of the attacks of the 90th Infantry Division. When the German counteroffensive in the Ardennes struck, the division was pulled out of the line and ordered to the VIII Corps, where Combat Command A fought alongside the 101st Airborne Division in the epic defense of Bastogne. The remainder of the division fought with other VIII Corps elements on the shoulders of the German penetration. The division continued to fight to reduce the German "Bulge" until January, when it was sent to the Seventh Army for rest and rehabilitation. Assisting there in another reduction of a German counterattack, the division was finally put in reserve in the Third Army area on 10 February. It was resting behind the lines of the XX Corps when it was selected by Generals Patton and Walker to help the 94th Infantry Division eliminate once and for all the Saar-Moselle Triangle.

The first tangible evidence that the men of the 94th had of the coming of the armor was the arrival at division headquarters of the commander of Combat Command A, Brig. Gen. Edwin W. Piburn, during the morning of 18 February. Colonel Bercquist conferred with Piburn to coordinate passage of the combat command through the infantry when the time came. Bercquist learned that Combat Command A, consisting of two task forces named Task Force Chamberlain and Task Force Richardson after their commanding officers, was available to assist the division clear the Triangle. Combat Command B, under Col. William L. Roberts, and Combat Command R, under Lt. Col. Wade C. Gatchell, were in the rear waiting for the word to advance through the hole to be punched by the infantry.

While the 10th Armored was moving forward, the men of the 94th were assembling as well. Within each regiment replacements were received, ammunition and supplies distributed, and the men rested as much as possible. It was believed that the 11th Panzer Division had left the area, because nothing had been heard from them since the debacle in Bannholz Woods on 9 February. There were some intelligence officers who argued that they could simply have been withdrawn into reserve behind the enemy lines and that they would quickly reappear when the attack opened. The findings of Sergeant Ramondini's patrol gave credence to this theory. Even without the presence of the enemy armor, there were still two enemy infantry divisions in prepared defensive positions opposing them. The division had its work clearly before it.

The morning of 19 February dawned with "low broken clouds." Air support scheduled had to be postponed until the afternoon, when nine squadrons of the Army Air Force flew ninety-seven sorties in support of the corps attack. On the ground, the first to attack was the 3d Battalion of the 301st Infantry. At 2:00 A.M. the battalion moved out in pitch darkness to the military crest of Münzingen Ridge. Along the way surprised enemy mortar crews were captured without resistance. This move, the only advance made without preparatory fires from the artillery, enabled the infantry to take up their line of departure without being discovered. The battalion's immediate objective, das Lee Woods, stood immediately ahead of them on the top of Münzingen Ridge.

Although the battalion had surprised the Germans to their immediate front, the LXXXII Corps itself was not surprised. The combat reconnaissance of the Germans and the increased sound of motors coming from the American lines had given sufficient notice to the Germans that something was going on in the American lines facing them. There was little they could do, however. The 11th Panzer Division, even if it had been available, was so seriously depleted that only a few of its tanks would have been of use. The defenders could only fight to the best of their ability behind stone and concrete fortifications, protected by minefields and barbed wire, and hope for the best.

The 3d Battalion waited in the darkness. Precisely at 4:00 the preparatory artillery barrage hit Münzingen Ridge. As soon as the artillery began impacting, the infantry moved forward. Company L encountered the usual minefield but fortunately found a clear path used by enemy tanks and lost no time in moving forward. Alongside Company L, Company K encountered the same field and used engineers with primacord to blast their way past it. By dawn the 3d Battalion had secured its objective.

Alongside the 3d Battalion, the 1st Battalion of the 301st was not so lucky. Moving from Butzdorf toward Münzingen Ridge south of its sister battalion, it encountered both mines and enemy mortar fire, which caused several casualties. Company C's commander elected to withdraw a slight distance from the edge of the minefield and circle around it. Coming out on the ridge too far north, the company swept the ridge from north to south, eliminating enemy opposition as they went. Second Lieutenant Howard Johnson, who went from platoon leader to company commander of Company C in a matter of minutes, explained, "The marching fire demonstration put on by our doughs was a thing of weird beauty. The men seemed to forget about mines or opposing fire as they kept their M1s hot. The roar of TD guns behind and to the sides was a pleasant feeling, and the tanks which opposed us were soon out of commission." Company B, attacking alongside, suffered casualties from "friendly fire" but continued on until it struck another minefield. More casualties resulted, but still the company moved forward. As dawn began to lighten the sky, tanks of Company B, 778th Tank Battalion, supported the battalion from as high on the ridge as they could climb, and shortly thereafter the battalion cleared the remnants of the enemy from its sector of Münzingen Ridge. Company A, assigned to mop up bypassed enemy positions, was ambushed by two machine guns that caught the platoon of Lt. Robert H. Wolf in the open. Sergeant Ichiro Matsuzawa crawled forward despite the crossfire and boldly attacked each in turn, killing or capturing both enemy gun crews. Matsuzawa's bold attack freed Lieutenant Wolf's men, who promptly proceeded to clear the remaining enemy from the rear of their battalion.

The 302d Infantry was assigned to capture the southern end of Münzingen Ridge. Attacking from Campholz Woods, the 1st and 3d Battalions also moved forward under the cover of darkness while the 5th Ranger Battalion, which had requested permission to participate in the attack, moved against the town of Oberleuken. With the first shells from the artillery preparation the 3d Battalion moved out of Campholz Woods into a storm of enemy small arms fire. Trying to advance despite this fire, the lead company ran into one of the ever-present minefields and stalled. The battalion dug in as best it could under the storm of enemy fire until daylight. Then tanks from Company B, 778th Tank Battalion, arrived in support and the attack began to move forward. Using a route cleared during the night by the 319th Combat Engineers, the armor of Company B fired directly into each individual enemy position, either destroying it or, in the case of bunkers, keeping the enemy in place until the infantry could get close enough to reduce the position.

The attack centered on the main enemy position in a bunker called Pillbox 153. Inside were both the enemy commander and the artillery observation party. Under the covering fire of the tanks, the men of Company I moved toward this position, which had fought the 94th Division since it had first arrived in the triangle. Privates First Class Alvin Cohen and Joseph J. Truss worked their way to the entrance of Pillbox 153, where Truss blew in the door with a demolition charge. Then Cohen emptied his Browning automatic rifle into the bunker. Using Cohen's fire for cover, TSgt. Edward Cardell threw fragmentation and white phosphorus grenades into the pillbox. The Germans quickly surrendered. Almost as soon as the Germans left the bunker, both the Americans and Germans rushed back inside to seek shelter from German artillery fire.

As the attack progressed the good news was passed back to division headquarters. By 8:30 A.M. XX Corps was informed by Colonel Bercquist that things "were going good" and that several pillboxes had been taken along with many prisoners. Progress was so rapid that within an hour General Malony called XX Corps and suggested that he might have an opening for the 10th Armored Division "before night."

The final objective, the seizure of Bannholz Woods by the 376th Infantry, went much as had all the other attacks that day. Advancing under artillery fire, and facing the same ever-present minefields, the 1st Battalion moved on Bannholz and Geisbusch Woods. Company B, still commanded by Captain Bowden, moved into Bannholz against light opposition. Those who believed that the 11th Panzer Division had left the area proved to be correct. Opposed briefly by 20mm enemy antiaircraft guns sited to fire on the advancing infantry, Company C used its attached tank destroyers to eliminate this only impediment to another successful attack. On the flank, Colonel Thurston's 3d Battalion seized the area around Geisbusch-Adenholz after a brief struggle in which, once again, mines were the main cause of casualties.

By midafternoon all of the division's objectives for the first day had been secured, with the sole exception of Oberleuken. There the 5th Ranger Battalion had run into a large electronically controlled minefield and been repulsed after heavy losses.

For the Germans the attack came as no surprise, so they had prepared as best they could. The removal of the 11th Panzer Division to other sectors resulted in the defenders' being reinforced with the 256th Volksgrenadier Division. Recruited from the Wehrkreis Four and Thirteen sections of Bavaria and Saxony and including a number of Sudeten Germans, the division had first been formed in the general mobilization of 1939. Replacements came primarily from Saxony, so the division took on a reputation as a Saxon division. After taking part in the campaigns in Belgium and Holland, it was a part of the massive force that Hitler sent into Russia in June of 1941. It spent three years on the Russian front, distinguishing itself before Moscow and during the battle of Rzhev. In the summer of 1943 the division suffered heavily during the battle of Smolensk, where its commander was killed and the division was considered destroyed. Surviving veterans of the eastern-front battles were combined with the newly raised 568th Grenadier Division to re-form the 256th Volksgrenadier Division. As a token of respect for the earlier accomplishments the division had its units carry the same numbers as the previous division. The newly reconstituted division was sent to the

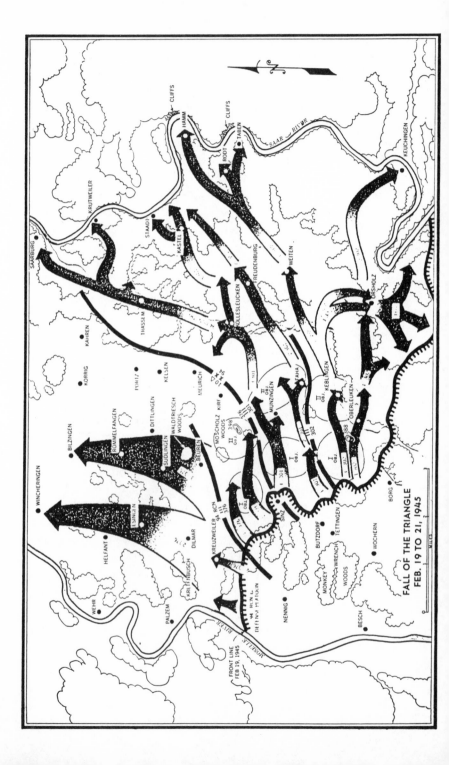

FALL OF THE TRIANGLE
FEB. 19 TO 21, 1945

western front, first to fight against the British at the battle of the Scheldt in November 1944 and then to eastern France, before being sent into the Saar-Moselle Triangle. Commanded by Maj. Gen. Gerhard Franz, it now faced the XX Corps attack.

All morning the phone wires between the XX Corps and 94th Division headquarters had been humming. Generals Walker and Malony constantly updated each other, growing anxious to pass the 10th Armored Division through the infantry. Indeed, it was still morning when Malony advised Walker that although the rangers had failed to take Oberleuken, a clear breakthrough existed and the armor could move forward. By midday, Walker had ordered General Morris to move.

Shortly after 4:00 P.M. Morris arrived at the headquarters of the 94th Division to coordinate with General Malony the passage of his division through the infantry. While there, both generals were advised that the 301st Infantry had seized the towns of Faha and Münzingen, the last objectives (excepting Oberleuken) assigned to the infantry in Corps Field Order Number 16. The Ghost Corps was within yards of the clear breakthrough demanded by General Patton.

The failure of the 5th Ranger Battalion to seize Oberleuken shifted that burden onto Colonel Johnson's 301st Infantry. Johnson swiftly redirected his 1st Battalion, which was in the middle of an attack on the town of Keblingen. Companies A and B had seized at some cost the outlying hills defending Keblingen when Company C, which was about to assault Keblingen proper, was advised to shift its attack toward Oberleuken. The company had to recall its armor support, which was already moving toward Keblingen, and focus the entire effort toward Oberleuken. Supported by the 301st Field Artillery and tanks from the 778th Tank Battalion, Company C stormed into the town and by late afternoon had it, along with 110 prisoners and seven 120mm mortars.

Lieutenant Colonel Cloudt's 3d Battalion seized Keblingen's outposts and then moved on toward the hills beyond it, from which enemy fire poured into the town. A patrol from Company I, again led by Pfc. Alvin Cohen and supported by tanks, secured the hills and captured two German women who had been firing an antitank gun against the Americans. Back in Keblingen, Company L was clearing the town. Lieutenant Charles C. Misner's platoon moved into the town against heavy resistance. Tank support allowed the infantry to enter the town, and clearing operations began. Resistance remained desperate and Lieutenant Misner crossed the open fields outside of town once again to personally direct his supporting tanks into the town. While his lieutenant was bringing forward the tanks, TSgt. Francis E. Kelly, the platoon sergeant, was wounded severely in the neck. Despite this wound he continued to lead the attack, refusing evacuation. When Lieutenant Misner returned to lead the platoon in the house-to-house struggle, Kelly personally directed each tank against those positions holding up the platoon's advance. By late afternoon Keblingen had been cleared.

The LXXXII Corps grew increasingly concerned as the day progressed. The 256th Volksgrenadier Division had joined the 416th Infantry Division in the defense. Yet although both divisions were experienced and, in the case of the 256th Volksgrenadier, relatively fresh, with an average age of twenty-seven years, rated "suitable for defense," the Americans had captured vital territory. The heavy and accurate American artillery fire had prevented the Germans from bringing forward critical reserves, and within moments of the artillery fire shifting, LXXXII Corps was receiving reports of American penetrations near Tettingen. Although the 416th Infantry Division reported repelling an American attack, it later admitted that a major penetration had been made and that there were no reserves left to counterattack. Reviewing its situation at the end of 19 February, LXXXII Corps decided that its main line of defense was at the breaking point. No reserves were available to restore the situation, so it was time to give serious consideration to abandoning the position entirely. Thought was given to retiring to additional West Wall positions "behind the Saar in the Wiltingen-Mettlach sector." The corps feared that if this retirement was not undertaken swiftly, the defenders of the Saar-Moselle Triangle, especially the "artillery and heavy infantry weapons units" would be lost and even the infantry might not be able to reach the next line of defense before the Americans. Already some of the crossing sites had been bombed and were either unusable or suitable only for walking infantry units. LXXXII Corps felt it imperative to get as many of its veteran troops back to the Saar defenses as possible, because only two battalions of Volkssturm manned those defenses. These home-guard type of battalions were notably unreliable once they came under fire. Quickly LXXXII Corps made their position known to Army Group G. Despite the logic of the appeal, it was denied and orders came down to hold the Orscholz Switchline by a counterattack to regain the lost ground. But by then the Germans in the remaining positions of the Orscholz Switchline could hear the rumbling sound of American tanks moving forward.

By that same evening of 19 February all of the 94th Division's first and second series of objectives had been taken. In its first full-scale divisional-sized attack since entering combat nearly seven months before, and for the first time with appropriate armor support, the division had taken all its objectives. The breakthrough sought by General Patton was provided for him by the XX Corps and especially by the men of the 94th. There remained now the business of exploiting what had been gained at such cost.

CHAPTER 16
BREAKTHROUGH!

For the 94th Infantry Division, 20 February began with good news. The XX Corps chief of staff called to tell Colonel Bercquist that General Patton had phoned and was quite pleased with the progress the division had made so far. Then, of course, came the typical Patton injunction to clear the remainder of the defenses by the end of the day. Although fulfillment of Patton's new directive was highly unlikely, both divisions pushed off aggressively that morning. The 10th Armored Division's Combat Command A moved out at dawn and was briefly delayed by a minefield, but continued forward. One of the difficulties experienced by U.S. armored divisions in the European campaigns was again evident as the 10th Armored moved into the Triangle. The structure of the American armored division as it existed in 1945 did not provide sufficient infantry within the division to adequately support the tanks. This became apparent, especially when fighting in built-up areas such as the Saar-Moselle Triangle, with its many fortified towns and villages. Shortly after the 10th jumped off, the 376th Infantry Regiment was attached to them to assist in clearing the Triangle.

Colonel McClune's 376th Infantry had itself been reinforced the night before by the division's reconnaissance troop and the headquarters defense platoon. One of the last objectives that had been assigned to the regiment was the seizure of the towns of Thorn and Kreuzweiler. Taking these towns would be the final step opening up the breach needed to launch the tanks of the 10th Armored Division. McClune ordered the 2d Battalion to take Kreuzweiler, while the reconnaissance troop and defense platoon were sent to Thorn.

Lieutenant Frank A. Penn's headquarters defense platoon had what most infantrymen consider a safe job. They protected the division headquarters personnel and guarded it wherever the headquarters was located. They rarely were shot at and usually were far enough in the rear to be safe from enemy action other than air and artillery attacks. Despite all that the division had suffered in the last month, morale was still sufficiently high that the platoon requested a chance to participate in the big attack. Because the division was attacking, it was unlikely that the headquarters would need any protection and so permission was granted. The platoon joined with the reconnaissance troop to assault the town of Thorn.

The reconnaissance troop had held various parts of the line during the past month and had made limited-objective attacks as well. Captain Scott T. Ashton's men had also maintained contact with other XX Corps units on the line. With the shortage of infantry and the need to make the final break in the enemy line, the reconnaissance troop and the headquarters defense platoon were given a big mission.

One section of the assault force, led by Lieutenant Penn, successfully avoided minefields and artillery barrages to enter Thorn. The rest of the troops, under Captain Ashton, were delayed by enemy artillery and mortar fire. The armor supporting them lost one tank to a mine, but the tank crew joined the unit to advance as infantry. The defense of Thorn was centered around the usual château, which came under direct fire from the armor and the bazookas of the defense platoon. After nearly half an hour of this shelling, the defense platoon assaulted the château, taking the position along with twenty-five prisoners. One of the men later explained their interest in participating in the attack by saying, "For weeks the Germans wouldn't let us walk guard in peace back at division by shelling us all hours of the night. It was a distinct pleasure to help pour some lead into them for a change." The defense platoon was relieved once the objective had been secured, missing the intense shelling that cost the reconnaissance troop fourteen casualties. Both units later returned to their usual duties.

Meanwhile, the 2d Battalion of the 376th moved on Kreuzweiler. The two assault companies, Companies F and G, left the line of departure and cleared two large wooded areas protecting the town. Overcoming the usual opposition of minefields, machine guns, and infantry rifle fire, the Americans moved through the woods and reached the town's edge. Here they stopped briefly to reorganize and then stormed the German defenses. Despite heavy mortar and artillery fire, the attack nevertheless succeeded in clearing most of Kreuzweiler by midmorning. The struggle continued, however, into the afternoon in order to overcome stubborn holdouts in several fortified houses. During this struggle, the 376th Infantry claims to have captured a Japanese soldier.

The Germans were not willing to let Kreuzweiler fall to the Americans. They understood that this was the last barrier between the Americans and open access to the Saar-Moselle Triangle. While the 2d Battalion was still mopping up, an enemy force of four tanks and one hundred infantry counterattacked down the road leading into Kreuzweiler. The 919th Field Artillery Battalion had prepared for such an eventuality, so when the enemy force reached a previously designated crossroads, a storm of artillery fire fell upon them, disrupting the counterattack and causing several casualties. Before the Germans could reorganize, Combat Command R of the 10th Armored Division moved into Kreuzweiler. Seeing that the situation was well in hand, the American tankers swept up the road lately used by the Germans and captured their jump-off point, the village of Dilmar, sending over a hundred Germans into prisoner-of-war cages.

Combat Command A had also moved into battle. Attacking along the right flank of the 94th Division, it moved on the village of Kirf. Minefields delayed the advance until engineers from the 55th Armored Engineer Battalion cleared a path. Moving swiftly, the tanks and armored infantry ran into an ambush, but soon overcame the German assault guns supported by machine guns and seized Kirf. The tankers then moved off the roads and assaulted Meurick. Here again they were stopped by "murderous antitank fire," but continued to attack with mortar fire. Later the tankers captured the command post of the 456th Infantry Regiment of the 256th Volksgrenadier Division and again took more than one hundred prisoners.

General Walker visited the headquarters of the 94th Division early on the twentieth. Knowing that General Patton was pleased with the breakthrough and that the armor had entered the battle, he awarded General Malony another Bronze Star, saying, "In giving this to you, Harry, I am honoring the decoration more than I am you." General Malony felt differently, knowing who had won the battle for XX Corps and later complimented his regimental commanders on a "splendid effort all the way thru" and instructed them to personally pass on his compliments to their soldiers.

Indeed, all the infantry and their supporting arms within the 94th Division were having the best day they had experienced since entering the Triangle. Colonel Johnson's 301st Infantry attacked the key town of Freudenberg and its defenses. Sweeping through woods and crossing streams that delayed its supporting armor, the infantry of the 2d Battalion swept into the village and, after overcoming artillery, machine guns, and snipers, declared the town secure by nightfall. The 3d Battalion moved to protect the flank of the 2d and at midday ran into a powerful force of the enemy retreating from Kirf, which had just been taken by CCA's Task Force Richardson. The battalion was on a hill overlooking the enemy's escape route. Opening a devastating fire on the retreating Germans, the men of the 301st drove them off the roads into woods where they hoped to find shelter. Company K, under heavy fire, cleared the woods, and later that morning the battalion established contact with the 10th Armored Division at Kirf. "One squad of the 301st knocked out six 88s and their crews in a stretch of two hundred yards." Continuing forward both battalions had by afternoon cleared their sectors completely, and established defense positions along the bluff overlooking the Saar River.

The 302d Infantry also had a successful day, although they drew the most difficult assignment. Their initial objective was the village of Weiten. The 3d Battalion moved against this fortified town, finding minimal resistance. Company K was even fortunate enough to seize intact a bridge across one of the streams in its path after driving off the bridge guard, who had not had time to set off the prepared demolitions. Bringing up the quadruple-mounted .50-caliber antiaircraft guns of Battery A, 465th Antiaircraft Artillery Battalion, the Americans raked the town before moving to assault it. Despite this preparatory fire, when the 3d Battalion and its supporting armor from the 748th Tank Battalion moved into the open they were immediately engulfed by antitank-gun fire from Weiten. The tanks withdrew into the cover of nearby woods while the infantry of Lt. Carmen L. Ramirez's platoon of Company I knocked out the enemy guns. The attack then resumed and the battalion secured the town, capturing several German officers in a command post along with their armored-vehicle escort. Simultaneously, the regiment's 1st Battalion under Major Stanion seized Oberleuken, which had previously defied the 5th Ranger Battalion.

There remained the problem of Orscholz. This thorn in the division's side had been assigned to Task Force Gaddis, commanded by the 302d Infantry's regimental executive officer, Lt. Col. John W. Gaddis, and composed of Major Maixner's 2d Battalion of the 302d Infantry and the 1st Battalion of the 301st. This force followed Colonel Cloudt's 3d Battalion, 302d, in its attack on Weiten, then branched off along a road that led to Orscholz. In a wooded area selected as the unit's assembly point, the lead scout, Pfc. Robert S. Karlix, encountered an enemy force of nineteen, which he quickly captured. Supported by the guns of the 301st Field Artillery and both infantry battalions' mortars, the task force attacked Orscholz in the early afternoon hours. With a platoon each of medium and light tanks, Task Force Gaddis fought through the town, house by house. Private First Class James Heard, of Company H's heavy machine-gun platoon, set up his gun in the center of the town's main street and swept the street with fire to prevent the Germans from moving between defensive positions. Although one of his crew was wounded by sniper fire, the gun remained in action, contributing to Orscholz's fall. By late afternoon, the town and its defenses were in the hands of Task Force Gaddis.

Colonel Bercquist called General Walker to inform him that Orscholz had fallen. Walker told him that he was "enthused" about the work of the division to date, and that "Army" (i.e., Patton) was "very well pleased."

Task Force Gaddis continued to secure its position in and around Orscholz for the remainder of the day and into 21 February. On that day 1st Sgt. William M. Kelley, one of the few survivors of the original Company B, 301st Infantry, which was destroyed in the first attack on Orscholz, accompanied a patrol into the woods where his comrades had last been seen. Here he found "several pieces of clothing bearing serial numbers which he recognized." The patrol also discovered "the graves of several men of the first Company B."

The 10th Armored Division continued to clear the Triangle with the 376th in support. Resistance varied from negligible to fierce. Team Richardson of CCA encountered problems at Kirf from mines and antitank guns, while Team Billet faced much the same at Meurick. The other teams of CCA and CCR met varying resistance and within forty-eight hours had, for all practical purposes, cleared the Saar-Moselle Triangle of organized enemy resistance. As a fitting climax to this struggle, and in typical Patton style, the purpose of the campaign was brought closer to realization when General Patton appeared at the command post of the 10th Armored on 21 February. After examining the dispositions of XX Corps, General Patton turned to General Walker and ordered, "Johnnie, cross the Saar and take Trier." Walker then turned to General Morris and ordered the 10th Armored to make the attack.

Walker returned to his headquarters and had his staff draw up Field Order Number 17. Following Patton's instructions, the corps order designated the 10th Armored to cross the Saar and seize Trier. The 94th Division was also to cross the Saar between Saarburg and Hamm on the night of 21–22 February and establish a bridgehead. It was then to be "prepared to continue the advance to the NE on Corps order," while being responsible for maintaining contact with both the 3d Cavalry Group and the 10th Armored Division. The 26th Infantry Division and the 3d Cavalry Group, with the 5th Ranger Battalion attached, were to maintain their defensive positions.

As the Saar-Moselle phase of the operation drew to a close, the price continued to remain high. During 19 February the 319th Medical Battalion of the 94th Division processed 611 wounded men, and on the twentieth another 344. The final day's cost in wounded was an additional 173. Against this, the division had cleared the Saar-Moselle Triangle, captured 1,469 prisoners, and put XX Corps in a position to enter the heart of Germany. It had gutted the 11th Panzer Division, making it incapable of performing its next counterattack against the American bridgehead at Remagen. It had destroyed the

416 Infantry and 256th Volksgrenadier Divisions, killing an unknown number of irreplaceable German infantry. The combined
cost of conquering the triangle since the first day the XX Corps had
entered the dangerous ground had made this one of the bloodier
battles of Third Army's career.

While higher command was already looking ahead to the con-
tinuance of the operation, the troops were pleasantly unaware of
their plans. The men of the 94th were particularly anxious to establish their defenses along the Saar, for they believed that "the corps
commander himself had indicated that with the clearing of this area,
the division would belly up to the Saar, outpost the river, and enjoy
a well-earned rest."

Hardly had the soldiers taken their first good look at the Saar
when word began to filter down that their planned rest and recuperation period was about to be postponed. Early on the afternoon
of 21 February, Lt. Harold J. Donkers, a division liaison officer at XX
Corps headquarters, called division headquarters to tell them that
"back here they're talking about a river crossing, and if it's made,
we'll be making it." Twenty minutes later Colonel Bercquist was on
the phone with Colonel Hagerty, telling him to have his men make
a detailed reconnaissance across the river and adding by way of ex-
planation that the division "might be on other side tomorrow." A few
minutes later Colonel Johnson received a similar call with instructions for his 302d Infantry. The final approval for an assault crossing of the Saar came with a call from General Walker, who explained
to General Malony that this was the "opportunity of a lifetime" for
the division, the corps, and Third Army.

Late that same evening Walker called again to let Malony know
that he could expect another visit from General Patton the following afternoon. Once again he expressed the belief that the opportunity to cross the Saar on the run was an opportunity of a lifetime,
but that if the division proved unable to accomplish this new task,
he was "not going to blame you, because you carried out the most
wonderful masterpiece, and the Boss [i.e., Patton] appreciated it and
I do too."

The men of the 94th, those very few who ever heard about the
commanders' good opinion of them, appreciated the kind words.

They would have appreciated a rest even more. Nevertheless, XX Corps, led once again by the 94th Division, was about to make an assault crossing of a river that would lead toward one of Germany's major industrial bases.

CHAPTER 17
TAKE TRIER!

The order to cross the Saar River and seize Trier gave XX Corps only one night to prepare for the assault. Although there had been speculation for days regarding the possibility of continuing the attack, no confirmation had been delivered until General Patton's dramatic order to General Walker at 10th Armored Division headquarters on the afternoon of 21 February. This left only the night between 21 and 22 February to organize, regroup, and begin the operation.

Crossing sites had to be selected within the boundaries given in the corps field order, units moved into position to include artillery battalions, and supplies such as food, ammunition, and gasoline brought forward. The night was one of constant movement for the staffs and troops of the 10th Armored and 94th Infantry Divisions. Despite the haste, the 94th was ready to assault before dawn of the twenty-second. In the 10th Armored, however, things began to go awry before the crossing.

The Saar River in February 1945 was between 120 and 150 feet in width and averaged a depth of fifteen feet. It could not be forded anywhere in the sector of the Ghost Corps. The river's current was swift, still swollen from the late winter thaws. The east bank, known to be defended by the Germans, dominated the west bank, giving every advantage to the enemy. "Great wooded, clifflike slopes" further dominated the area, and these were dotted with the usual concrete pillboxes and other fortifications, some three miles deep in areas that the Germans believed might be used as crossing sites. American intelligence knew that elements of the 416th Infantry Division and the 256th Volksgrenadier Division had escaped from the

Triangle and taken up positions on the east bank of the Saar. Once again XX Corps would have to face these enemy forces, although depleted, waiting in concrete defenses. The advantage still lay with the Germans; the XX Corps's units, though no more depleted and tired than the Germans, were attacking once again into prepared defenses.

The 10th Armored Division selected the 376th Infantry to make their assault crossing of the river, near Ockfen. Combat Command B's tank destroyers would provide covering and supporting fires, and once a bridgehead was established, CCB would pass through and attack toward Trier. CCA was detailed to assault across the Saar by using the intact bridges at Kanzem and Wiltingen. CCA would pass through the 376th Infantry's second bridgehead and join CCB in the attack on Trier.

Getting bridges across the Saar for both divisions was essential if the infantry were to be able to maintain any bridgeheads they established. In order to accomplish this, XX Corps ordered the 1139th Engineer Group to provide both boats and bridging equipment to each division to facilitate their crossings. The 1139th Engineer Group was understrength, however, with most of its equipment being used by other divisions of Third Army farther north. The 10th Armored engineering officer, Lt. Col. Wadsworth P. Clapp, sent an officer to meet the 1139th Engineer Group and lead the boat battalion to its destination. He found the group's headquarters and started back to the division, leading the boat battalion behind him. However, upon his arrival back at division only three trucks were still following him, the rest having become lost in the darkness. Without boats there could be no crossing of the Saar by the 10th Armored on 22 February.

General Patton was en route to XX Corps on the morning of the 22 February. On the way, he stopped off at an army hospital to decorate twenty army nurses with the Bronze Star. Then he made a brief stop at the 4th Armored Division of XII Corps to make an award of the Medal of Honor to an officer of that division, before continuing on to XX Corps.

Upon his arrival at XX Corps, Patton's mood quickly darkened when he was informed by General Walker that the 10th Armored Division's attack had been delayed a day due to a lost bridging train. At a meeting with Generals Walker and Morris he "found that Morris had let his train get lost, and therefore was not across at Saarburg, and that, at a late hour in the afternoon when I met him, he was being held up by small-arms fire from the far side of the river." Patton's furious temper vented itself once again, this time on Walker and Morris. To Walker he said, "You should have seen that it was in place. So should I. We have all three fallen down on the job." By the time he departed XX Corps, his anger had increased to the point where he blustered that "General Morris will lead his division across the river in the first boat, or, if necessary, swim." Later, the historian of the 10th Armored would declare that this incident was the cause of the "only critical remarks directed at the division by General Patton during the war."

Although the 10th Armored was delayed until its boats and bridges came forward, the 94th had proceeded with its own crossing of the Saar. Having only two infantry regiments left to it after the attachment of the 376th to the 10th Armored, General Malony assigned to each a sector of his front and ordered them to prepare for an assault crossing. The 301st Infantry was to cross in the vicinity of Serrig-Kreuzweiler and advance to establish a bridgehead some six thousand yards in depth. Similarly, the 302d Infantry was to establish its bridgehead in the area Serrig-Hamm and also establish a secure bridgehead. The 301st was charged with maintaining contact between the two divisions.

Colonel Hagerty directed his 3d Battalion, under Lieutenant Colonel McNulty, to reconnoiter the town of Stadt while Lieutenant Colonel Dohs's 2d Battalion checked out the town of Kreuzweiler. They were expected to be jumping-off points for the assault crossing. Each had a road leading into it from positions held by the division and could thereby support an attack. The 94th Division Reconnaissance Troop reported that Kreuzweiler was still held by an enemy force that outnumbered them. Colonel Dohs made a personal reconnaissance, which confirmed the report of the troop, leaving only Stadt as a crossing site. Because the 3d Battalion was already located near Stadt, it was designated as the assault force for the entire regiment.

The 302d Infantry also had difficulties in selecting a crossing site. The town of Hamm had no usable road and was under fire from across the river already. The men of the regiment found that the only other choice was the village of Taben, which under any other circumstances would not have been selected, as it was out of the assigned area allocated to the regiment. The west bank was poor in all respects as a crossing site, while the enemy-held east bank was dominated by a large hill mass known locally as Hocker Hill. This hill, rising some four hundred feet above the river, was protected by a twelve-foot vertical retaining wall, a highway, and a railroad. Despite all the obvious drawbacks, Colonel Johnson had no alternative. The 1st Battalion was ordered to move from Oberleuken to Taben to make the assault crossing before dawn on the twenty-second. Johnson hoped that because the site was so obviously impractical the enemy would not defend it in strength.

The enemy situation across the river was, in fact, largely unknown to the Americans, as no patrols had yet had time to cross the river. The division did know that the enemy had his usual Siegfried Line concrete defenses spread throughout the area. In addition, the Germans had unlimited observation from the eastern heights, which dominated the west bank. The usual minefields and prepared artillery fires were expected. The XX Corps's 7th Artillery Observation Battalion had not had time to identify accurately enemy artillery positions across the river, and so the 94th Infantry Division would be attacking with practically no knowledge of the enemy defenses other than that they would be formidable. Like the 10th Armored Division, the 94th was to be aided by the 1139th Engineer Group, which attached its 135th Engineer Combat Battalion directly to the division. Lieutenant Colonel Ellis, the division engineering officer, contacted the engineer group to arrange coordination between the division and the bridging battalion.

Unlike the 10th Armored, the 94th was prepared for the failure of the bridging battalion to arrive. When it had not arrived by midnight, Colonel Ellis sent the operations officer of the organic 319th Engineer Combat Battalion, Maj. Albert R. Hoffman, out to look for them. Two miles from the town of Freudenburg, Major Hoffman found the trucks bearing the boats snugly bedded down for the night. Acting quickly, Hoffman got the convoy back on the road and then split the trucks between the two divisional crossing sites. After ensuring that the trucks arrived, Major Hoffman returned to his other duties.

At the Taben site, Major Stanion, commanding the 1st Battalion, had to prepare without a chance to look over the location chosen. Arriving in darkness, the 1st Battalion, 302d Infantry, detrucked and prepared for the attack. They learned from the division engineers that the boats were not yet there, so they settled down to wait. One hour after the designated assault time, the boats arrived at Taben. The infantrymen, assisted by the engineers, manhandled the thousand-pound assault boats down to the river's edge. There was a thick fog rising off the river, which, in addition to the darkness, gave additional protection to the assault force. It nevertheless took the battalion more than an hour to move and prepare the first six boats. With many more boats to be brought down to the river's edge and time passing quickly, Lieutenant Colonel Ellis determined to take a risk with the remaining boats. Counting on the fog and the darkness to cover the movement, he ordered the drivers of the loaded trucks to drive them down the hill leading to the crossing site, then turn off their engines and let them roll quietly to the water's edge. This was done without difficulty or enemy interference, and soon the battalion was ready to attack.

Company C had been selected to make the first crossing. Shortly before dawn on 22 February, Sgt. John F. Smith's squad from Company C boarded an assault boat manned by two combat engineers and crossed successfully to the enemy-held bank. Here they encountered the retaining wall, but their luck held and they discovered a scaling ladder left in place by the retreating enemy. Having crossed undetected, they scaled the wall quietly and surprised two Germans guarding a pillbox covering the exact route they had just crossed. Seven more soldiers emerged from this pillbox and were added to Sergeant Smith's haul. By this time, the rest of the 2d Platoon had arrived and they succeeded in clearing the remainder of the landing site, capturing two more pillboxes and several prisoners. The 94th Infantry Division was across the Saar.

Companies A and B of the battalion quickly followed Company C into the newly established bridgehead. Clearing operations began and Company C, led by TSgt. James Cousineau, climbed and secured Hocker Hill. The major terrain obstacle to the Taben bridgehead was taken by the infantry, using skill and surprise unsupported by armor or artillery. Meanwhile Company A moved on the town of Serrig, the center of the planned bridgehead. As it moved out, the artillery observer with the battalion, Captain Bruhl of the 356th Field Artillery, noticed about one hundred Germans moving forward against the company's advance. Quickly adjusting the fire of his battalion on the enemy force, the Americans witnessed the nearly complete destruction of the counterattacking enemy by the first artillery concentration fired since the crossing. The assault on Serrig continued until it reached an orchard just outside of the town, where enemy troops dug in to the orchard fired on the Americans. Using marching fire, the men of Company A quickly routed the enemy force, which left twenty-seven dead behind. Supported by Company B on its flank, Company A soon entered and secured Serrig.

Back at division headquarters, things were tense due to the pressure put on by XX Corps, which needed a swift and successful crossing to avoid another of General Patton's outbursts. General Malony personally observed both river crossings and by early morning Colonel Bercquist could report that they had been successful. The next matter of concern was the vitally needed bridges, and Bercquist turned the tables by pressuring the XX Corps engineer to expedite their delivery.

Although both crossings were successful, the crossing at Stadt was no less difficult than that at Taben. Like those of its sister regiment, the 301st Infantry's boats were delayed due to lack of urgency in the boat battalion and to a traffic jam in the rear of the 301st Infantry. Two companies, I and K, were planned to make the crossing side by side. However, confusion in the darkness and the loss of a boat truck made the plans useless. Instead, Lieutenant Colonel McNulty, commander of the 3d Battalion, changed plans and adjusted the order of attack to a column of companies, led by Company I. Unlike the crossing at Taben, the Stadt crossing was detected by the enemy before the troops put their boats in the water, and machine-gun fire began to land on the west bank. The troops waited for a lull in the enemy fire, then launched the boats. Covered by artillery fire, Company I paddled swiftly across the river. Although both sides were firing blindly into the fog, the distraction sufficed for the company to cross safely. In some confusion, from boats landed in disorder, the company managed to get ashore in reasonable condition, only to face barbed wire along the water's edge, which snared some of the assault boats. In order to save the boats for following waves, the wire had to be cut by hand rather than by use of explosives. Still protected by the fog, the attackers breached the wire and the boats returned for the next wave. Several, now manned only by two engineers each, were swept downstream by the current and never seen again.

Meanwhile, Company I continued to consolidate its tiny bridgehead. Breaches in the barbed-wire barricade were marked with toilet paper for following companies, as were detected minefields. Near Serrig some infantrymen from Company I were pinned down by enemy fire in an antitank ditch. Alone and cut off from the main body of Company I, this group faced disaster until Pfc. Robert L. Chapman leapt from the ditch with his Browning automatic rifle and charged the closest pillbox. Working his way to the back of the fortification, he captured a prisoner, then had him talk the remaining occupants of the pillbox into surrendering. Chapman's comrades then came forward and occupied the captured pillbox. Other Germans soon moved on the pillbox, threatening to capture the occupants. Rather than risking that, the squad returned to the antitank ditch, covered by Private Chapman's BAR (Browning Automatic Rifle). As he turned to join his comrades in the ditch, Chapman was struck down by a concussion grenade thrown at close range. The blast threw him into the ditch and then he was wounded in the shoulder. Chapman struggled to his feet and killed the enemy threatening his squad, then covered the squad as it organized its defense of the antitank ditch. Chapman survived to wear the Distinguished Service Cross he won that morning.

While Company I struggled to maintain its foothold on the eastern bank, the rest of the battalion struggled to cross and support their fellow infantrymen. However, only six of the sixteen boats used in the initial crossing managed to return to the west bank. This was not sufficient to move many soldiers at a time, and to make matters worse, boats that had returned were short of oars, as many men, in the excitement of an assault crossing, had carried their oars with them into battle. As usual, the resourceful soldiers of the 319th Combat Engineers at the crossing site managed to find outboard motors to expedite future crossings.

While awaiting the arrival of the motors, the battalion continued to attempt to cross. Using the boats and paddles available, Company K next tried to cross. With only six boats available, and with the fog being burned off by the rising sun, Company K's crossing was more costly than the earlier attempt. German artillery and machine-gun fire now fell with more accuracy, so the 4.2 mortars of Company B, 81st Chemical Mortar Battalion, attempted to cover the attack with smoke. Two of Company K's boats were lost to enemy artillery fire, however, and only one managed to return to the west bank intact.

Shortly after this attempt, the engineers arrived with both the outboard motors and more boats. Although the motors had to be serviced under enemy fire, causing more casualties of both boats and personnel, the rest of Company K and Lieutenant Colonel McNulty's battalion headquarters managed to cross the river in the next attempt. The battalion quickly established itself in and around Stadt. Under continuing enemy fire throughout the day and night, it nevertheless was established firmly across the Saar River.

With the two crossings successfully established, the rest of the division moved into follow-up positions. The remaining battalions of the 301st and 302d moved toward the crossing sites to take their turns crossing the Saar. The 94th Reconnaissance Troop mopped up bypassed enemy resistance along the west bank, while the 5th Ranger Battalion relieved elements of the division to enable them to move over the river.

General Patton arrived in midafternoon at the division's forward command post to observe the operations. After the scalding review of the 10th Armored Division's efforts, the general could not have been other than pleased at the infantry's efforts, yet he left no recorded comments of his view of the Saar River crossing. Perhaps his reticence was due in part to the news that the afternoon attack of the 10th Armored had been postponed once again due to the inability of the 81st Chemical Mortar Battalion to get its smoke generators positioned in a timely manner, as well as the delay of the 376th Infantry at the crossing sites caused by enemy automatic weapons fire.

Colonel McClune had established his regimental command post immediately adjacent to the 10th Armored's command post. After receiving orders to begin his assault crossing of the Saar, he sent forward Companies C and L to the crossing sites. They had more than fifteen hundred yards of open ground to cross before even reaching the river. As they approached, they discovered that the smoke screen was fading fast because the enemy fire from the now alerted enemy positions across the river was so heavy and accurate that it prevented the chemical mortar battalion from refueling the smoke generators or repairing them when they stopped working. Company C managed to struggle down a ditch to within two hundreds yards of the river, but Company L was forced to take shelter in an apple orchard near the line of departure. Colonel McClune, accompanied by his driver, Cpl. John R. Hills, and his radioman, T/4 Grade Richard J. Scheibner, attempted to get the attack moving by personal example, but enemy fire was too accurate for an advance over the remaining open ground. Captain Brightman, commanding Company L, was killed in the attempt, and Lt. James W. Cornelius, commanding Company C, was wounded. The 376th Infantry would have to wait for the cover of darkness.

General Patton, never known for his patience, determined that he would not rely on the 10th Armored alone. The bridge sites captured by the 94th Infantry Division would be of no immediate help to a rapid exploitation by the 10th Armored, which had yet to gain its own beachheads over the Saar. During a tour of his XII Corps to the north of XX Corps, he visited the headquarters of the 76th Infantry Division. Determined to achieve his immediate goal of conquering the former Roman city of Trier, he impressed his desires forcefully on the men of the 76th. "It was a cold, gray, damp morning. General Patton, in parka, glistening helmet, spotless tan boots, and armed with the famed two pistols, drove up to the 76th Division CP, strode brusquely into the inner sanctum, placed a huge fist on a map of Trier. That was all. It was an order." The race for Trier was on.

CHAPTER 18
ACROSS THE SAAR

In order for the Ghost Corps to position itself to accomplish the latest directive from General Patton, the 10th Armored Division had to cross the Saar River. The 94th Infantry Division, at less than two-thirds strength, could not possibly drive on Trier alone. The operations officer of the 10th Armored quickly drew up a new plan to cross the Saar. Lieutenant Colonel Joseph A. McChristian selected the 1st and 3d Battalions of the attached 376th Infantry to make the assault crossing. Two separate crossings were to be made to divide the enemy's resistance between them and to increase the chances of at least one attempt succeeding.

To ease the infantry's way, CCA ordered its two task forces to seize the towns where bridges over the Saar existed. Task Force Chamberlain was directed against the towns of Kanzem and Wiltingen, each with a bridge, while Task Force Richardson was sent to Tawern at the tip of the Triangle with a view toward Trier.

The attempt at a coup de main by the charging tankers of the 10th Armored failed. Racing toward the bridge at Wiltingen, the leading armored elements ran headlong into an enemy minefield that covered the road and extended into the fields on both sides. The tankers had to call up the engineers of the 55th Armored Engineer Battalion. Working in the pitch darkness of the night of 21–22 February, they cleared a path before dawn. Just as the armored infantrymen raced through the gap, a "tremendous explosion on the river rocked them with the knowledge that the enemy had blown up their objective." Moments later the second bridge at Kanzem was also destroyed by the Germans. The 10th Armored Division would not capture a bridge across the Saar.

General Morris had only the infantry part of the plan left to get his division across the river. Colonel McClune was doing his best to get his regiment set for the crossing. During the night of 22 February the colonel and his driver rode to the town of Ayl, one of the crossing sites selected by the 10th Armored Division, to give himself a picture of how to deploy the regiment later that night. McClune had been told by the 10th Armored staff that the town was in their hands, and so he drove to Ayl to ascertain the best location for his battalions to assemble for the river crossing. As they were about to pull into the town, the colonel's driver noticed that the sentries about to challenge them did not appear to be wearing American helmets. Probably some of the engineers, the colonel thought, and told his driver to slow down. As they approached he leaned out, expecting the familiar hushed command to "Halt!" But it didn't come. It was then that they noticed the distinctive German helmet on the sentry. The driver slammed the jeep into reverse, getting safely away before the enemy could react. McClune immediately contacted the headquarters of the 10th Armored to learn that the armored infantry really had not yet cleared Ayl.

The colonel's men, awaiting orders to move to the river, fared little better. The regiment's cooks managed to prepare the first hot meal the infantry had seen in days, but just as the meal was about to be distributed, orders came to rush to the river to meet the boats they would use to cross the Saar. The hot meal was left uneaten and the men waited at the river's edge for the boats that never came. Throughout the day false alarms came and went but no crossing developed. First the boats failed to arrive, as did the smoke generators. After spending most of the night and half the day waiting for the boats, McClune pulled his regiment back from the river to rest pending the next developments. Meanwhile, he sent the regimental liaison officer, Lt. Jess L. Long, out looking for the boats.

The next development, as we have seen, was General Patton's arrival at the 10th Armored's headquarters. A result of this meeting was that immediate orders were sent to Colonel McClune to "cross at once." The 376th Infantry tried their best to comply, but just as the troops had organized themselves at the water's edge, the protective cover of the smoke generators failed again. At the same time, a breeze blew through the valley of the Saar, dispelling what little smoke cover remained. Within minutes the two assault battalions were exposed to unobstructed enemy observation. As always, the Germans reacted swiftly and decisively. Observed artillery, mortar, and machine-gun fire ripped into both the soldiers and their equipment. All of the boats that were available were destroyed. The majority of the smoke generators were also useless. Casualties among the troops and the supporting engineers were heavy, including the death of Capt. William A. Brightman of Company L, and the wounding of Lt. James W. Cornelius, of Company C, the two assault companies.

With no boats and no protective smoke, McClune withdrew his men from the river, immediately notifying the 10th Armored. In response, he was asked how soon he could renew the attack. He replied that as soon as he had enough boats and one hour to position them, the 376th Infantry would try again.

The replacement boats arrived after dark. As the troops struggled to move the heavy craft to the water's edge, a heavy fog again began to rise off the river. Finally, one hour before midnight, all was in readiness and the assault troops pushed off into the river. Company C, now commanded by Lt. Ben R. Chalkley, crossed without opposition but once ashore faced machine guns firing along preplanned lines. In the fog, the troops manning the pillboxes could see very little, however, and the Americans quickly noted where the fire was coming from, then followed it to its source, attacking and capturing each enemy position in turn. Although enemy mortar and artillery fire began to fall as the attack progressed, the beachhead had been secured sufficiently that this did not deter consolidation.

Meanwhile at the adjoining beach, Company I, which had replaced the hard-hit Company L as assault company, landed without opposition. The fog and the stealth of the infantrymen achieved what might have been impossible, surprise. The soldiers of Company I, led by Lt. William R. Jacques, managed to reach the pillbox line without being fired upon. They then proceeded to reduce the positions one by one. Some resisted, while others surrendered upon demand. Company I's beachhead was secure.

The seizing of the beachheads did not remove the opposition, however. Colonel McClune, concerned that the 1st Battalion was still contesting the enemy defenses, went to the shore to observe and give what assistance he could. As his jeep approached the launch sites it was caught in a mortar barrage. This time the colonel's driver, Corporal Hills, couldn't get out of the way in time and all the jeep's occupants were wounded. Hit again while in a roadside ditch, Colonel McClune was later evacuated. The first and only commander the 376th Infantry had known in World War II was gone. The regimental executive officer, Lt. Col. Raynor E. Anderson, assumed command.

The 376th Infantry's 2d Battalion now moved forward to follow its sister battalions across the river. Lieutenant Colonel Martin learned that opposition in the 3d Battalion's area was considerably less fierce than at the 1st Battalion's crossing site, so he moved his battalion there with few casualties. Crossing in the darkness of 23 February, the 2d Battalion had Ockfen as its objective, the major town in the immediate area. "It was so dark you couldn't see more than fifteen feet in front of your face, and you had to part the smoke with your hands to walk through it." Although moving through the fog, smoke, and darkness was difficult, the battalion managed to follow the riverbank until close by the town. Heading inland, the Americans began the attack still cloaked by darkness and were soon involved in a house-to-house struggle. Just as dawn promised to simplify their advance, the men heard approaching armor. Knowing that no bridge had yet been constructed across the river at their backs, the Americans prepared to battle German tanks. Despite their bazooka teams' attempts to destroy or cripple them, the 2d Battalion soldiers were forced to surrender their gains in the town and withdraw to the surrounding hills. Colonel Martin said later of his battalion's withdrawal, "Nothing but mountain goats or scared infantrymen could ever climb this hill, and my whole damned battalion is up here."

The withdrawal was only temporary, however. The artillery of the 919th Field Artillery Battalion, the 10th Armored Division, and corps artillery batteries placed a devastating barrage on Ockfen. "It looked as if the town just blew up." Eight battalions of artillery ranging in caliber from 105mm to 240mm blasted the town for five minutes, after which the infantry called for a cease-fire, as it was affecting the front-line troops. Companies E and F quickly assaulted the town to find that only shell-shocked survivors remained. The rest of the enemy force, including the armor, had fled. Colonel Martin ordered his mine platoon of the battalion antitank company to mine the road leading into Ockfen from the enemy position to protect against any enemy armor that might reappear. The repulse of the enemy had been so decisive, however, that only scattered artillery fire hit the battalion the rest of the day, but even this cost it the services of its executive officer, Maj. John R. Dossenbach, who was wounded by shell fragments.

While the 2d and 3d Battalions were making progress, the 1st Battalion was still struggling to preserve its meager beachhead. After Company C had crossed, Company B followed. Before all of the company could cross, however, there were no boats left. A call quickly went out for more boats, but until these arrived those infantrymen on the west bank were isolated. Colonel Minor was soon advised that no more boats were immediately available but that he could cross with the 3d Battalion's to get the remainder of his battalion across the Saar. Minor moved his men swiftly to the new crossing site, crossed successfully, and united his battalion. He found that Company C, the assault company, was now commanded by TSgt. Thomas D. Huthnance, all officers having become casualties. Appointing Capt. Frank Malinski, a battalion staff officer, as the new commander of Company C, Colonel Minor began to organize his attack.

At the end of daylight on 23 February the 376th had accomplished its initial missions. It had established a bridgehead over the Saar and held Scharfenberg Ridge, the immediate objective on the eastern bank. Ockfen was secured. Now it was up to XX Corps, and the 10th Armored Division.

General Walker was thinking about improving the security of the bridgeheads gained by the 94th Infantry Division and Combat Team 376. A solution he decided upon both to secure the beachheads and speed up operations was to establish a blocking force behind enemy lines at the village of Zerf, astride their main supply route (MSR). By cutting the enemy's MSR, Walker hoped to require him to withdraw his forces to other positions, thus freeing XX Corps to move against Trier. He had the ideal unit available within XX Corps to accomplish this task, the 5th Ranger Battalion, so he released it from attachment to the 3d Cavalry Group and attached it to the 94th Infantry Division. Having had their skills as elite assault troops wasted since the early days in Normandy, the unit was about to embark on a mission that one historian would later call the only one performed after D-Day that was "appropriate to the rangers' original purpose."

CHAPTER 19
"YOU CAN'T BE HERE!"

The 5th Ranger Battalion owed its existence to two men who never served with it. Early in the war, Gen. George C. Marshall, the U.S. Army chief of staff, ordered several officers to England to observe and report on the various organizations within the British military forces. One of these was Brigadier General Lucian K. Truscott, who was greatly impressed with British commando forces. These light infantrymen were used for raids, special reconnaissance operations, and spearheading major attacks, being trained to a highly professional standard. Truscott recommended that the U.S. Army establish a similar force, if not for raids, then train qualified men to return to their own units and pass on new skills to their comrades. As a result of his recommendation, the 1st Ranger Battalion was created in England.

Selected to command this unit was Maj. William O. Darby. So successful were Darby's efforts that after leading his battalion in the assault on North Africa, he was directed to raise and train two more battalions. These he led in the invasions of Sicily and Italy. Known by this time as "Darby's Rangers," or officially as the Ranger Force, they were unfortunately deployed on the beachhead at Anzio, where they were virtually destroyed in a battle against enemy armor.

The success of the Ranger Force in North Africa and Sicily stirred the creation of other battalions for use in other theaters. Two ranger battalions were trained for use in the European Theater of Operations specifically to participate in the Normandy invasion. These battalions, the 2d and 5th Ranger Battalions, assaulted enemy strongpoints on the flank of Omaha beach, where they were instrumental in securing their objective of the most bitterly contested beach of the entire operation. Once the beachhead was secured there were few appropriate missions for them. Both participated in the Brittany campaign, where they performed as line infantry. Later, after training replacements, the 2d Rangers were assigned to First U.S. Army, where they were bled white in the Huertgen Forest. The 5th Rangers were assigned to Third U.S. Army, and finally were now to perform "the only deep infiltration mission assigned to the two battalions after D-Day."

Lieutenant Colonel Richard P. Sullivan commanded the 5th Ranger Battalion, having served with the unit since before the Normandy landings, where he had been the executive officer of the battalion. Now, as commander, he had already led it in several combat operations. On 22 February the Rangers were spread out, holding defensive positions behind the front of the 94th Infantry Division. Two of their six companies were in Orscholz, two others at Taben, and the remaining two near Wieten. Shortly before noon, Sullivan was ordered to report for instructions to Colonel Bercquist, from whom he learned that XX Corps had ordered his unit to assemble without awaiting relief in their present positions, and prepare for an infiltration mission behind enemy lines; objective was the Irsch–Zerf Road.

Sullivan immediately ordered his battalion to assemble at Taben to cross the Saar into the 94th's beachhead. Sullivan and his battalion operations officer, Capt. Edward S. Luther, tried to obtain as much information on friendly and enemy forces as they could but were disappointed with the information available at division headquarters. Sullivan then took Lt. Louis J. Gambosi and his platoon of Company B as an escort and proceeded to the beachhead. Still looking for information, Sullivan, Luther, and the escort platoon crossed the river and climbed Hocker Hill to confer with Colonel Gaddis. He was disappointed to learn that the 302d Infantry was still struggling to maintain its precarious beachhead, but acquired what information he could while sending Gambosi back to bring up the battalion. During the time the battalion took to pass through the 94th's route to combat, Capt. Charles E. Parker's Company A had six men killed and another eighteen wounded by enemy fire.

At midnight of the twenty-second Sullivan assembled his company commanders at the advance command post of the 302d Infantry and briefed them on his plans for the infiltration. Having learned that the 302d Infantry was not yet at its planned line of departure, he determined to pass through its present lines and proceed on an azimuth heading of ten degrees.

At 2:00 A.M. on 23 February, the battalion moved off into the darkness in front of the 302d Infantry. Keeping an interval of fifty yards between companies, it advanced in two columns. Captain Jack A. Snyder's Company C led the left column, while Capt. George R. Miller's Company D was on the right. Trouble began even before the battalion left Hocker Hill. The second echelon in the column consisted of 1st Lt. James F. Greene Jr.'s Company E and Capt. Bernard M. Pepper's Company B. As they moved down Hocker Hill an artillery barrage mixed with small arms fire hit both companies. The artillery forward observation party attached to the battalion was hit hard and rendered ineffective, while Company B suffered several casualties. The barrage separated the bulk of the battalion from the lead elements, and Sullivan was soon aware that Companies C and D were alone. He sent Captain Luther back to determine what had happened, while contacting the missing companies by radio. Half an hour was lost while the battalion reunited itself.

The battalion then continued on its mission. Harassing fire continued to strike around them as they moved in the darkness. Sullivan noticed that the enemy seemed to be firing at the sound made by his Rangers as they moved in the brush and woods. Later, when moving in more open areas, he realized that the enemy was attracted to the noise made by the antitank mines his men were carrying. These had been brought along to help establish a roadblock at the objective and could not be abandoned. There was nothing the rangers could do to muffle the sounds of the rattling mines. The battalion then encountered a large group of Germans in their path, whom they quickly captured. Although the prisoners slowed the unit and drained its fighting strength by the need for guards, Sullivan "just couldn't kill that many, so we had to take them prisoner." By daylight the battalion found a place to rest and reconnoiter the next part of the route.

After the reconnaissance patrols returned, Sullivan formed the battalion in a square formation with 1st Lt. John M. Carter's Headquarters Company in the center and moved off in the direction of Zerf. Using artillery-spotting rounds to maintain direction, the men kept to wooded areas as much as possible. As they proceeded toward their objective, they encountered three pillboxes, from which they captured another thirty prisoners. Shortly afterward the rear of the column, headquarters company and Company B, were attacked by about fifty Germans. Apparently the enemy took them for a patrol and charged across open ground into the Americans' fire. After decimating the attacking force, Sullivan found himself saddled with over one hundred prisoners. Company B, which had lost contact with more than a platoon and a half during the night, also had several casualties, leaving only sixteen men, so it was assigned to guard the growing numbers of prisoners.

As they advanced into enemy territory, more Germans were encountered. While crossing a stream, Captain Parker's Company A was attacked by some enemy soldiers whom they chased away, leaving a few German casualties in the field. Shortly afterward, a German Red Cross vehicle came along and stopped to look over the wounded. A German doctor and four medical aidmen were taken from the ambulance by Company A. The doctor was brought to Colonel Sullivan, to whom he complained, "This is four thousand yards behind the lines—no, no—you can't be here."

Throughout the day the rangers continued their advance. Each time they encountered enemy forces, they changed direction to prevent them from getting a chance to predict the route and prepare an ambush. Company B's meager forces continued to guard a growing number of prisoners. The German doctor, now recovered from his surprise at becoming a prisoner so far behind his own lines, was treating both American and German wounded and continued to do so throughout the mission.

During the night of 22–23 February, the battalion alternately moved and rested. At each halt, patrols were dispatched to check on the surrounding area for enemy positions and to check the route ahead. During these halts the number of prisoners taken by the battalion continued to grow. Several pillboxes, fortified houses, and field fortifications were taken by these patrols. Early on the morning of the twenty-third, an enemy self-propelled artillery piece opened direct fire on the battalion but withdrew when the rangers returned fire. Finally, shortly after dawn, the battalion arrived near their objective.

Colonel Sullivan dispatched 1st Lt. John T. Reville's Company F to search and clear the area. They captured fortified houses and brought back another thirty prisoners. An artillery battery had been reported in the area, but they did not find it. Sullivan then set about establishing his roadblock, the purpose of the rangers' mission to Zerf. It was to be located where the Irsch–Zerf road entered some woods, giving the rangers some concealment. As the battalion approached the final objective, Company B, bringing up the rear, came under enemy fire. Despite this last-minute delay, the battalion reached its designated location and Sullivan issued his orders, disposing his battalion for the fight that was sure to come.

Lieutenant Greene's Company E was ordered to place the anti-tank mines on the road, then to establish themselves in position where they could cover the road with small arms fire. Greene also positioned a bazooka team to cover the road. Basing themselves on Company E's position, the rest of the battalion set themselves up in a rough circle for all-around defense. As they settled in, an enemy self-propelled gun came down the road. Seeing the rangers and the roadblock, its crew "jumped out and ran like hell" before the rangers could react. After failing to destroy the gun with bazooka fire, the men poured gasoline on the vehicle and burned it.

After this incident the Germans in the area became aware that the rangers were on the road. Company A, withdrawing from an outlying position, was nearly overrun by an enemy force that had approached their position unseen. It took over two hours for the combined fire of the battalion to extricate Captain Parker's command. As the day wore on, more and more attention was directed at the surrounded rangers, who maintained the crucial roadblock against all attacks.

While they were infiltrating the enemy lines to establish their roadblock, the 94th Infantry and 10th Armored Divisions were trying to break those same lines. The 301st and 302d Infantries were still struggling across the Saar. Boats were still a problem, with enemy artillery and automatic weapons fire disabling them almost as quickly as the Americans could get replacements. Casualties continued to mount, and in the 2d Battalion, 301st Infantry, the seventy survivors of Companies F and G were combined into a composite company under the command of Capt. Otto P. Steinen. Company E of this battalion had fifty men left in it. So exhausted were several men that, once across the river, several had to be medically evacuated, including the commander of Company E, Captain Stokstad, who was ordered by medics to hand over command and report for treatment. Lieutenant Edmund G. Reuter assumed command of what was left of Company E.

Hocker Hill was still not completely secure. The rangers had found to their detriment that the enemy still controlled the approaches to the hill and held strong positions on its flanks. As the battered remnants of the 2d Battalion, 301st, moved up the left side of Hocker Hill, they were struck by enemy fire from several strong-points. Not strong enough to attack these enemy positions directly, the troops made several attempts to outflank them. When this failed, the 356th Field Artillery Battalion was called upon to direct fire on known positions. While the artillery was doing its work, the battalion Antitank Platoon was ordered up to the line to act as reinforcement for the depleted ranks in the infantry. With the support of the 356th Field Artillery and the additional strength provided by the antitank platoon, the battalion secured its flank on Hocker Hill that afternoon.

Because of the disorder in which the attack had developed after the initial problems with the crossings, the battalions of the division were all intermingled. General Malony gave control of whichever battalions happened to be in their sectors to Colonels Hagerty and Johnson and ordered them to clear the east bank of enemy opposition, so as to permit bridges to be constructed at the crossing sites. The attachment on 24 February by Corps of the 1258th Engineer Combat Battalion permitted the return of the 3d Battalion, 101st Infantry, to the 26th Division, but did not improve the strength of the attacking battalions. Confusion increased as leaders fell to enemy fire or exhaustion. One shell killed Lieutenant Colonel Dohs, commanding the 2d Battalion, 301st Infantry, and the commander of Company F, and wounded several of the battalion staff officers. So numerous were the casualties among the officers that regimental headquarters had to send down its own operations officer, Maj. George W. Brumley, to take command.

It was not until late morning of 24 February that an organized assault to clear the east bank could be launched by the 3d Battalion of the 301st. Although opposition remained fierce, and positions captured were sometimes lost and recaptured, the attack succeeded in clearing enough of the east bank to permit the ferrying of vehicles across the Saar. Accurate enemy fire still plagued the crossing site at Stadt until it was discovered that an enemy artillery observation party was concealed on a cliff overlooking the bridgehead. Once discovered, the observers quickly surrendered and admitted to directing the accurate enemy fire. The enemy fire naturally became less accurate, so the 135th Combat Engineer Battalion, assisted by Company A, 319th Combat Engineers, constructed a treadway bridge at the Taben crossing site. The trucks carrying the bridge sections had to run a gauntlet of long-range enemy machine-gun fire. Although several trucks were hit, none was disabled enough to block the access road. On the eastern bank, the retaining wall had to be breached to prepare a road off the incoming bridge. Once the basic work was completed, units of the 778th Tank Battalion crossed the bridge to support the troops on the east bank. Throughout the night, the engineers worked hard to keep the bridge in operation. Repeatedly, the floats that supported the bridge were punctured by enemy fire and had to be refloated. The bridge and the arrival of the tank support for the beleaguered infantry on the east bank opened the restricted bridgehead that had been up holding the 94th Division. Gradually, over the next few days, the division enlarged its bridgehead, pushing the enemy out of his prepared defenses and advancing deeper into Germany. Resistance remained fierce to the end, and ominous signs of enemy reinforcements began to appear when Company A, 301st Infantry, found itself being counterattacked on Hocker Hill by the 506th Panzergrenadier Battalion. Other signs, however, were more encouraging. On 27 February, as the 302d Infantry was moving forward to a series of hills on their front, one unit came under heavy automatic weapons fire from the Germans. During the firing one soldier who spoke some German called to the enemy, who immediately ceased fire and entered into surrender negotiations. As it turned out, the American and German company commanders were able to converse in German, and soon settled on terms. The Germans marched into the American rear area while the 302d Infantry climbed the recently evacuated hill. Lieutenant Baumgaertner was also still at it. Commanding Company A of the 302d, he was questioning some freshly captured prisoners in a pillbox when the phone rang. Answering it in perfect German, he told an inquiring German officer that the recent action had been a patrol that had been successfully repulsed. This deception saved Company A from the usual three hours of artillery fire that usually fell on recently captured positions.

Things remained just as confused in the 10th Armored Division's zone of operations. Although the 376th Infantry had successfully crossed the Saar, the armor still remained on the west bank. Without armored support the depleted units could not advance. For a while it seemed doubtful they could even retain the bridgehead. Lieutenant Colonel Thurston's 3d Battalion came under attack on the twenty-fourth, with the enemy penetrating its lines until Capt. Ralph T. Brown, commanding Company K, used his personal skill as a sharpshooter to kill the enemy soldiers who had entered the American positions. Several days later, during an attack on the village of Bierfeld, Captain Brown found an enemy World War I 77mm artillery piece firing directly on his company's line of advance. Picking up a grenade launcher, he advanced alone against the weapon holding up his command. Fighting his way past several enemy rocket-launcher teams protecting the artillery position, he managed, although seriously wounded, to clear the way for supporting tanks to move up and silence the enemy obstacle.

When his attack stalled, Lieutenant Colonel Thurston learned that the supply parties bringing up vitally needed food and ammunition simply could not keep pace with expenditure, so he arranged to have artillery observation planes drop supplies to the troops, with twenty Piper Cub planes dropping food, ammunition, radio batteries, and medical supplies. While they were engaged in this effort, two

German planes attacked them, but although aircraft were damaged, none was shot down. A heartening reinforcement appeared, as Company B, 61st Armored Infantry Battalion, arrived. The 10th Armored was finally sending its infantry battalions across the river.

Company B was attached to Lieutenant Colonel Martin's 2d Battalion, still struggling to hold the regimental objective of Ockfen, as battles raged back and forth over the hills and fields. Casualties continued to mount, and both Colonel Martin and his executive officer were wounded and evacuated. Captain Frederick D. Standish, next in line, somehow escaped from a position surrounded by enemy forces, but was so exhausted he, too, had to be evacuated. Things were so desperate that Lieutenant Colonel Anderson, the 376th Infantry's new commander, appealed to General Malony for aid. Sending a teletype directly to 94th Division headquarters, he explained that "our lines are so extended that we cannot prevent enemy infiltration" and "I have no reserve." Colonel Anderson went on to complain that he had "no support or direct fire of heavy weapons." Only two platoons of tank destroyers were on the west bank supporting his regiment. The 376th had lost fourteen officers and 161 enlisted men since crossing the Saar, and was now understrength forty-seven officers and 506 enlisted men. There was little General Malony could do, however, as his own bridgeheads were held precariously.

It was not until the twenty-fifth that the 10th Armored Division managed to cross three tanks into the 376th's bridgehead. These were immediately attached to Colonel Martin's depleted battalion, which was able to move against several pillboxes threatening its position. Second Lieutenant Ernest N. Dyrlund's Third Platoon, Company E, consisting in total of seventeen men, moved with the tanks. Two tanks became bogged down and the remaining one soon became the target of every German gun in the vicinity. The tank commander was wounded and had to crawl out of his vehicle, as the tank crew halted and ceased fire. Lieutenant Dyrlund was killed as he directed his men. Technician Fifth Grade Paul E. Ramsay of Company E ran through the enemy fire to the tank commander to give him first aid, and brought him safely back to the rear. He then returned to the tank and took command of the ongoing battle. He directed the fire of the tank's guns while using its radio to report to the battalion command post on the situation. Due to Technician Ramsay's actions the survivors of the attacking force were able to withdraw safely without further loss. Ramsay survived to wear the Distinguished Service Cross he earned that day.

The 10th Armored Division was doing all it could to help. Frustrated at the inability to get a bridge across the Saar, General Morris formed a task force under Brigadier General Piburn, consisting of the three armored infantry battalions. They were sent into the 376th's beachhead early on the twenty-fifth to help hold the bridgehead, and moved rapidly to attack the Germans. Shortly after, Company B of the 61st Armored Infantry Battalion was surrounded in the village of Schouden. Colonel Minor's 1st Battalion, 376th Infantry, was ordered forward to relieve them with Companies A and B attacking and the decimated Company C in reserve. The attack jumped off on 27 February, supported by the 919th Field Artillery and the regimental cannon company. Determined opposition from hidden enemy pillboxes delayed it until Sgt. Leon D. Crutchfield of 2d Platoon, Company A, discovered how to locate the hidden enemy, by changing the direction of his platoon's attack directly toward the town. This revealed the hidden pillboxes, camouflaged from the flank, and supporting tank destroyers could suppress their fire from across the river while the infantry reduced each one in turn. While these attacks were in progress, Generals Morris and Malony conferred and agreed to send the tanks over the bridge now established at Taben in the 94th Division zone. General Walker, anxious for success, quickly supported the plan.

While the armor crossed the Saar and took its casualties as had the infantry before it, the armored elements of Task Force Riley crossed at Taben and maneuvered to attack the enemy from the flanks and rear. Meeting up with their armored infantry elements, the task forces moved to join the 94th Division's struggling infantry and the combined force soon cleared Irsch, putting pressure on the Germans holding the front of the 376th Infantry.

The constant American attacks had finally borne fruit. The relief sought by Colonel Anderson finally arrived on 26 February, when an attack by the 376th directed at a link up between the 10th Armored and the 94th Infantry Divisions found that the enemy had withdrawn during the night. The 10th Armored attacks had threatened the enemy flanks facing the 376th Infantry. Added to this was the fact that the rangers had cut their supply lines and were threatening their rear, while the 94th Division was outflanking them on the south. Pounded on all sides, the Germans withdrew to their next line of defense. Wearily the infantry loaded up their equipment and moved east once again. The rangers were still out there somewhere, and they needed relief.

CHAPTER 20
THE TIGER STRIKES

The delay in getting the 10th Armored Division across the Saar, and the ongoing struggle facing the 94th Infantry Division, did not please General Patton. Determined to find an opportunity for Third Army to lead an assault into the heart of Germany, he kept the pressure on his subordinates while at the same time pleading and dealing with his superiors. When he learned that the 12th Army Group commander, General Bradley, was coming to visit Third Army on 25 February, Patton "coached the three corps commanders" on how to behave during Bradley's visit. He particularly instructed them to try to convince Bradley "to let us continue the use of the 10th Armored Division for the purpose of taking Trier."

Overall the visit went well from Patton's viewpoint. He believed that he had convinced Bradley against his will to let Third Army keep the 10th Armored Division and attack toward Trier, while circumventing orders from SHAEF. Actually, Bradley had every intention of clearing out all enemy opposition west of the Rhine, using both Third and First Armies, and in fact, he was under orders from General Eisenhower to do just that. Eisenhower had already advised General Marshall that he was going to "abandon temporarily the general attack in the Ardennes and throw our entire weight into a rapid closing of the Rhine below Düsseldorf." Although Bradley believed the Ardennes attack could lead to a breakthrough, he conformed to Eisenhower's directive. This operation, which he code-named "Lumberjack," was "designed to advance Hodges and Patton to the Rhine River, clearing out all Germans north of the Moselle River and west of the Rhine in the triangle formed by Cologne-Coblenz-Trier."

General Bradley was very well aware that his plan, and those of his subordinate army commanders, "clearly exceeded even the loosest definition of "aggressive defense," which was what had been ordered by General Eisenhower's directive of 1 February. Unlike General Patton, General Bradley did not attempt to deceive General Eisenhower, who authorized Operation Lumberjack on 20 February. Clearly Patton had jumped the gun on Bradley's plans, but he was knowingly or otherwise acting in full accordance with them when he launched the XX Corps into the Saar-Moselle Triangle and then on Trier.

The meeting on 25 February resulted in approval being given by General Bradley for the 10th Armored to continue its attack while the 90th Infantry Division, then resting and refitting within the Third Army's zone, would be designated as the reserve required by SHAEF. The objective officially was now Trier.

The 10th Armored Division had adopted the nickname "Tiger Division." Now that the bulk of the division had crossed into the 94th Division's bridgeheads, they would be given a chance to show how appropriate the name was. General Walker ordered both divisions across the Saar to drive on the central town of Beurig. Once this was secured, the 10th Armored would send a force to relieve the 5th Ranger Battalion and then dash for Trier. This plan was to be executed on 25 February, just as Generals Bradley and Patton were discussing its future.

When XX Corps attempted to execute General Walker's plans, however, they found that the deep belt of enemy defenses, particularly the concrete pillboxes and bunkers, prevented rapid exploitation as envisioned. Both the infantry of the 10th Armored and the regiments of the 94th were still struggling to get past this enemy line of defense. For the 94th Division it was the second time it had been required to make a frontal attack on the Siegfried Line.

When Col. William L. Roberts's Combat Command B moved out in the direction of Beurig, they were stopped by infantrymen of the 94th Division and guided around the town, which they were still trying to capture. The infantrymen directed them to a wooded trail that bypassed the town and put them out on the Beurig–Zerf Highway on its eastern side. This resolved one of Roberts's problems, putting his force beyond the prepared enemy defenses. But he still had no infantrymen to support his tanks, as the infantry of the 10th Armored were still heavily engaged in assisting the 94th Infantry clearing the bridgehead. This second problem resolved itself when, as the combat command passed through the Beurig area, the lost platoons of Company B, 5th Ranger Battalion, attached themselves to his command.

When the rangers had departed Hocker Hill to begin their infiltration, they had been under heavy attack. During this time 1st Lt. Louis J. Gambosi and his 2d Platoon of Company B, 5th Rangers, lost contact with the rest of the battalion. Company B had moved off with the 1st Platoon in the lead, followed by a machine-gun section, followed in turn by the 2d Platoon. "During the shelling the men in the 1st Platoon lost contact with the leading part of the company." The group did not immediately realize that contact had been lost and remained "on the west slope of Hocker Hill waiting for word to move." It was shortly before dawn that they realized that their battalion had left without them, and they attempted to catch up by following the 10-degree azimuth ordered by Colonel Sullivan. Reaching a stream north of Hocker Hill, they received artillery, mortar, and machine-gun fire, so they withdrew and later that morning made another attempt to join their battalion. This time they successfully crossed the stream that had earlier delayed them but, once across, were fired on directly by an antitank gun. Mortar and artillery fire again came down on them, and again they withdrew. At about this time, Lieutenant Gambosi was contacted by battalion headquarters, who told him to return to Hocker Hill and rejoin the battalion at the first opportunity.

Gambosi and his reinforced platoon returned to Serrig and spent the day awaiting developments. Later that afternoon "a major from the 10th Armored Division came through Serrig at the head of a tank column. He said that he had no infantry. We joined his column (21st Tank Battalion)." Gambosi had another officer and twenty-four Rangers with him. These were loaded onto two half-tracks and moved with Task Force Riley to Irsch. Here they were to meet their armored infantry elements, Lt. Col. Miles L. Standish's 61st Armored Infantry Battalion, after which the united task force was to move to Zerf and relieve the rest of the beleaguered 5th Ranger Battalion.

The 61st Battalion, unknown to Lt. Col. John R. Riley, commanding Task Force Riley, was not in Irsch. In fact, they were still struggling alongside the 376th Infantry to get off Scharfenberg Ridge. When Task Force Riley approached Irsch, accompanied only by twenty-four Rangers, the first thing they encountered was an enemy roadblock. The leading Sherman tanks blasted through the roadblock, bypassed the remnants, and entered the town. However, as the third Sherman tried to bypass the roadblock, a German 88mm dual-purpose gun opened fire and knocked it out. The fourth tank in line was destroyed by an enemy bazooka team, as was the fifth Sherman. As if this was not enough opposition for Task Force Riley, "a German Tiger tank moved up and hit two of our Second Platoon light tanks, which were farther back in the column." The tank company commander sent for Lieutenant Gambosi, ordering him and his rangers into the town to clear it and protect the two leading Shermans that were somewhere up ahead.

The rangers quickly moved to clear Irsch. They soon cleared three roadblocks and chased the Tiger tank out of town as they approached. The rangers reached the far, or north, end of town, where they discovered a fourth roadblock covered by another Tiger tank. The rangers called for artillery support, but none was available as there was an ammunition shortage. Despite this, they cleared the roadblock, taking sixty prisoners. The Tiger tank, not wishing to close with the infantry unsupported, did not attack. As the Rangers were clearing Irsch, help finally arrived as Company B, 20th Armored Infantry Battalion, joined them. Company B, which had just crossed into the bridgehead, captured some three hundred prisoners from the 416th Infantry Division and claimed five enemy tanks as well. By the time Irsch was secured, Task Force Riley had lost five tanks, five men killed, and another twenty wounded.

During the night, Companies A and C of the 20th Armored Infantry Battalion also fought their way into Irsch, assisted by the attacks of the 376th Infantry, trying to clear its area and rejoin the 94th Division. At about midnight, Task Force Riley was ordered to move "immediately" east to relieve the 5th Ranger Battalion at Zerf. Reorganized as Temporary Team A, the 10th Armored elements in Irsch, still reinforced by the orphan ranger unit, moved out of Irsch along the road that led to Zerf and the 5th Ranger Battalion. The tanks moved off, each carrying two of Lieutenant Gambosi's rangers aboard. The other rangers followed in half-tracks. At the edge of Irsch, a Tiger tank blocked the road and with its first shot set the leading American Sherman on fire. The second Sherman followed the fate of the first, and the Tiger turned its attention to the half-tracks carrying the rangers. Just as they jumped out, the half-tracks exploded into flames. Because Task Force Riley had moved out "bumper to bumper" it could not maneuver to attack the Tiger. The American force was obliged to withdraw into Irsch to sort itself out. The crew of the Tiger, however, did not wait around and went off of its own accord, rather than face infantry unsupported.

Task Force Riley reported back to headquarters that they could not advance in the darkness. The reply was that they had to move out immediately, even if they did not have infantry support. Two companies of the 20th Armored Infantry Battalion were then sent on foot to clear the road leading out of Irsch. By the time everything was organized, it was dawn, and so the attack took place in daylight. This time opposition was slight and the tanks, followed by the armored infantry's half-tracks, moved down the road unimpeded. An observation plane supporting the column reported antitank guns along the road ahead, so the infantry moved out on foot to capture sixty prisoners and the guns. After this, the task force moved swiftly along a skyline drive to where the ranger battalion had been reported. Stopping there, Riley dispatched Lieutenant Gambosi and his rangers to make contact with their battalion, while they proceeded on to Zerf. The column was once again ambushed by antitank guns and lost another tank. The gun, located in a pillbox alongside the road, was then destroyed and Task Force Riley proceeded into Zerf. Here, as at Irsch, they had to fight their way past ambushes by antitank guns, enemy infantry, tanks, and roadblocks. Led by the infantry, the task force secured Zerf by midnight on 25 February. Over one hundred more enemy soldiers entered prisoner-of-war enclosures at the end of the day.

Meanwhile, Lieutenant Gambosi and his men were trying to make contact with their battalion, but once again they were adrift. They found that they could not locate their parent battalion as the rangers were either not where they were reported to be, or Lieutenant Gambosi was in the wrong place. Rather than remain alone in a confused situation, with friendly and enemy units moving through the area, Gambosi and his platoon rejoined Task Force Riley in Zerf.

Actually, while Lieutenant Gambosi was unaware of it, contact had been made by the armored infantry with the 5th Ranger Battalion just before noon on the twenty-sixth. The infantry's half-tracks were used to transport wounded rangers to the rear, after which the task force moved off toward Zerf. The ranger battalion was left to maintain its position until other forces could catch up.

The rangers had already had quite a struggle since arriving at their roadblock position. Setting it up early on the twenty-sixth, they soon benefited from enemy ignorance of their presence. After their initial encounter with the self-propelled gun, they captured an enemy tank destroyer, which they destroyed with rocket fire, and knocked out an enemy half-track.

Enemy walking-wounded continually entered their position, withdrawing from the fighting along the Saar, and were added to the prisoners held by the battalion. The rangers' good fortune held until just minutes before they were relieved by Temporary Team A, when the Germans began an attack on their position. Enemy artillery fire preceded the attack by more than six hundred Germans, which came from two directions. These attacks were driven off, but losses required that more men be put on the defensive lines. Company B, which had been guarding prisoners, was moved on line, leaving only a skeleton guard. Shortly after this attack, an attempt at supplying the rangers by airdrop failed when enemy ground fire kept the planes too high to be effective, but the later resupply by Temporary Team A helped alleviate the problem. Another attack by a scratch unit of enemy infantry forced the rangers to give up about one hundred yards of their position along with the loss of fourteen rangers as prisoners, but with the help of XX Corps Artillery they held the rest of their position and turned back the enemy force. On the following morning Task Force Riley arrived, relieving immediate pressure by the enemy on the rangers.

Later on the twenty-sixth the rangers ambushed a retreating column of enemy infantry, capturing 145 and killing several others. And finally on the same day, Lieutenant Gambosi and his wandering platoon rejoined the battalion. The 5th Rangers had spent more than two days behind enemy lines, not including the time it took to reach the block. Late that afternoon General Malony contacted the battalion and attached it to the 301st Infantry. The siege was officially over.

While the rangers blocked the Irsch–Zerf road, the 94th Division to which they were attached was trying to relieve them, as was the 10th Armored Division. The 301st Infantry faced one pillbox after another; reduction of them took time, especially as the infantry was understrength and exhausted. There were still support elements on the west bank that were vitally needed on the east side. The division commander ordered Company A, 319th Engineers, to put in another treadway bridge at the bridgehead site near Stadt. Enemy opposition was less in this area, and the Americans held the eastern bank securely. By midafternoon the bridge was taking traffic. The division's military police platoon sent Sgt. Clifford G. Bailey and three men to control traffic at the Taben bridge site, still under accurate enemy fire. Transporting enemy prisoners safely across the river also became a problem for the military police platoon. About three hundred prisoners were present on the east bank of the river; and they were in danger from German fire, and also in the way of the attacking troops. Major John Schaub, commanding the military police, arranged for an engineer truck to winch a ferry across the river, transporting the prisoners safely out of harm's way. The river's current, however, soon capsized the raft being used as a ferry, but shouting his orders across the river, Schaub had the remaining prisoners marched down the bank to the other bridge site, where they were safely escorted across. Later, as the 10th Armored crossed, Sergeant Bailey escorted each armored vehicle down the steep slope to the bridge to ensure that none would become disabled and block the only access road.

Meanwhile, across the river, the 94th Division was attacking north, while the 376th Infantry attacked south to effect a continuous link between the bridgeheads. The fighting was the same as it had been since the division entered the Saar-Moselle Triangle. Enemy positions consisted of numerous concrete pillboxes, trenches, and fortified towns and villages. There were also roving tanks and self-propelled guns in the area, as the 10th Armored was learning to its cost at Irsch. After two days of struggling through these types of defenses, the 3d Battalion, 301st Infantry, was again about to attack the critical village of Beurig on the morning of 26 February. Prepared for a vicious fight, the infantry was surprised to find no resistance as they entered the town. Checking houses and streets as they moved, the troops became concerned that they were walking into an ambush. As they approached the northern end of the town they saw troops they thought to be enemy moving about in the area. After carefully checking them out, the soldiers of Lieutenant Colonel McNulty's battalion were relieved to learn that they saw members of the 3d Battalion, 376th Infantry. The bridgeheads were now linked.

The linkup gave the infantry a brief respite. Kitchen trucks were brought up and hot food was served for the first time in five days. Some lucky soldiers even received belated Christmas packages from home. The respite was brief. Soon the infantry returned to the fight still going on around them.

While the 10th Armored and the 94th Division struggled toward Trier, the remaining division within XX Corps, the 26th, continued with its series of limited objective attacks in the Saarlautern area. The 101st Infantry relieved the 328th Infantry to continue attacks designed to keep enemy forces in the area occupied, and thus prevent them from moving against the Ghost Corps's bridgeheads over the Saar.

To the north of XX Corps, XII Corps continued its attacks. The 5th Infantry Division attacked across the Prüm River successfully. Adding the relatively new 76th Infantry Division to the troop list, XII Corps set about establishing a firm bridgehead. The remaining unit of Third Army, General Middleton's VIII Corps, was in the process of refitting and reorganizing after their operation to reduce the last of the enemy Ardennes counteroffensive penetrations. The corps was preparing to join in what was fast becoming a general offensive by Third Army.

While XII Corps and XX Corps were fighting their way to the Rhine, General Patton was still fighting off SHAEF. Occasional reminders arrived at Third Army headquarters that 10th Armored

Division was designated to return to SHAEF reserve; these re-minders were viewed with anxiety by Patton and his staff. Despite occasional temper tantrums designed to push his troops to their lim-its, Patton was well aware that the 10th Armored and the 94th In-fantry Division were doing all they could to get to Trier. The 26th Division was in no position to help, other than to provide the same diversionary attacks they had been doing. General Patton therefore turned his attention to the XII Corps. It was positioned north of XX Corps and contained some of the general's most favored units—the 4th Armored and 5th Infantry Divisions, both of which had been with Third Army since Normandy. It also contained the freshest di-vision in Third Army, the newly arrived 76th.

The 76th Infantry Division was activated at Fort George Gordon Meade, Maryland, on 15 June 1942. Shortly thereafter, it was desig-nated as a replacement-pool division. After training thousands of re-placements, it entered the usual series of training maneuvers until it departed the United States on 10 December 1944. After staging in England, it moved to the continent and was attached to Third Army on 19 January 1945. Further attached to XII Corps on 25 Jan-uary 1945, the 76th Division relieved the 87th Infantry Division in positions along the Sauer and Moselle rivers near Echternach, Lux-embourg. A week later it was ordered to assist the 5th Infantry Divi-sion in an attack across the Sauer and into the Siegfried Line.

The division was commanded throughout its wartime career by Maj. Gen. William Richard Schmidt. Schmidt was born in Nebraska in 1889, and graduated from West Point with the class of 1913. Com-missioned in the infantry, he served at a variety of posts, but was not sent overseas in World War I. After the First World War, he served as an assistant professor of military science and tactics at the Univer-sity of Illinois, and then performed the same duties at Ohio North-ern University. Later he taught at West Point, and he attended the Infantry School at Fort Benning, Georgia, and the Command and General Staff School. After commanding infantry battalions, he graduated from the Army War College in 1931. Further schooling at the Chemical Warfare School and the Army Industrial College was followed by a four-year tour of duty on the War Department Gen-eral Staff. Prior to assuming command of the 76th Division in December 1942, General Schmidt had commanded the 21st and 39th Infantry Regiments, and had served as the assistant division commander of the 81st Infantry Division.

XII Corps was directed to take the enemy city of Bitburg, north of Trier. On 7 February, the 5th Division's 2d and 10th Infantry Regiments led an assault crossing of the Sauer River. The 76th Division assigned its 417th Regimental Combat Team (RCT) to the attack in support of the 5th Infantry Division. The 417th commander, Col. George E. Bruner, in turn, ordered his 1st Battalion to lead the regiment across the river. Its commander, Lt. Col. Clarence A. Mette Jr., ordered Companies A and B to lead the assault, followed in the second wave by Company C. In a scene similar to that in the 94th Infantry Division's sector, the assault boats manned by three engineers of the 160th Combat Engineer Battalion and ten to twelve infantrymen of the 417th Infantry struggled to carry the heavy assault boats in darkness some five hundred yards to the river's edge. The enemy was quickly alerted to the struggling Americans and opened fire even before the first boat hit the water. As the boats pushed off into the river, casualties began to mount. "The boat behind one in which rode Private Harry Goedde sank under a direct hit, its occupants swept downstream. His own boat started to drift toward the very spot where a Nazi machine gun was spitting fire from the bank. The men tried frantically to restrain their course by grabbing for rushes along the water's edge but swamped the gunwales."

Despite this heavy enemy fire, the surviving infantrymen of the 76th Division landed and began clearing out enemy defenses on the east bank. They overcame the usual minefields, pillboxes, and field fortifications, as additional troops attempted to cross in support. As would happen in XX Corps, boats were lost, reducing the number available for follow-up waves, and enemy artillery fire became more accurate as dawn rose, causing the landings to be suspended. The 160th Combat Engineers tried to get a cable across the river, but after three attempts were thwarted by enemy fire, they put in a bridge instead. The bridge was quickly destroyed by the swift current, stranding Companies A and B across the river.

As usual, the Germans quickly counterattacked. A tank-supported infantry attack was repulsed by the novice infantrymen without loss of ground or casualties. The division's own combat engineers, the 301st Engineer Combat Battalion, tried to get bridges and cables established across the Sauer River, but each attempt was a failure due either to enemy fire or the river itself. More boats were brought up to replace the first group, and reinforcements were soon paddling across the river. Finally, after two days of hard work, the engineers bridged the river. The bridgehead was secured and the 76th Division, along with the rest of XII Corps, attacked the main Siegfried Line defenses.

For the next two weeks, XII Corps struggled through the same type of in-depth defense that had been tying up XX Corps. Just as the corps fought its way through the defense line, General Patton arrived at General Schmidt's headquarters. As I mentioned earlier, he made one of his dramatic gestures when he thrust his fist on a map of Trier without saying a word, a statement Schmidt understood. The 76th Division immediately "concentrated on making contact with the XX Corps to the south." The 417th Infantry moved off in a column of battalions, supported by detachments from the 702d Tank Battalion, 808th Tank Destroyer Battalion, 301st Engineer Battalion, and 76th Reconnaissance Troop. Their objective: Trier.

CHAPTER 21
TRIER TAKEN!

Lieutenant Melvin I. Mason led his Company C, 20th Armored Infantry Battalion, across the Saar River on 24 February. Together with the rest of the 20th Armored Infantry Battalion, it was ordered to pass through the lines of the 376th Infantry Regiment and advance along the main road to Irsch. The task force was commanded by Lt. Col. Jack J. Richardson, the 20th Battalion commander. The 21st Tank Battalion units attached to the task force were still struggling to get across the Saar when orders to proceed to and seize Irsch were received by Colonel Richardson. The crossing was under heavy artillery and machine-gun fire, so the battalion had to cross "singly and in small groups," disorganizing the companies. Once they were across, enemy opposition, combined with the terrain, contributed to further disorganization. The battalion's assembly in preparation for the attack on Irsch "finally took place on the crest (Scharfenberg Ridge) during the early morning hours of 25 February."

Moving through the lines of the 376th Infantry, the 20th Battalion moved some two thousand yards before encountering serious opposition as "the battalion ran into the fire of a series of pillboxes, eleven in all," which halted forward movement. The command located itself in a vineyard to reorganize and get some rest while Colonel Richardson planned his attack.

How structurally sound these east-bank pillboxes were had recently been proven when the 778th Tank Battalion had made five direct hits into one of them, thinking the enemy still occupied it. They were told, in no uncertain terms, that members of Company B, 301st Infantry, were in occupation and didn't appreciate the attention. Fortunately, none of the Americans inside was even slightly injured.

Colonel Richardson assigned Lieutenant Mason's Company C to assault four pillboxes on the left, Company A four on the right, and Company B the remaining pillboxes flanking the road to Irsch. An artillery barrage was ordered, after which the companies attacked, similarly to those attacks made throughout the Saar-Moselle Triangle campaign. Machine-gun sections were set up where they could fire on the pillboxes, causing the defenders to seek shelter. Covered by the machine guns, the infantry advanced to each in turn, using satchel charges and bazooka fire to seal the firing ports. Once pillboxes began to fall, the others, observing the fate of their comrades, became more likely to surrender. Company C's four assigned pillboxes yielded thirty-six prisoners after being attacked by artillery, machine guns, bazooka, satchel charges, and bangalore charges. The pillboxes were conquered in one and a half hours with no losses to American soldiers.

As soon as the prisoners were sent rearward, the battalion moved forward again. Moving across country and avoiding the road, they reached Irsch at midnight. Here they found Task Force Riley fighting its way into the town. Companies A and B moved into Irsch to help clear its east side, while Company C cleared the northeast section where Lieutenant Gambosi's ranger platoon was operating. The 20th Armored Infantry Battalion rounded up 290 prisoners from the German 416th Infantry Division during its sweep of Irsch.

While the Americans secured the town and rested during the hours of darkness, new orders were sent from 10th Armored for the commanders of Task Forces Richardson and Riley. Task Force Richardson was moved from Combat Command A to Combat Command B. They further stated that the two task forces would combine their efforts to relieve the 5th Ranger Battalion at their roadblock in front of the division. As we have seen, these orders resulted in the formation of Temporary Team A, which went on to relieve the rangers the following day.

While Temporary Team A ran down the road to Irsch, Task Force Richardson moved on foot on the flanks of the main road. Lieutenant Mason's Company C experienced only light opposition, and captured a German command car and a pillbox containing twelve soldiers and fifty civilians. After this easy start, things went badly. Enemy artillery took a hand against their advance, pouring "exceptionally heavy" and "severe" artillery fire into the American forces. The armored infantry advanced during lulls in the fire, soon reduced to an "interdictory nature all along the road and the vicinity of the road." As they approached Zerf, they came under direct enemy small arms fire from pillboxes, so the men went into a draw that ran about five hundred yards from the road and advanced using it for protection. They passed the rangers, who sought assistance in evacuating their wounded. Colonel Richardson sent over five half-tracks.

While the wounded were being evacuated, the leading elements of Task Force Richardson were coming under renewed heavy-artillery and small arms fire. A heavy fog also had risen, making observation difficult. Lieutenant Mason, leading Company C, fired at a German soldier, only to find that there were three more Germans facing him who, fortunately, surrendered.

As soon as the soldiers started forward again they found themselves pinned down in a machine-gun crossfire. The company dropped into nearby ditches and returned fire. Setting up their own machine guns, they soon suppressed the enemy fire, which enabled them to withdraw. Tanks were called for, and these sprayed the enemy area with cannon and machine-gun fire, and then withdrew. The position was bypassed and Company C moved into Zerf, where it was attached to Temporary Team A.

While Company C was being deflected from the northeast, Company B had more luck to the southeast, where they successfully cleared the area against minimal opposition. They, too, rejoined the battalion in Zerf. While these companies had been clearing the area surrounding Zerf, a task force was assembling just outside the town. This new force consisted of the 21st Tank Battalion, elements of the 51st Armored Infantry Battalion, and two platoons of the 609th Tank Destroyer Battalion. The new task force was placed under the command of Colonel Richardson. While Colonel Richardson was organizing his force into combat teams, another group of Americans fought their way into Zerf. Task Force O'Hara arrived after fighting their way forward from the Saar. Like the other task forces, it had been divided up to help the 10th Armored cross the river. Reunited now, it had followed the other task forces north until arriving in Zerf. Lieutenant Colonel James O'Hara's team consisted of his own 54th Armored Infantry Battalion, Company B of the 21st Tank Battalion, a platoon of Company B, 55th Armored Engineer Battalion, and a light tank platoon from the 21st Tank Battalion.

There were now three task forces in and around Zerf, meaning that Zerf and the surrounding area were securely in American possession. The task forces were once again reorganized, leaving a reduced task force commanded by Lt. Col. Thomas C. Chamberlain behind to secure Zerf, while the others moved out in the direction of Trier. Task Force O'Hara's forward movement was slow due to the enemy artillery, mortar, and machine-gun fire along the road. Just beyond Zerf was a turn in the road leading to Trier, which quickly became known as the "hot corner" because the Germans had at least one dual-purpose 88mm antitank gun sited to fire on it. Attempts to pass this point were costly, and Lt. Col. James O'Hara was killed when his vehicle was hit and destroyed by the enemy gun.

Task Force O'Hara, now assisted by Task Force Chamberlain, continued to attack along the direct route into Trier. Resistance was fierce, and progress difficult. "The operation from Irsch around the hot corner at Zerf and on into Trier was worse than Bastogne. We lost more vehicles and men. The enemy was sitting on the hills where we couldn't find them or get at them with artillery. They had their artillery zeroed in on the roads. They would hold their fire until we were close and sometimes they would allow the first column to bypass their position and then open up on the second column. The infantry in the half-tracks were vulnerable to the air-burst artillery. There was not enough infantry left at the end to flush out the hills and clear out the gun positions." Despite this intensity of opposition, the Tiger Division continued to attack. Clearing out one position after another, some heavily defended, others less so, the task forces moved toward Trier. Senior officers led from the front, resulting in more losses among battalion commanders. Lieutenant Colonel Wadsworth P. Clapp, who had so recently been blamed for the bridging delay by General Patton, was killed by mortar fire while supervising at the crossing site, and Lt. Col. Miles L. Standish, eleventh direct descendent of illustrious Pilgrim forefathers, also fell in battle at the head of his 61st Armored Infantry Battalion. Progress remained slow and costly.

While the 10th Armored struggled along the roads and ridges toward Trier, the 94th Division had cleared and secured its bridgehead, enabling all elements of XX Corps to cross in support of the continuing attack. As its next objective, the division was assigned a series of eleven hills, which were needed to expand and secure the lodgment. Colonel Johnson's 302d Infantry was assigned most of them, but a few went to the 301st Infantry. Accordingly, its 3d Battalion moved on the morning of 27 February to secure Hill Number 4, situated along the Irsch–Zerf road, one of the positions that was making life miserable for the 10th Armored. As the tankers had road priority, the infantry had to march across country carrying all their heavy equipment. After moving nearly two miles forward, the leading company, Company K, came to a wooded area some fifteen hundred yards deep, which had to be cleared to allow the battalion to approach its next objective.

The infantrymen were exhausted after the long march, but even if they had been fully alert, they were uninformed as to who was in the woods to their front. Similarly, the men of the 5th Ranger Battalion had spent four days now in those woods, under intermittent attack the whole time, and they were thus inclined to believe that all approaching forces were enemy. Colonel Sullivan had earlier advised Colonel Hagerty that any forces approaching during darkness would be fired upon. The combination of exhaustion and caution caused Company K to approach the woods in attack formation. The rangers opened fire after the briefest of attempts to identify them. One ranger platoon leader demanded the password, which was correctly given, but another platoon challenged, received no answer, and opened fire. The approaching darkness and the nervous state of both units combined to start a slowly growing firefight between friendly forces. Lieutenant Robert L. Vinue, of Company K, was certain that he had heard an American voice raise the challenge, so at great personal risk he ran toward the ranger lines, shouting orders to cease fire. After a few minutes the American forces recognized each other and the firing ceased. Company K lost three men killed and another seven wounded.

Other battalions of the 94th continued to clear their areas as well. Lieutenant Colonel Cloudt led his 3d Battalion, 302d Infantry, forward to relieve elements of the 376th Infantry, which were still isolated on Scharfenberg Ridge. During this attack, Company L encountered one of the ever-present enemy pillbox nests. Attempting to negotiate a surrender, the Americans were asked by the enemy sergeant in charge to "stage a mock battle" in order to preserve his reputation. Obligingly, the infantry fired their weapons in their general direction, after which the sergeant and his men duly surrendered. Near Company L, Company K discovered a large cave filled with enemy civilians, and sent them to the rear under guard. The column was attacked by a German patrol. When fired upon by the force guarding the civilians, the enemy patrol members quickly changed their minds and joined the prisoners.

Things were progressing well indeed in the 94th Division's sector. General Malony had earlier remarked to General Walker, when observing his new area of operations in the hill country, that "I need mountain infantry here." On the morning of 27 February Brigadier General Collier called Malony to tell him "General, you have your wish for mountain troops! The German 2d Mountain Division is now in front of you." XX Corps had learned from prisoners captured by the rangers during their siege at Zerf that a new enemy formation was arriving on the corps front in an effort to save Trier. Army Group G had attached the 2d Mountain Division to LXXXII Corps with instructions to use it to stop the advance of the Ghost Corps.

The 2d Mountain Division, or 2d Gebirgs Division, was formed on 1 April 1938, in Innsbruck, or Wehrkreis Eighteen, from the former 6th Division of the Army of the Federal Republic of Austria. It consisted of the 136th and 137th Gebirgsjäger (Mountain Infantry) Regiments and the 11th Gebirgs Artillery Regiment. It served in Poland in 1939 and Norway in 1940, where it distinguished itself by relieving its sister 3d Mountain Division, which was encircled by British forces at Narvik. For the next three years it was a part of the German effort to sustain Finland in the war, fighting in the frozen north near the approaches to Murmansk. At the end of 1944, seriously depleted in strength, it was sent to Denmark for reorganization, where the two infantry regiments were reinforced with supply and other noncombatant units. Most replacements were also Austrians, whose interest in saving Germany from defeat varied with their political affiliation. The division, commanded by Maj. Gen. Hans Degan, had just arrived from Denmark when Army Group G directed it to save Trier. A scratch force of this unit had attempted to reduce the ranger roadblock, but without supporting arms or armor that attempt had proved a costly failure. The bulk of the division could not get between Trier and the 10th Armored Division in time, so the mountain troops found themselves facing the veterans of the 94th Infantry Division and the 5th Ranger Battalion.

While the Germans' newest addition to the battle faced off against XX Corps, XII Corps contributed to the battle for Trier by moving south. General Schmidt's 76th Infantry Division had "attacked north from Echternach, turned east to cross the Prüm and Nims, and then swung south for its second attack through the Siegfried wall, but this time taking it from the rear." The division had made nearly a circular attack, which now was directed at Trier. As with XX Corps, pillboxes and prepared defenses still faced the infantrymen. The 385th Infantry Regiment moved to attack a position known as Katzenkopf, or Cat's Head. The main feature of this mutually supporting defensive position was Seeckt Number 1520, of which only the top was visible from the Americans' line of approach. It contained three turrets, which "housed five machine guns, an automatic machine mortar, and a disappearing-type flamethrower. The two machine-gun turrets, projecting three feet four inches above the earth, had steel walls twelve inches thick. Hit by 90mm high-explosive projectiles fired from M36 tank destroyers, these walls had been penetrated to a depth of no more than six inches." Against such positions the advance of the 76th Division was as slow and costly as that of the XX Corps to the south. Nevertheless, the 1st Battalion, 385th Infantry, and the 808th Tank Destroyer Battalion combined to reduce this fortification, and the advance continued.

Minefields plagued the 76th Division as they had the Ghost Corps to the south. During a minefield clearing operation in its advance, Pfc. Herman C. Wallace of Company B, 301st Combat Engineer Battalion, stepped on an antipersonnel mine. He knew that he had tripped the activation device and that the instant he moved, the mine would jump aboveground and spray the area with fragments. Since this might kill or maim the other members of his squad, the Texan decided to place his other foot directly on the mine to prevent its rising above ground, even though he was aware that his only chance was to fall flat on the ground. The mine exploded and killed Private

Wallace, but no other member of his squad was injured. Private First Class Wallace was posthumously awarded the Medal of Honor.

As his troops struggled toward Trier, General Patton protected his rear. During 27 February he called General Bradley and told him that while he had not yet taken Trier, if he could keep the 10th Armored Division, he would soon have it. Bradley, who already knew that SHAEF would not seriously intervene, gave him permission to keep the division, while promising that he would not "listen for the telephone" from SHAEF.

The Tiger Division certainly was trying to attain the general's objective for him. No fewer than three task forces were advancing on Trier. The attack of the 76th Division in the north had drawn off the major enemy defending force in Trier, the 212th Volksgrenadier Division, which had moved to stop XII Corps. Left in Trier and its environs were two local defense battalions (known as Volkstrum), the city police, and the crews of several dual-purpose 88mm antiaircraft/antitank guns. The usual minefields and field fortifications also served to frustrate efforts of the task forces on the approach to Trier. In an effort to clear one of these minefields on 28 February, a platoon of the 55th Armored Engineer Battalion advanced into the field, covered by the guns of Task Force Chamberlain. As it went to work, enemy machine guns, waiting for just such a moment, opened fire. The engineers did clear the field, but left 40 percent of their men behind at casualty clearing stations.

Task Force Haskell, formerly O'Hara and now commanded by Maj. Warren Haskell of the 54th Armored Infantry Battalion, fared little better. As they advanced along the road leading to Trier, enemy observation brought constant artillery and mortar fire down on them. Vehicle after vehicle was hit and knocked out. Even resting was not easy on the road to Trier. One team of Task Force Haskell stopped to rest on the night of 27–28 February. Unaware that they were in sight of an enemy artillery battery, they were rudely awakened at 3:00 in the morning by an artillery barrage into their position. The enemy, knowing the Americans were in the open, sleeping, used air-burst fire to wound fifteen of them before their artillery could return fire. An enemy infantry attack was beaten off, and just as the tankers felt that the worst was over, dawn brought direct fire from two 88mm dual-purpose guns, which destroyed the last of the team's remaining half-tracks.

Major Haskell sent out Company B, 54th Armored Infantry Battalion, to encircle the enemy battery position, while his tank destroyers kept them busy with fire. Two other tank destroyers moved around to a flank and opened fire. Together they captured thirty prisoners, four 88mm guns, and twelve automatic weapons. Almost before this fight was over, Major Haskell was receiving urgent orders from Colonel Roberts to move on Trier. Task Force Haskell tried to comply. During the move forward, after reequipping, the task force's casualties continued to mount. "The terrain was a series of hills and deep valleys which offered excellent positions for enemy gun positions." Shooting from high ground, the enemy batteries knocked out five more half-tracks and an armored car. Towns blocking the approach to Trier were captured, but at the end of the fight Task Force Haskell had only four tanks and five half-tracks left in operation. Infantry losses were so severe that communications men, assault gun troops, and headquarters personnel were pressed into service as infantrymen.

While Combat Command B struggled forward, the last elements of the 10th Armored crossed the Saar. Combat Command Reserve crossed on 27 February and moved up to release elements of both Combat Commands A and B for the advance on Trier. One freed up was Task Force Richardson, still securing Zerf. Relieved from this duty by the 1st Battalion, 301st Infantry, during the afternoon of 28 February, the task force organized itself for an advance toward Trier. Consisting now of only Company B and Headquarters Company, 20th Armored Infantry Battalion, and Company B of the 21st Tank Battalion, Task Force Richardson moved out of Zerf during the afternoon of 1 March.

Shortly after leaving Zerf, Lieutenant Colonel Richardson received orders from Combat Command B to proceed directly toward Trier, using a narrow route between task forces Haskell and Norris, both of which were still struggling toward Trier. Ordered to "get into Trier tonight and seize intact, if possible, the two key bridges over the Moselle," Task Force Richardson moved off under the cover of darkness. "It was a clear night, with a full moon and excellent visibility." The "column shot up to the village of Irsch, where a roadblock was encountered that was to have been defended by three 88mm guns." Fortunately for Task Force Richardson the position was unmanned, and after they fired two tank rounds into the position, enemy soldiers quickly came out of the houses where they had been sleeping and surrendered. After having the prisoners remove the roadblock, the task force moved toward its objective. With no further opposition, Richardson led his force into the city limits of Trier. Here the Americans surprised and captured a company of enemy infantry and four antitank guns. "Evidently the Americans had not been expected in that part of the city that soon." Richardson learned from one of his new prisoners that he was to have alerted the guard at the bridges when the Americans arrived so that the bridges could be destroyed in a timely manner. Deciding to try to continue with his surprise, Richardson detailed one team under Captain Billet to attack the northern bridge, while another under Lieutenant Riley was to advance through the city to the southern bridge. Billet reported to Richardson at 2:00 A.M. that his objective had been destroyed before he arrived. Task Force Richardson's only chance now was to hope that the remaining bridge was still standing.

Riley's team moved out along an avenue that followed the bank of the Moselle River and shortly radioed back to Richardson, "Have reached bridge. Bridge intact. Am receiving small arms fire." Task Force Richardson hurriedly moved to the aid of Team Riley, where Lieutenant Colonel Richardson carefully directed the seizure of his main objective, a bridge over the Moselle. With Team Riley pinned down at the bridge approaches by machine-gun fire, a platoon of armored infantry under Lieutenant Fletcher raced across the bridge, covered by machine-gun fire from Richardson's tank. Expecting the bridge to blow up under them at any moment, Fletcher and his men crossed safely to encounter at the far end "a German major and five enlisted men rushing toward the bridge with detonating caps and an exploder. The German major was drunk."

Quickly, Lieutenant Colonel Richardson assigned men to cut all wires leading to the bridge while the rest of the task force crossed to form a bridgehead on the other bank. The captured German major, fearful over his dereliction of duty, quickly revealed the presence of another seventeen German officers attending a party down the street from the bridge. These were quickly captured without a struggle. As the presence of the task force became known to the enemy, more and more Germans surrendered, until by 10:00 A.M. of 2 March, they had over eight hundred prisoners on their hands. Throughout the day more parties of enemy soldiers appeared to participate in the defense of Trier only to learn they were a day late, and these were soon added to the prisoner-of-war tally. For the rest of the day Task Force Richardson rested around their bridge, letting the rest of the Tiger Division mop up Trier. They had earned it.

General Patton was thrilled. He recorded in his diary that General Walker had reported the capture of Trier and described it as "a very fine operation and has netted us over seven thousand prisoners." Patton tried to notify both Generals Eisenhower and Bradley of his accomplishment but neither was available, so he left a message with Eisenhower's chief of staff. Later, Bradley returned his call, and Patton recorded that he was "very much pleased" and that both Eisenhower and his chief of staff, Bedell Smith, were equally happy with his triumph. He was disappointed that Eisenhower didn't "take the trouble" to speak with him personally, but felt once again that his "military ideas are correct" and that he had been vindicated in pushing across the Saar. Believing he had "fooled them again," he relished his triumph. The following day, 2 March, he had an opportunity to gloat over his victory, as he was handed two messages. The first came from SHAEF, ordering him to bypass Trier as it would take four divisions to capture it, while the second was from General Walker, confirming the capture of Trier with one of its vital bridges intact. Patton immediately sent for Sergeant Rosevich and dictated an urgent telegram to SHAEF via 12th Army Group. "Have taken Trier with two divisions," the message read. "What do you want me to do? Give it back?"

CHAPTER 22
LAMPADEN TO THE RHINE

The 76th Infantry Division reached the north bank of the Moselle River on 3 March and made contact with the 10th Armored Division. Mopping-up activities were still going on in the town and the 1st Battalion, 376th Infantry Regiment, which had begun the campaign six weeks before, was called in to finalize the capture. Despite the last-ditch defense in the vicinity of Trier, the capture of that town had ruptured the German defensive line immediately to General Patton's front. The Germans had not given up, however.

With usual German adaptability, battle groups of various units were hastily thrown together to restore the ruptured front. Remnants of both the 416th Infantry Division and the 256th Volksgrenadier Division, along with fortress battalions, reinforcement battalions, and rear-area units, were hastily organized to present a defensive line against the American thrusts. The bulk of the 2d Mountain Division arrived and took its place in the defense line. Indeed, it was on 3 March that the 94th Infantry Division identified its first prisoners from that new unit. These men, from the 13th Company, 3d Battalion, 137th Mountain Infantry Regiment, were quick to tell their captors that they were the advance of an attacking force that would strike early on 4 March.

The attack came against Maj. Gilbert N. O'Neill's 3d Battalion, 301st Infantry. It hit Company L, which had only fifty-four men present for duty on Hill 5. In accordance with division policy, a reinforcement group of forty men was ready but was being held in Zerf under the company first sergeant until they could be briefed on combat conditions. As the attack caused casualties, these new men were

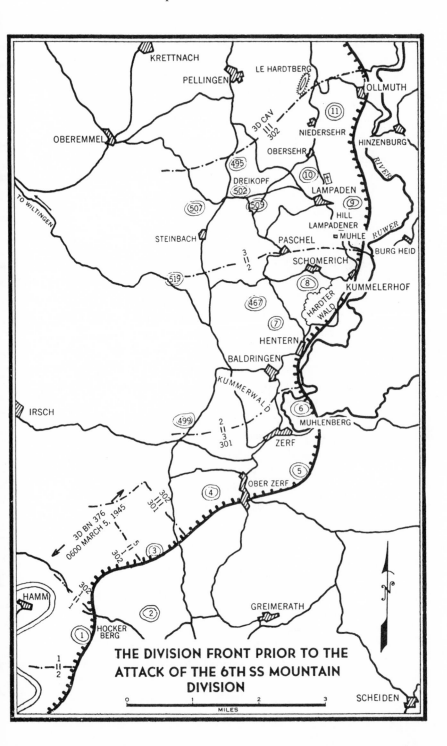

KRETTNACH

LE HARDTBERG

PELLINGEN

OLLMUTH

3D CAV
III
302

11

NIEDERSEHR

HINZENBURG

OBEREMMEL

OBERSEHR

RIVER

495

TO WILTINGEN

DREIKOPF

502

10

LAMPADEN

507

509

9

HILL
LAMPADENER

STEINBACH

PASCHEL

MUHLE

RUWER

BURG HEID

3
II
2

SCHOMERICH

519

8

KUMMELERHOF

467

HARDTER
WALD

7

HENTERN

BALDRINGEN

KUMMERWALD

2
II
3
301

IRSCH

499

6

MUHLENBERG

ZERF

5

OBER ZERF

302
301

4

3D BN 376
0600 MARCH 5, 1945

302
5

3

302

HAMM

2

GREIMERATH

1

HOCKER
BERG

**THE DIVISION FRONT PRIOR TO THE
ATTACK OF THE 6TH SS MOUNTAIN
DIVISION**

1
II
2

0   1   2   3
MILES

SCHEIDEN

N

filtered forward into the foxholes thereby vacated, a particularly difficult way to enter combat conditions. Within hours, the Austrian mountaineers had knocked out the company machine guns, as well as the reinforcing heavy machine guns from Company M, 301st Infantry. Toward dawn four enemy self-propelled guns moved up the hill and drove one platoon off the vital height. As the armor roamed at will along the hillside, the enemy infantry returned and captured the company command post. Lieutenant Henley, the company commander, had gone back to guide up reinforcements, but 2d Lt. Sylvester M. Beyer of the 356th Field Artillery and two sergeants were captured. Moved down the hill for questioning, the three soldiers refused to divulge any information. One of the enemy soldiers opened fire on the trio, killing one of the sergeants and severely wounding Lieutenant Beyer and the other sergeant. Before anything further could be done, Pvt. Irving S. Clemens noticed the group and opened fire, permitting Lieutenant Beyer to escape to American lines, where he refused treatment until he could contact his battalion and direct artillery fire on the enemy infantry. This fire separated the enemy infantry from its armor support, causing the attackers to withdraw. Lieutenant Beyer survived to wear his Silver Star.

The repulse of the attack coincided with new orders received by the 94th Infantry Division. These called for a replacement of the tired and depleted 94th by the 26th Infantry Division, which in turn was to be replaced on its front by the new 65th Infantry Division. XX Corps provided trucks and instructed all units to remove unit patches and vehicle identifications for secrecy. The rotation was to take place over the three nights of 6–8 March.

The Germans, however, still did not admit defeat. A new unit was brought forward to prepare for a counterattack to restore the German line. The LXXXII Corps received orders that its newest addition would join with its already assigned units for a massive counterattack. The objective was to cut the main American supply axis, the Zerf–Pellingen road, and reach Trier to relieve units thought to be holding out behind the lines. Leading the new attack would be the new arrival, the 6th SS Mountain Division.

The 6th SS Mountain Division was a Waffen SS formation unlike the 2d Mountain Division. It was composed of both native Germans and ethnic Germans from Tyrol, the Balkans, and Denmark, who had volunteered to serve Germany. It had a battalion of Norwegians, which it had left behind while passing through that country on its way to LXXXII Corps. It had originated as a unit of the SS Totenkopf ("Death's Head") detachments, which the leader of the Schutzstaffel (SS), Heinrich Himmler, sought to enlarge into a private army. In order to get the arms, training, and respect he needed for these units, a battalion of the SS Totenkopf was formed in 1940 for the German occupation of Norway. From this modest beginning, Himmler managed to raise the unit to a motorized regiment, known as SS Regiment "Nord," and finally to a division. Formed in April of 1941, the 6th SS Mountain Division "Nord" was by June of 1941 fighting along the Russian front alongside the Finns. It operated in this forbidding arena until German forces began to withdraw late in 1944. It managed to withdraw into Norway and later spent two days rehabilitating in Denmark. Commanded by SS Lieutenant General Karl Heinrich Brenner, it took part in the German Alsace counterattack, but when that attack failed, it returned to reserve status until called upon to stop the Ghost Corps.

General Hahm, commanding LXXXII Corps, protested "the impossibility and the senselessness of this task." Ordered to attack despite his objections, Hahm decided to launch a coordinated three-direction attack, one by each of the divisions available. The 6th SS Mountain Division was to attack and seize the Zerf–Pellingen road, the 2d Mountain Division was to capture Muhlenberg and protect the southern flank of the attack, while the 256th Volksgrenadier Division was to take the commanding heights around Gutweiler and be prepared to push forward from them. The artillery units of all three divisions were combined with and under command of LXXXII Corps artillery to ensure strong supporting fire. The initial objectives of all the units were heights that were part of a formation known as Lampaden Ridge. The attack was to strike on the night of 5 March.

Using infiltration tactics and attacking without artillery preparation, the enemy started filtering into the lines of the 94th Infantry Division and 3d Cavalry Group about 1:00 A.M. on the morning of 6 March. The Second Battalion, 12th SS Mountain Regiment "Michael Gaismair" began to infiltrate the lines held by Company G, 302d Infantry. The Americans, who had been introduced to infiltration tactics by the 11th Panzer Division in January, began to pull their outposts back for consolidation. Some outposts were cut off and killed or captured, but many returned to the main force successfully. The Germans did, however, manage to infiltrate between widely spread units of the 94th Division.

The 11th SS Mountain Regiment "Reinhard Heydrich" struck directly at Lampaden Ridge and the positions of the 3d Battalion, 302d Infantry. The opening moves of the attack were shielded by thick woods through which the Germans advanced, but most of the American outposts managed to return to the main line of resistance successfully. At about 2:00 A.M. of 6 March, Sgt. Max L. Ledesma of Company K, 302d Regiment, moved forward to run a one-man contact patrol with Company L. As he approached a cemetery he was challenged by several soldiers who gave the correct password. Before he could reply, Sergeant Ledesma recognized the peculiar German helmet silhouette and opened fire. Return fire severely wounded the sergeant, who survived long enough to crawl back to his position and notify his men about the compromised password.

Major Harold V. Maixner's 2d Battalion, 302d, also came under attack. In the village of Obersehr a sentry from Company B, 774th Tank Destroyer Battalion, was approached by a group of men who gave the correct password and announced that they would return in a moment with more men. When these returned they surrounded the sentry and took him prisoner before he realized they were the enemy. Now both Colonel Cloudt's 3d and Major Maixner's 2d Battalions, each defending several villages, were infiltrated by SS troops. By 4:00 A.M. the Germans attacked openly. Company K, 302d, was heavily hit in the village of Ollmuth. Elements of the 774th Tank Destroyer Battalion, reinforced by the 3d Platoon of the 302d Infantry's Cannon Company, held on to Obersehr despite the enemy's seizing many village buildings. In Lampaden a reinforced Company I was fighting for possession of that village.

The Germans pushed back some American positions, but others of their attacks failed. In one instance, a group of Germans, failing in their attack on the village of Baldringen, sent Sgt. Richard W. Finkbone, whom they had captured earlier, into the town to arrange their own surrender rather than attack again. Unfortunately, this netted them little when, a few moments after surrendering, many were killed by German artillery fire. To the north the 256th Volksgrenadier Division succeeded in driving in the outposts of the 3d Cavalry Group, but soon lost every gain when the irate cavalrymen returned with their considerable firepower. Most of this group soon surrendered as well. By dawn of 6 March the situation was extremely confused. There were Germans attacking Americans, Americans attacking Germans, and small groups of each side out of touch with anyone.

Lieutenant Colonel Cloudt, commanding the 3d Battalion, 302d, decided to clear things up in his area. He ordered a platoon of Company L supported by three tanks to relieve Obersehr. Lieutenant Ramirez's 3d Platoon moved out in squad formation, with one squad approaching from the east while the remaining two came directly from the south. One tank was quickly disabled and the others withdrew. Going back to Lampaden, Ramirez started over again. This time all squads attacked together supported by the tanks, but heavy and accurate automatic and antitank fire decimated the attackers. Ramirez went down with wounds, the platoon aidman was killed, and many others fell to the enemy fire. Platoon Sergeant Albert I. Orr took command and pressed the attack. Finally one of the supporting tanks managed to get a clear shot at the main enemy defensive position, and the survivors of 3d Platoon cleared the hill crest and captured fifty enemy prisoners. For the next three days, under constant enemy fire and living off rations taken from the dead, the platoon's survivors would hold the hill they had so dearly won.

Messages began arriving back at division headquarters by early afternoon of the severity of the attack. At first General Malony felt that the attack was of a minor nature and could be held easily. Within moments, however, messages from Colonel Cloudt stressing that he was facing "good troops of a mountain division" caused Malony to alert Colonel Minor's battalion of the 376th Infantry. After conferring with Colonel Bercquist, Malony ordered Minor forward. General Walker contacted Malony to inform him that the relief would be postponed "until position of Colonel Cloudt had been restored." General Paul, commanding the adjacent 26th Infantry Division, also called to give Malony permission to use at his own discretion any of his units that happened to be near the scene of the counterattack.

While reinforcements were being alerted, the battle at Lampaden continued with renewed ferocity. Colonel Johnson ordered his Company C and the attached 1st Platoon, Company A, 778th Tank Battalion, to relieve Company G in the village of Schomerich. This village was under constant attack by troops from the 12th SS Mountain Regiment. After gaining control of some outlying houses, these troopers stripped American prisoners, donned their uniforms, and attempted to infiltrate American-held buildings. They also pressed civilians into service as snipers. Despite these efforts the Americans held.

At the village of Lampaden, Colonel Cloudt learned his battalion was surrounded when members of his ammunition and pioneer platoon returned from a mission to the rear with German prisoners. A force sent to clear the road to the rear captured some additional prisoners. Sergeant Eugene T. Hack of the battalion's intelligence section quickly identified these men as members of the 2d Battalion, 11th SS Mountain Regiment. Shortly afterward additional confirmation of his surrounded condition came to Cloudt when three members of the 7th Field Artillery Observation Battalion came into Lampaden to report that the convoy they had been with had been attacked by Germans and the other members had been captured.

The fighting at Obersehr continued while Lampaden was being surrounded. Private First Class Paul L. Zaring, a member of the 3d Platoon, 302d Infantry's Cannon Company, became involved in a personal duel with SS troopers attempting to overrun his position. With the rest of his platoon either wounded or trapped in a house nearby, Private Zaring spent the day protecting both his comrades and their guns. While administering first aid to a wounded friend he dodged artillery, small arms, and antitank fire and kept the attackers away from his guns and trapped platoon. At one time, a German officer managed to get within ten yards of Zaring and was about to hurl a grenade when the American spotted and shot him. His one-man stand, which saved both his platoon and their guns, earned him the Distinguished Service Cross, one of six the division would earn on the ridge.

Lieutenant Colonel Otto B. Cloudt Jr. was a man beset with difficulties, but he responded to each as it arose. One was the wounded and prisoners crowding the area. As he wasn't able to spare guards for the unwounded prisoners, they had to remain. But a convoy of wounded consisting of twenty-five Americans, including Lieutenant Ramirez, and fourteen Germans was dispatched with a guard detail of six able-bodied men of the 3d Battalion. They were to deliver the wounded and return with an ammunition resupply. They were stopped near Dreikopf by enemy soldiers. The Germans were inclined to let the convoy pass until one of the German wounded complained of his treatment. The whole group was taken prisoner and herded into a nearby gun emplacement.

Lieutenant Colonel Cloudt next addressed the issue of Obersehr. He organized a scratch platoon made up of two squads, which he mounted on two 778th Battalion tanks and sent crashing into Obersehr. The surprised Germans, whose antitank ammunition had been expended on the houses sheltering Obersehr's defenders, were caught off-guard and unprepared. The combined force of Americans cleared the town. Outside, a similar force of infantry and tanks roamed the German rear areas and captured seventy prisoners. Signs of progress became more numerous when a German noncommissioned officer, accompanied by a sergeant from the 7th Field Artillery Observation Battalion, approached Cloudt with a request for a prisoner exchange. Delaying as long as he could, Cloudt finally rejected the exchange out of concern that the released prisoners could advise the enemy about the weakness of the 3d Battalion's positions.

Meanwhile the battle around Lampaden continued. Lieutenant William J. Honan commanded the heavy machine-gun platoon of Company M, 302d Infantry, which was emplaced around the town to help repel the enemy attack. Having lost contact with his individual squads, he went forward to restore contact with them and withdraw his men to better positions, accompanied by Sgt. Walter L. Cranford of Company L, also seeking some of his men. Carrying a light machine gun, Lieutenant Honan went first to the position held by a machine-gun squad commanded by Pfc. (later Sgt.) Wallace M. Gallant. Gallant, a twenty-four-year-old native of Maine and a former ASTP student, had sited his gun in "the best position available, because there were no significant terrain features to which we could have otherwise safely and effectively deployed." In order to conceal their position the squad had let several infiltrating groups pass undisturbed. Later they opened fire on larger groups of the enemy, "but it didn't seem that the Germans had pinpointed our location— fortunately." Concerned that his limited supply of ammunition would not last the day, Gallant chose his targets carefully. Armed with an M1 carbine and M1 Garand rifle, which he used on small groups to conserve machine-gun ammunition, he could hear the rising sound of battle in Lampaden to his rear. Trying to learn what was happening, he found that his phone line had been cut. It was this loss of communications that prompted Lieutenant Honan to seek him out. Gallant's squad had, however, captured the squad of infiltrating Germans who were rolling up his communications wire and who walked, unsuspecting, right into his position. The prisoners were sent to the rear, guarded by two of the squad who had been wounded.

Next to approach were a group of about twenty German officers. Taking careful aim, as he had been taught in training at Camp Phillips, Gallant scattered this group. It was then that Lieutenant Honan found the position. Gallant had held the forward position, and until Honan appeared, no one had ordered him to leave. Now, with his three surviving men, he was ordered into Lampaden, where his diminished squad set up their two guns on a manure pile. Here he assisted an unidentified sergeant setting up a daisy chain of mines to stop enemy armor. Things began to blur after that, but he fired nearly constantly for the rest of the day, remembering, "I was getting low on ammunition and the barrel of my gun was red hot." Another of his men was mortally wounded and the building in which he had taken shelter was wrecked by direct fire, but the position was held and "the whole area to my front was covered with German bodies. I was surprised to note the number of different uniforms they wore." Private First Class Gallant was the second member of the 3d Battalion to earn the Distinguished Service Cross this day.

Lieutenant Honan had gone on to his other squad, led by Pfc. Paul W. Chapman. They, too, were still in action and holding their assigned position. Covered by Lieutenant Honan, who stood erect to attract the enemy's attention while firing his machine gun from the hip, this squad also withdrew into Lampaden. Lieutenant Honan continued to search for his last squad unsuccessfully, but upon his return to Lampaden found that they had withdrawn on their own. Not all groups outposting Lampaden made it back successfully, however. One squad from the first platoon of Company L was cut down by enemy machine-gun fire. The SS troopers then came up and machine-gunned the survivors. Two wounded men, who had pretended to be dead, survived and crawled into Lampaden to report the atrocity.

As darkness fell on 6 March, both sides prepared to attack. General Malony's orders to the 376th Infantry to relieve the 302d were being fulfilled. The German commanders also decided that they would renew their attack in the morning. Although the 11th SS Mountain Regiment was down to one-battalion strength, the remaining battalions of the division could still possibly crack the American defenses along Lampaden Ridge with one more attempt.

The new enemy attack began in the early morning fog of 7 March. Supported by self-propelled guns, mortars, rockets, and artillery fire, the attack came in against the eastern and southern avenues leading into town. A vicious fight ensued and quickly became very personal. Technical Sergeant James T. Chapman of the battalion's antitank platoon manned a lone gun against the self-propelled guns leading the eastern attack, using every round of ammunition available. He then found a bazooka and began sniping at enemy armor, destroying four enemy vehicles. Private First Class Gallant again manned his gun from the manure pile and cut down attacking infantry as he had the day before. Lieutenant Honan and Pfc. William T. Baxter each fired a 60mm mortar singlehandedly to stop the attack coming in from their direction. Private First Class Baxter then made an exposed ammunition-resupply run, during which he killed one German and captured three others. He then joined Sergeant Chapman in destroying another enemy armored vehicle. Lieutenant Douglas LaRue Smith, an original member of the division and now commanding Company M, adjusted 81mm mortar fire directly on attacking SS troopers with such accuracy that their attack faltered. The Germans did not seize Lampaden.

Still anxious to get his tired division out of the line, General Malony continued to work for its relief while the battle around Lam-

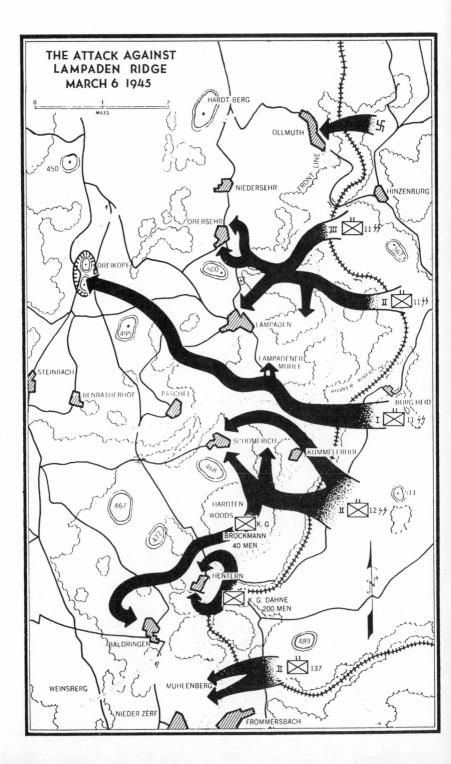

paden raged. While General Cheadle and Colonel Bercquist monitored the fight for him, he arranged with General Walker and General Paul that the relief, delayed by the counterattack, would take
place on the nights of 8 and 9 March. Once two regiments of the
26th Division had replaced the 301st and 302d Infantry, the 94th Infantry Division could pull out for its delayed rest.

Lieutenant Colonel Minor's 1st Battalion, 376th Infantry, had
pushed out patrols on 6 March to try to contact Lieutenant Colonel
Cloudt's 3d Battalion, 302d Infantry. Despite their inability to make
contact, the American attack began as scheduled on 7 March. The
operation was fiercely opposed with heavy losses, including the loss
of four supporting tanks, so the attack was postponed to 8 March.

Things were equally bad for the Germans. The staunch defense
of the 3d Battalion, 302d Infantry, for which it received a Presidential Unit Citation, and now the attacks of the 1st Battalion, 376th Infantry, had depleted the Germans' ranks and equipment severely. Resupply was impossible, the only route of withdrawal was threatened,
and all medical supplies were exhausted. Ammunition was low, and
in one unit only one of the original six mortars remained operational. A second attempt at prisoner exchange offered to Lieutenant Colonel Cloudt was again rejected. Just as the German commander around Lampaden was again about to attack, in a last
desperate attempt, orders came to withdraw. The battle of Lampaden
was over.

Finally, 8 March brought both relief and more work for the 94th
Infantry Division. Even before it became clear that Lamapden was
secure, Colonel Bercquist received a call from XX Corps to halt the
relief efforts. Shortly afterward General Malony confirmed to General Cheadle that no additional units were to be relieved. The following day, General Walker appeared at division headquarters and
ordered the division to participate in a corps attack to the Rhine to
begin 13 March.

The sudden change in orders affected not just the 94th Infantry
Division, but the entire Third Army. General Patton now had the
breaches he needed in German defenses before the Rhine, and he
determined to race for that final natural barrier protecting the German heartland. Having taken Trier from the Germans, who had used

it as a springboard for the Battle of the Bulge, he would now use it as a base for his move to the Rhine. Although he was racing the Germans, he was at least as interested in winning the race against his fellow Allied Armies.

Third Army now consisted of Maj. Gen. Troy H. Middleton's VIII Corps, Maj. Gen. Manton S. Eddy's XII Corps, and General Walton H. Walker's Ghost Corps. Each was directed toward the Rhine at all possible speed. It was the kind of war that Patton relished the most, pursuit. Eddy remarked, "The heat is on like I never saw before." Patton was going to push his three corps across the Palatinate area straight on for the Rhine. He was aware that both Field Marshal Montgomery and General Patch were preparing operations to cross the Rhine, and above all he wanted to be waiting for them when they arrived. The seizure of the Remagen Bridge by General Hodges's First Army made the rush to the Rhine even more urgent in Patton's eyes. As often happened, his impatience took the form of anger vented upon his subordinates. General Eddy was called to explain delays by the 4th and 11th Armored Divisions in his corps, who had dared to stop and to draw breath. General Walker's corps, now reinforced by the 12th Armored Division under Maj. Gen. Roderick R. Allen, began to race across the Palatinate in such random order that General Hodges remarked while looking at a situation map that it reminded him of "an intestinal tract."

The Ghost Corps led one wing of the pursuit. Reinforced now to a strength of six divisions, it was in effect a small army. The 94th Division was to be in the forefront of the attack and on 14 March received another visit from Patton, who told General Malony, "Keep up the good work, you are doing fine." He went on to stress that he wanted battalion commanders up front with their leading companies warned about a new German practice of leaving behind time bombs, and decried unnecessary destruction on the part of American soldiers. Not to be outdone, Walker spoke with Malony and told him, "I want you to give them the works right now, night and day keep pushing forward, don't stop, give them everything you got until we get to the river."

Now began the race to conquer the Saar-Palatinate and reach the Rhine. Army Group G, now under General Paul Hausser, still defended in front of Third Army. He quickly requested permission to withdraw behind the Rhine, knowing that his depleted forces and the loss of the defenses of the Siegfried Line all but eliminated any chance of successfully defending the Saar-Palatinate. Field Marshal von Rundstedt, passing on Hitler's orders, denied the request. Because Seventh Army was still engaged in pushing a strong force back from the West Wall, General Bradley suggested that Third Army, now well behind the enemy's main defenses, strike the main blow. General Eisenhower approved and Patton was unleashed. He arranged for Generals Walker and Eddy to make converging attacks toward the Nahe River while missing no opportunity to rush forward to the Rhine and, if at all possible, seize a bridge.

General Walker was to attack first to draw off any hidden German reserves while General Eddy's corps would follow to take advantage of the situation. The 3d Cavalry Group led off with a diversionary attack along the Moselle and Ruhr Rivers. Then the three infantry divisions of the Ghost Corps moved forward, supported by some thirty-one battalions of divisional and corps artillery. The 94th Division led the XX Corps along the left flank, while the 80th Division drove down the corps center and the 26th Division drove south, protecting the corps right flank. The 65th Division staged diversionary attacks in the Saarlautern bridgehead.

The terrain was ideal for defense, with many hills, villages, ravines, and forests scattered along the area, but the Germans were too weak to do more than defend at isolated places. Although this could cause a brief flurry of combat, nowhere did it seriously delay the drive of XX Corps to the Rhine. Pillboxes briefly slowed the 26th Division's advance, and a counterattack by the remnants of the 6th SS Mountain Division delayed the 80th Infantry Division for a day. But just as General Patton was again getting impatient, knowing General Patch's Seventh Army was breaking out of its bridgehead, the 302d Infantry of the 94th Infantry Division plunged forward four miles in one day, indicating a clear break in the enemy defenses. A similar break by a battalion of the 80th Infantry Division's 318th Infantry signaled to General Walker that the time had come to release his armored elements. He ordered the 10th Armored Division to pass through the 94th and race for the Nahe River. Just as the Tiger Division jumped off, General Eddy's XII Corps launched its attack at dawn on 14 March. The following day Seventh Army opened its attack to crack the West Wall in its sector and form a front fully along the Rhine.

The 10th Armored Division raced forward toward the Nahe River as directed. Alongside them the 12th Armored Division, with elements of the 94th Division attached, moved forward. Using searchlights to brighten the dark night, the Tiger Division raced night and day toward its objectives, also assisted by units of the 94th. Together the three divisions, two armored and one infantry, made "spectacular gains" in the race for the Rhine. Yet despite the startling difference between the battle a month ago and in mid-March, the German defenses still took a toll. In the 65th Division's attack near Saarlautern an aidman in the 259th Infantry Regiment, Pfc. Frederick C. Murphy was hit in the shoulder by enemy automatic weapons fire. Disregarding his wound and refusing evacuation, he entered a minefield to help wounded and set off a mine that severed one of his feet. Despite these crippling wounds, he continued to crawl around aiding wounded men until a second mine explosion killed him. He was awarded a posthumous Medal of Honor.

Between the racing XII and XX Corps, the enemy had no chance to form a firm defensive line. Towns and villages were defended stoutly, while others were surrendered meekly. The German forces facing Third Army were disorganized and depleted. The rampaging 10th and 12th Armored Divisions scattered the enemy fragments while the infantry of the 80th and 94th Divisions rounded them up or pushed them aside. The thrusts of XX Corps threatened the only feasible routes of withdrawal for those German units facing Seventh Army, and so now came permission for them to withdraw to avoid encirclement. General Walker, aware of the opportunity as well as the Germans, turned the 10th Armored Division south to help encircle the enemy facing Seventh Army while the 12th Armored and 94th Infantry Divisions continued the race for the Rhine. Both divisions were targeted on the industrial city of Ludwigshafen. Here they came under heavy attack by some three hundred planes of the Luftwaffe, including the new jet-propelled planes. Although the jets escaped, Battery D of the 465th AAA Automatic Weapons Battalion claimed some hits on the accompanying propeller-driven machines.

The infantry of XX Corps was hard pressed to keep pace with the armored task forces, but quickly the same trucks that had been intended to take the 94th Infantry Division to rest areas were used to rush them forward alongside the 12th Armored. Supplies, food, and rest were nonexistent, but by Saint Patrick's Day 1945, XX Corps was firmly on the Rhine.

Ludwigshafen remained a problem, however. With a population of more than 145,000 civilians and a large I. G. Farben industrial plant, it was a large and easily defended city. Defended by the 9th Flak Division, veterans of the French, Russian, and Crimean Campaigns commanded by Lt. Gen. Wolfgang Pickert, it was armed with heavy antiaircraft weapons that could now serve equally well against armor. Stopped cold by the strong antitank defenses, the 12th Armored tried to rush the town unsuccessfully. Unable to breach the defenses, the division turned for assistance to the 94th Infantry Division. The 376th Infantry was assigned to assist in clearing the enemy from Ludwigshafen.

The 1st Battalion, 376th Infantry, also the recipient of a Presidential Unit Citation and now led by Lt. Col. Eskel N. Miller Jr., after Colonel Minor's promotion to regimental executive officer, drew the initial task of clearing the city. Initial reconnaissance determined that the enemy intended to defend the city. After passing a line of eleven burned-out half-tracks of the 12th Armored Division, patrols entered the city only to be driven to cover by automatic weapons fire. Company C dispatched a night patrol under SSgt. Robert E. Trefzger "to reconnoiter the area for enemy defenders." If the patrol found a way into the enemy defenses, it was to send back two guides to bring up the rest of the company.

"The patrol was to cross a very large, open field west of the city's outskirts," after which it had to cross a lake and then attempt to get into a row of houses. "The field contained many very large bomb craters and the patrol carefully and quietly advanced from crater to crater. It gradually became obvious from the widespread coughing and an occasional unshielded cigarette 'light-up' flare that the area between the patrol and the lake and houses was heavily defended by awake and presumably alert enemy troops." Sergeant Trefzger concluded that no infiltration was possible on this site and returned with his report.

With attempts to infiltrate the Ludwigshafen defenses impractical, and after hearing the destruction of its Rhine bridge, General Malony created Task Force Cheadle for the job of securing the city. Consisting of the 376th Infantry, Combat Command A of the 12th Armored Division, Company B, 774th Tank Destroyer Battalion, Battery D of the 465th AAA Battalion, and Company B (less one platoon) of the 81st Chemical Mortar Battalion and commanded by General Cheadle, the task force proceeded to methodically clear the town. For the next two days the infantry fought against an enemy liberally equipped with automatic weapons and high caliber artillery used for downing planes but now turned against them on the ground. On the twenty-third, Malony added the 301st Infantry to the battle and dissolved Task Force Cheadle, placing the operation directly under division headquarters. Just as the additional forces were moving into place the Germans fled across the river or faded into the civilian population. On 24 March General Walker declared Ludwigshafen secured. The Ghost Corps was firmly on the Rhine.

EPILOGUE

General Patton did not get across the Rhine before all others, as he had fervently hoped when he noted, "We are in a horse race with Courtney [Hodges]. If he beats me [across the Rhine] I shall be ashamed." He learned on 7 March, just as XX Corps was beating off the last attack of LXXXII Corps at Lampaden, that III Corps of First Army had seized intact a bridge over the Rhine at Remagen. Instead of being ashamed, he felt admiration and appreciation of the difficult accomplishment of First Army. For General Patton, the task now became one of not being the last across the Rhine.

Patton was aware that 21st Army Group under Field Marshal Montgomery was planning an elaborate crossing of the Rhine in the north, while Seventh Army was alongside his own Third Army and fast approaching the Rhine all along its zone. If either of those forces crossed before Third Army, then Patton's cherished publicity opportunity, already partially eclipsed by First Army, would have passed.

Patton hoped for a swift conquest of the Saar-Palatinate region as a springboard for an "on the run" leap across the Rhine River. In this he was supported by General Bradley, who, in a meeting on 19 March, had authorized precisely that objective. First Army, already across, was to secure its bridgehead, while Third Army was to beat the British. The Sixth Army Group under Lt. Gen. Jacob Devers, to Patton's south, was not considered a threat. Devers was not considered the equal of the group of longtime friends commanding the major units of 12th Army Group.

General Patton now had both an objective to his liking and a timetable. Bradley's permission to cross the Rhine and the knowledge that 21st Army Group's set-piece attack across the Rhine was scheduled for 23 March put Patton in a position in which he thrived. He had already collected an assortment of assault boats and engineer troops for the crossing, including navy assault boats and crews. Now he went to General Eddy of XII Corps and demanded that he rush the Rhine. Eddy demurred, asking for an additional day, but Patton refused and conferred with him to select the best crossing site in his area.

The two generals originally studied the area at Mainz but quickly concluded that a crossing attempt would be expected there and defenders were probably in place. Patton continued to study the map until his gaze settled on the village of Oppenheim, about fifteen miles upstream of Mainz. While establishing diversionary movements at Mainz, General Eddy ordered one of Third Army's most experienced divisions, the 5th Infantry, commanded by Maj. Gen. S. Leroy Irwin, to cross in secrecy on the night of 22 March.

Irwin selected Col. Paul J. Black's 11th Infantry to make the crossing. Given less than twelve hours to prepare an assault over Germany's premier river after having earlier been told his regiment was going into a reserve position, Colonel Black switched priorities and prepared for his new mission.

The enemy was even less prepared. Having lost vast quantities of men and materiel in the Saar-Palatinate battle, they were still in the process of reorganizing their shattered commands. While Colonel Black was preparing his assault, there was not even a division-sized unit available to oppose him on the opposite bank. This quickly became apparent when 1st Lt. Irven Jacobs led Company K across just before midnight of 22 March. They found only seven Germans, completely surprised, to oppose them. The rest of the 3d Battalion followed and found no serious opposition in their area. Downstream, the 1st Battalion encountered more determined opposition, but after a fierce hour's battle the bridgehead was secure. Third Army was across the Rhine.

Patton quickly contacted General Bradley to tell of his success, and after a brief delay to ensure his beachhead was secure, Third Army's first crossing of the Rhine was made public. But General Patton wasn't finished. The crossing at Oppenheim was not located in an area that would readily establish Third Army in an advantageous position for future operations. General Middleton's VIII Corps was ordered across the Rhine in a second assault crossing designed to protect the established XII Corps crossing and to project Third Army past the Mainz River, which faced XII Corps. Middleton's 87th and 89th Infantry Divisions were to cross at Boppard and St. Goar, respectively.

These crossings faced more opposition, and some fighting was required before this beachhead was secured. All of Third Army's objectives along the Rhine had now been fulfilled. Yet General Patton was not content. He had one corps still on the "wrong" side of the Rhine. Exactly why he ordered a third assault crossing has never been made clear, but Walker's Ghost Corps was ordered to cross between Third Army's other two corps at Mainz. Originally scheduled to be supported by XII Corps's flanking units, this part of the plan failed to materialize, and General Walker sent the 80th Infantry Division across the Rhine on the morning of 28 March. They faced the same disorganization as had the other two corps and swiftly established a beachhead at nominal cost. Germany lay open to Third Army.

To the south, Seventh Army also crossed the Rhine. General Devers at Sixth Army Group, concerned initially that dams that controlled the flow and level of water in Seventh Army's area would be opened and delay matters, was relieved to learn before the approach to the Rhine that these dams, jointly controlled by German and Swiss commissions, would remain closed due to diplomatic pressure put on the Swiss. Having eliminated this threat, Seventh Army selected its XV Corps to cross above and below the city of Worms. The 45th Infantry Division, followed by the 63d Infantry Division, would assault above the city while the 3d Infantry Division, supported by the 44th Infantry Division, would cross to the south.

The crossings went in before dawn on 26 March and met initially heavy but sporadic resistance, but disorganization and lack of support on the German side ended the battle after a few hours. Seventh Army was across the Rhine to stay.

To the north 21st Army Group launched a massive ground and airborne assault which, after fierce resistance, overwhelmed the defenders. Against the opposition by some of the best remaining troops in the German Order of Battle, including the First Parachute

Army, overwhelming Allied might turned the tide quickly, and by the end of the first day, 24 March, all doubt as to success had vanished.

The last remaining campaign, that of central Germany, was accomplished swiftly. For the Ghost Corps, the assault crossing of the Rhine was followed by the seizure of the city of Kassel, then a month-long race alongside its longtime companion, XII Corps, deep into Germany and finally into Czechoslovakia where the end of the war found it. The 10th Armored Division, never one of General Patton's favorites, was traded to Seventh Army for the 6th Armored Division, which was attached to XX Corps. The 10th Armored, still under General Morris, assaulted Kirchheim, crossed the Danube, and ended the war in Austria. General Malony's 94th Infantry Division went for rest and recuperation to the new XXII Corps of the new Fifteenth Army and, together with two U.S. Airborne Divisions, held one flank of the American effort to reduce the Ruhr pocket. It performed occupation duties around Düsseldorf while reorganizing, and later it, too, moved to Czechoslovakia, where it served on occupation duties.

Although overshadowed by the much larger Battle of the Bulge and later the Remagen Bridge crossing, the campaign in the Saar-Moselle Triangle and the resulting Saar-Palatinate Campaign were fine examples of the U.S. Army at its best. The XX Corps's struggle in the triangle is in itself a compelling argument that the U.S. soldier was the equal of the German, with or without the material advantages so often given as the reason for his victories. Clearly these advantages did not exist in the first weeks of the Saar-Moselle battle. Supplies, particularly proper clothing and food, did not reach the front-line troops in sufficient quantities to prevent heavy-weather casualties. Armored support, another common item often pointed to as the reason for American victories, was usually unavailable. Artillery support was effective and available, but the German opposition had an equal resource and used it effectively. Moreover, the German defenders in January and early February had a first-class and fully equipped panzer division available for defense and counterattack, supported by two infantry divisions whose quality the German commanders themselves rated as suitable for defense.

Yet the 94th Infantry Division, with brief support from the 8th and later the 10th Armored Divisions, overcame this defense. That the struggle was costly and could have been more swiftly concluded had more resources been allocated is not in dispute. But it does point to the fact that in 1945 the American soldier was quite capable of accomplishing his mission under circumstances no better than those affecting his German counterpart. The infantry cracked the newest segment of the vaunted Siegfried Line in an area that was both well defended and well supported. It did so by and large with its organic artillery and supporting troops. Air support played a minimal role because of weather restrictions. Armor was rarely available, and then only in small numbers allocated for brief periods. Indeed, for much of the battle, the Germans held armor superiority, both in quality and quantity.

These same troops, once across the Saar River, then proceeded to become pursuit columns, swift and easily motorized, to take advantage of the resulting disorganization of the enemy brought on by their earlier efforts. This picture of American soldiers mounted on tanks and trucks often obscures the earlier picture of the hard and difficult fighting that brought on the pursuit. In this the Saar-Moselle Triangle campaign is again a good example. Its early stages are often ignored or slighted, while the pursuit to the Rhine is highlighted as a classic example of American pursuit tactics.

General Malony recorded that his division lost 1,087 men killed in action, 4,684 wounded in action, and 113 missing. He also noted that some 5,868 men had been evacuated "for trench foot, frozen feet, or other nonbattle causes." Additional wounded remained at their posts, while many of the ill or injured men also returned to duty. Nevertheless, this is a high toll for a unit whose most intense combat was at a period when the war was well on its way to conclusion. Against that toll General Malony recorded some 20,547 enemy soldiers taken prisoner, untold thousands of others killed, three enemy divisions decimated, the vaunted Siegfried Line twice breached, and American forces advanced to the heart of Germany.

There were other, unreported, losses as well. Young Edmund H. Lessel was born and lived in Orscholz for the first fifteen years of his life. He was about nine years old when the battles raged about his home. His father had just been reported missing in action in Russia, his home was under American fire, and he and his mother and sisters had been evacuated across the Moselle River. When they returned after the war, of the five hundred houses in Orscholz, "not a single one was untouched, about 45 percent were totally destroyed including our home." He came home to find destroyed German and American armored vehicles scattered all over the area. "The killing must have been awful, dead bodies were found long after the war was over." He reports finding four dead soldiers, two German and two American, while playing in abandoned positions. It appeared that the four had encountered each other, fought to the death, and then been covered with snow and leaves until found years later by children playing. These and many others were reported and properly interred.

There are still men missing in action in the Saar-Moselle. On 27 March 1990, Alex Arendt, a twenty-one-year-old university student, was using his metal detector between the villages of Sinz and Weis when it picked up what turned out to be an identification bracelet reading "PFC John W. Thompson, 32718032, U.S. Army." Research indicted that Private First Class Thompson had been reported killed in action on 26 January 1945 while a member of the 376th Infantry Regiment.

There were other casualties as well. In the summer of 1945 Edmund Lessel and eight friends were playing in the fields around Orscholz when they discovered abandoned weapons and ammunition. The group, ranging from eight to twelve years of age, had no idea what they had found and treated the items as toys. Apparently an antitank rocket exploded in the midst of the group and three were killed and the rest horribly mutilated. American troops stationed nearby rushed to the scene and saved those who had been injured by rushing them the thirty miles to Trier, where a U.S. military hospital was in operation. At least 173 of Orscholz's original population of 1,988 people perished in 1945.

General Malony later noted what he felt were the reasons for his division's success. One factor of importance was morale. The division had trained and served together for years before being sent overseas, and despite the serious disruption caused by the drafting of replacements from it several times, it retained its morale throughout its service. This is in large part a tribute to its leadership. Malony recalls that as the division was preparing to leave the United States he conducted an inspection of every unit to determine if each member could speak and understand English. In a society where multiple languages were still widely spoken, this was an important matter. In one battalion the general discovered a soldier of Chinese ancestry. He approached the soldier and began asking him routine military questions. He received a blank stare in reply. Immediately the soldier's sergeant came to his defense, asserting both the soldier's competence and his value to the sergeant's squad. Again General Malony tried to solicit a response, without success. This time the battalion commander urged, even pleaded, with the soldier to respond to the general. This time the soldier gave out a monologue in what Malony later recorded as "the beautiful five-toned language of the North Chinese" but not one word of English. Reluctantly he ordered the soldier transferred from the division.

Many months later, during the bitter struggle for the town of Nennig, General Malony was visiting the front line positions of one battalion of the 302d Infantry Regiment. Together with the regimental commander, Col. Earle A. Johnson, they were observing operations when he noticed a messenger come in from a surrounded unit. All communications with that unit had been cut off and every attempt to reach it had failed. Yet this wounded messenger came in with vital information. "His helmet was gone; he was slightly wounded in the head and neck and the blood which is so plentiful from such wounds flowed down his cheek onto his clothing; he staggered slightly and held out his hand, which we could all see held a yellow telegramlike Field Message form. No one moved; we all stared at him. 'Me come,' he said proudly." It was the same Chinese soldier whom the general had ordered from his division back in the United States. As he was being taken out to the first-aid station, Malony complimented him on getting his message in, only to once again hear the same Chinese language response he had first heard back at the port of embarkation. "But I didn't care. My conscience was perfectly easy. He could speak and understand English; more than that, the sergeant who had thought him to be a good soldier was quite right."

Clearly the morale of the American infantrymen in Europe was generally not a problem. Moreover, the leadership, so often decried in later years, was equal to the task of commanding motivated soldiers. General Malony was later to remark on how the mix of experienced professional soldiers and the newly trained civilian officers worked so well to balance the leadership given to the soldiers of World War II. Some fifty years later former Capt. Douglas L. Smith, a civilian soldier of Company M, 302d Infantry, would recall with admiration the leadership of his professional battalion commander, Colonel Cloudt, and deeply regret the inability of Colonel Cloudt to present his story to a student of the battle.

General Malony analyzed the success of his division, and by inference all U.S. Army divisions, after his retirement. His was a draftee division, "average age twenty-six, initially officered by a nucleus of regulars about whom were gathered officers who came principally from the reserve corps and the National Guard, most of whom had had no combat experience and very little idea of what it meant." He believed that the group of West Point graduates, and most particularly his three combat-experienced regimental commanders, were key factors in his unit's success. In addition to seeing combat in World War I, his key officers "had all been through the army educational system, to include the Command and General Staff Course at Fort Leavenworth." For the commanding general this was an advantage in that "all they required was to know what they were to do, not how they were to do it." He particularly relied on his two general officer assistants, General Cheadle and the artillery commander, General Fortier. Malony had been associated with both officers before activating the 94th Infantry Division. He had served at West Point with Cheadle and on the staff in Washington with Fortier.

On the negative side, he decried the limits of promotion available to commanders of supporting units. "If, for instance, my medical officer commanding was deserving of higher rank than that of lieutenant colonel, the only way he could get it was by leaving the division and getting a way-behind-the-lines job with a hospital or some other ex-combat job carrying with it an increased grade." The quality of the cadre also concerned him. "Our cadre came from the 77th Division, and I went down to look it over as the men were individually interviewed and transferred. Naturally enough, no commander wants to get rid of his best men and the 77th was no exception—but their commander, General Eichelberger, and I were present and there were a few turnbacks." Another negative factor was the support troops provided for the maintenance of the training facilities in the continental United States. General Malony found them to be "the poorest of the draft, not fitted for combat, undisciplined, untrained, of poor appearance and uniform. They were evil influences on the combat troops as well as on my disposition."

Malony also remarked on the value of outside support when he noted, "The ones who really suffered were the women who, desirous of being with their husbands until the last minute, had followed them to Salina. The city was not nearly large enough to provide accommodations for them in rentable homes. As one frustrated soldier put it, everything was rented, to include all the hollow trees." He abhorred the loss of trained men for the replacement system and decried the men sent to replace those ordered to North Africa. These he called "spit-backs," recovered wounded who were physically unfit for combat, and similar rejects. He was able to transfer most of these men to rear-area units outside the division before it departed for the active theaters of war.

Malony's personal observations and conclusions were borne out by an independent study done nearly a decade after his death. A private research firm, contracted by the Department of Defense, studied the 88th Infantry Division, which served in combat in the Italian Campaign from mid-1944 to the end of the war. It, too, was a draftee division, although it suffered less from replacement stripping than did the 94th Division, and also saw somewhat less combat. This study concludes that the quality of its enlisted cadre, the stability of the division's personnel and leadership, and its esprit de corps were critical factors in its performance. In effect this applied in varying degrees to all U.S. Army divisions of the Second World War.

It has been seen how the initial cadre was carefully screened by Generals Malony and Eichelberger when activating the 94th Infantry Division. Although that division suffered unusually from personnel stripping, its core of leadership remained intact. And Malony's tale of the Chinese soldier speaks well for its morale. In the 90th Infantry Division, leadership turnover was more intense than normal, and that division suffered accordingly until the situation was resolved and it developed its own esprit de corps. The study attributes to the morale factor the central position for good performance of a World War II division. It goes on to state that "to a large extent the result of Sloan's leadership and especially of the discipline he imposed, the esprit became the chief agent for sustaining high performance, developing new leaders, stimulating resourcefulness and innovation, and integrating replacements into the division. It was largely because of this esprit de corps that the character and quality of the division survived command changes and casualties."

The subject of casualties is another area of concern. General Patton's admonition to the division made it into his diary, and thereafter into the few accounts of the battle, as reflecting poorly on the performance of the 94th Infantry Division, especially as to nonbattle casualties. Yet much of the blame, as has been pointed out, for those casualties rests with Third Army headquarters, of which General Patton held personal responsibility. Inadequate footwear, inadequate rations, lack of sufficient warm clothing, and the general conditions under which the men fought all contributed to the nonbattle casualty rate. Because records of nonbattle casualties are not available for comparison purposes, no true study can be conducted. However, a veteran of the division, Leo Kohlner of the 302d Infantry, made a detailed study of the ratio of combat casualties per day of combat for all divisions that served in northwest Europe. In this study he took the days spent in combat for each division and computed the average casualty rate per day. Interestingly, this study shows that the 94th Infantry Division ranks fourth for casualties per combat day, coming after the 4th Infantry, 29th Infantry, and 80th Infantry Divisions but ahead of better known units such as the 30th Division, one of Patton's favorites, the 2d Infantry Division, 90th Infantry Division, and most others. Like the 88th Infantry Division and many others, because it did not participate in a widely known campaign, was not overrun by enemy forces, and did not make a spectacular chase, it is little known outside very small circles. Yet that division, and so many more like it, were the core of the U.S. Army in the Second World War.

APPENDIX

Number of Enlisted Men by State
94th Infantry Division, 1 January 1943*

State	Count	State	Count
Alabama	269	Nevada	6
Arizona	8	New Hampshire	5
Arkansas	28	New Jersey	799
California	128	New Mexico	23
Colorado	224	New York	2,565
Connecticut	72	North Carolina	478
Delaware	29	North Dakota	81
Florida	32	Ohio	1,125
Georgia	333	Oklahoma	59
Idaho	7	Oregon	17
Illinois	1,108	Pennsylvania	1,766
Indiana	751	Rhode Island	8
Iowa	109	South Carolina	416
Kansas	159	South Dakota	62
Kentucky	357	Tennessee	452
Louisiana	20	Texas	135
Maine	17	Utah	10
Maryland	229	Vermont	6
Massachusetts	177	Virginia	368
Michigan	719	Washington	31
Minnesota	289	West Virginia	353
Mississippi	15	Wisconsin	1,231
Missouri	1,180	Wyoming	10
Montana	15	No Record	28
Nebraska	140	Canada	14

*All charts with asterisks as reported to General Maloney, January 1943–1944, by the division statistitian. General Maloney's notebooks, dated January 1943–1944.

Age Distribution—94th Infantry Division*
1 January 1943

Age Group	Number of Men	Percent of Total
17–19	406	2.5
20–25	9,238	55.2
26–31	3,638	22.5
32–37	2,060	12.4
38–43	1,033	6.4
44–49	170	.99
50 and over	3	.01
Division Totals	16,548	100.00%

Breakdown by Specific Age*

Age	Number of Men	Age	Number of Men
17	7	34–35	692
18–19	399	36–37	543
20–21	4,924	38–39	424
22–23	2,484	40–41	345
24–25	1,830	42–43	264
26–27	1,498	44–45	154
28–29	1,177	46–47	11
30–31	963	48–49	5
32–33	825	50 and over	3

Division Total 16,548

Average Age of the 94th Infantry Division by Unit*

Unit	Jan. 1943	May 1943	Jan. 1944
301st Infantry	26.1	25.6	25.5
302d Infantry	26.1	25.6	25.2
376th Infantry	25.8	25.6	25.6
Div. Artillery HQ	26.9	26.9	26.4
301st Field Arty. Bn.	27.9	27.4	26.4

Unit	Jan. 1943	May 1943	Jan. 1944
356th Field Arty. Bn.	27.8	26.7	26.2
390th Field Arty. Bn.	27.6	27.2	26.5
919th Field Arty. Bn.	27.7	26.5	26.1
94th Quartermaster Co.	27.9	27.6	27.5
319th Medical Bn.	27.5	27.0	26.8
319th Engineer Bn.	28.3	26.9	26.6
Division HQ	29.1	28.6	26.8
94th Signal Co.	26.9	26.9	26.1
94th Recon. Troop	25.3	26.0	25.2
794th Ordnance Co.	27.9	26.4	26.0
Division Averages	26.7	25.9	25.9

Number of Men Over 40 Years of Age by Unit
94th Infantry Division, 1 January 1944*

Unit	Jan. 1943	May 1943	Jan. 1944
301st Infantry Regiment	52	20	18
302d Infantry Regiment	133	13	10
376th Infantry Regiment	128	5	11
Division Artillery Headquarters	10	4	3
301st Field Artillery Battalion	45	8	5
356th Field Artillery Battalion	57	3	5
919th Field Artillery Battalion	58	8	4
390th Field Artillery Battalion	52	11	12
94th Quartermaster Company	9	3	4
319th Medical Battalion	28	1	1
319th Engineer (Combat) Battalion	60	6	5
Division Headquarters	22	5	5
94th Signal Company	15	7	4
94th Military Police Platoon	0	0	0
94th Reconnaissance Troop	4	2	1
794th Ordnance Company	14	1	1
Division Totals	687	97	89

Average Years of Education 94th Infantry Division*

Unit	Jan 43	May 43	Jan 44
301st Infantry Regiment	9.3	9.2	9.4
302d Infantry Regiment	9.3	9.2	9.4
376th Infantry Regiment	9.4	9.4	10.0
Division Artillery Headquarters	11.2	11.1	11.2
301st Field Artillery Battalion	9.4	9.4	n/a[1]
356th Field Artillery Battalion	9.1	9.7	9.6
919th Field Artillery Battalion	9.8	9.8	9.6
390th Field Artillery Battalion	9.6	9.5	9.3
94th Quartermaster Company	9.4	9.4	9.6
319th Medical Battalion	10.0	10.4	10.3
319th Engineer (Combat) Battalion	9.4	9.2	9.1
Division Headquarters	11.7	11.1	11.5
94th Signal Company	10.8	11.0	10.5
94th Military Police Platoon	11.8	10.6	n/a[2]
94th Reconnaissance Troop	10.6	10.4	10.4
794th Ordnance Company	9.9	10.3	10.5
Division Averages	9.5	9.5	9.7

1. This unit, the 301st Field Artillery Battalion, is not listed on the final report to General Malony in January 1944. No reason is given, and it appears to be an oversight. General Malony's Notebooks, January 1944.

2. The cumulative report in January 1944 included the Military Police Platoon with division headquarters. Prior figures are from the previous reports submitted to General Malony in January and May 1943. General Malony's Notebooks, January 1944.

Illiterate and Non–English Speaking Enlisted Men
94th Infantry Division, 1 January 1944*

Unit	Illiterates (Rate per 1,000)	Non-English (Rate)
301st Infantry	70 (27.7)	14 (5.5)
302d Infantry	73 (29.1)	9 (3.6)
376th Infantry	52 (20.4)	8 (3.1)

Unit	Illiterates (Rate per 1,000)	Non-English (Rate)
Div. Artillery HQ	0 (0.0)	0 (0.0)
301st FA Bn.	12 (19.1)	1 (1.6)
356th FA Bn.	5 (8.2)	1 (1.6)
919th FA Bn.	7 (11.7)	1 (1.7)
390th FA Bn.	10 (17.2)	2 (3.4)
94th Quartermaster Co.	0 (0.0)	0 (0.0)
319th Medical Bn.	6 (13.8)	2 (4.6)
Div HQ	0 (0.0)	0 (0.0)
319th (C) Engineer Bn.	9 (13.5)	2 (4.6)
94th Signal Co.	0 (0.0)	0 (0.0)
94th Recon. Troop	0 (0.0)	0 (0.0)
94th Ordnance Co.	0 (0.0)	0 (0.0)
Division Totals	244 (19.8)	40 (3.3)

Comparison of Army General Classification Test Scores
94th Infantry Division Versus Normal Expectancy*
1 January 1943

Score Range	Grade	94th Division	Normal Expectancy
130–160	I	4.2%	7.0%
110–129	II	22.5%	24.0%
90–109	III	32.1%	38.0%
60–89	IV	34.4%	24.0%
30–59	V	6.8%	7.0%

Comparison of Army General Classification Test Scores
94th Infantry Division Versus Normal Expectancy*
1 January 1944

Score Range	Grade	94th Division	Normal Expectancy
130–160	I	3.8%	7.0%
110–129	II	27.1%	24.0%

Score Range	Grade	94th Division	Normal Expectancy
90–109	III	32.7%	38.0%
60–89	IV	31.9%	24.0%
30–59	V	4.5%	7.0%

Number of Noncitizens in 94th Infantry Division by Unit, 1 January 1943*

301st Infantry Regiment	113
302d Infantry Regiment	153
376th Infantry Regiment	128
Division Artillery Headquarters	9
301st Field Artillery Battalion	25
356th Field Artillery Battalion	27
919th Field Artillery Battalion	31
390th Field Artillery Battalion	40
94th Quartermaster Company	0
319th Medical Battalion	34
319th Engineer (Combat) Battalion	6
Division Headquarters (incl. MP Platoon)	17
94th Signal Company	12
94th Reconnaissance Troop	6
794th Ordnance Company	1
Division Total	602

Foreign-Born Enlisted Men of the 94th Division*

Country	Number of Enlisted Men
Italy	158
Germany	134
Canada	79
Austria-Hungary	69
Russia	65
Great Britain	54

Country	Number of Enlisted Men
Ireland	52
Poland	47
Greece	29
Mexico	27
Sweden	22
Cuba	19
China	19
Czechoslovakia	16
Turkey	14
Denmark	13
Yugoslavia	16
Norway	10
Division Total	843

The report noted that not all units had reported, and recommended that the totals be increased by ten percent.

Foreign Languages Spoken by Members of 94th Division*

Language	Number of Enlisted Men
Italian	470
Polish	369
German	258
Slovak	122
Yiddish/Jewish	107
Spanish	102
Greek	72
French	64
Finnish	53
Hungarian	52
Russian	47
Swedish	41
Lithuanian	33
Croatian	30
Czechoslovakian	28
Chinese	22

Language	Number of Enlisted Men
Norwegian	20
Ukrainian	15
Danish	12
Portuguese	12
Bohemian	12
Dutch	11
Syrian	10

Personnel and Ordnance Comparison U.S. and Germany Infantry Divisions 1944–1945

	U.S.	German Infantry Div.	German VGD
Authorized Personnel Strength	14,253	12,352	10,072
Rifles and Carbines[3]	11,722	9,069	6,504
Submachine guns	90	1,503	2,064
Machine guns[4] .30-cal. (U.S.) 7.92mm (German), MG34 or MG42	157	656	423
Automatic Rifles (BAR)[5]	243	—	—
60mm Mortars	90	—	—
81mm Mortars	54	48	42
120mm Mortars	—	28	24
Bazookas[6] 2.36" (60mm) (U.S.) 3.5" (88mm) (German)	557	108	216
50-cal. (12.7mm) Machine guns[7]	236	—	—
20mm Automatic Anti-aircraft Guns	—	12	—
37mm Automatic Anti-aircraft Guns	—	—	9
57mm AT Guns	57		–
50mm or 75mm Towed Antitank Guns	—	21	9

	U.S.	German Infantry Div.	German VGD
75mm Armored, Self-Propelled Antitank Guns	—	14	14
75mm Infantry Howitzers	—	18	38
105mm Infantry Howitzers	18	—	—
105mm Howitzers	36	36	24
105mm Guns (Rifles)[8]	—	4	4
Medium Howitzers 155mm (U.S.) 150mm (German) Howitzers	12	8	8

3. In the ETO, practically all .30-caliber rifles were semiautomatic M1s or M1 carbines; only snipers were issued the bolt-action M1903A4 Springfield with a telescopic sight. The vast majority of German rifles were Mauser 1898s, bolt-action weapons that held five bullets; by the autumn of 1944, however (and especially in the *Volksgrenadier* Divisions), German riflemen began receiving MP43 and MP44 automatic rifles, the precursors of the Soviet Kalashnikov family.

4. Includes M1917A1 water-cooled "Heavy" machine guns and M1919A4 or A6 "Light" machine guns.

5. The Browning Automatic Rifle was a magazine-fed (20 rounds) .30-caliber weapon fitted with a bipod. It was the squad support weapon, whereas the German squad support weapon was the belt-fed MG34 or MG42.

6. The German total does not include the quantities of Panzerfausts, or antitank grenade launchers, which were issued on an irregular but ever-increasing basis to German infantrymen throughout the war. With ranges of 30–250 meters, (depending on the model) and extremely effective shaped-charge warheads, they were particularly devastating in armor-restrictive terrain, such as built-up, heavily-forested or mountainous areas.

7. Although used for many purposes, these were intended primarily for anti-aircraft use.

8. These were flat-trajectory weapons with effectively twice the range of the 105mm howitzers (20,850 yards vs. 10,600).

(Chart courtesy Keith E. Bonn)

Headquarters 94th Infantry Division
APO 94   U.S. ARMY

General Orders

5 October 1945
Number   258

Unit Citation[9]

Under the provisions of Section IV, Circular 333, War Department 22 December 1943, the following Units are cited:

> 3d Battalion, 302d Infantry Regiment
> 3d Platoon, Antitank Company, 302d Infantry Regiment
> 3d Platoon, Cannon Company, 302d Infantry Regiment
> 1st Platoon, Company B, 774th Tank Destroyer Battalion
> 1st Platoon, Company B, 778th Tank Battalion

On 5 March 1945, after the assault crossing of the Saar River near Lampaden, a bridgehead five miles in depth was established. The German 82d Corps planned an all-out offensive to regain this vital ground, cut supply lines, and reestablish contact with troops believed to be occupying pillboxes south of Trier. On 6 March to 7 March 1945, these units, exhibiting unwavering fortitude and indomitable tenacity, successfully protected the division bridgehead in the face of overwhelming odds. Bearing the brunt of four fanatical assaults by the 11th SS Mountain Regiment (Reinhard Heydrich), supported by two assault-gun companies and two engineer companies which counterattacked with relentless ferocity, they refused to yield ground and, despite the savage onslaught, inflicted enormous losses on the enemy. When the sector was completely surrounded by an enemy envelopment and under continual shelling, although cut off from supplies and reinforcements, these gallant defenders remained in position and repelled all attacks by the numerically superior forces. To accomplish this it was necessary to order all personnel into the line. Cooks, mechanics, and drivers abandoned their normal duties and fought tenaciously as riflemen. Losses sustained were 116 officers and enlisted men killed, wounded, and missing in action. The enemy lost over 500 killed, 170 captured, and 7 assault guns destroyed. As a result of their tenacious stand and intrepid actions a severe enemy threat to the security of the bridgehead was eliminated, thus permitting the marshalling of our forces on the east bank of the Saar, making possible the devastating drive to the Rhine River.

—BY COMMAND OF MAJOR GENERAL BARNETT

9. Copy provided by Mr. Douglas LaRue Smith to the author. Captain Smith commanded Company M of the 302d at Lampaden. This citation was confirmed after fifty years languishing in the archives in permanent order 224-1 of 12 August 1997, awarding the Presidential Unit Citation to the units listed.

Order of Battle
German Army in the Saar-Moselle Triangle

Oberbefehlshaber West
Generalfeldmarschall Gerd von Rundstedt, Commanding

Army Group G
Colonel General Johannes Blaskowitz, Commanding

LXXXII Corps
General der Infanterie Walther Hahm, Commanding
Colonel Graf von Ingelheim, Chief of Staff
    Mobile Artillery Corps
    Corps Signal Battalion
    Corps Supply Company
    Detachment, Military Police

416th Infantry Division
Lieutenant General Kurt Pflieger, Commanding
Colonel Karl Redmer, Chief of Staff
    712 Infantry Regiment (3 Battalions)
    713 Infantry Regiment (3 Battalions)
    714 Infantry Regiment[10]
    416 Artillery Regiment (6 Batteries)
    416 Panzerjäger Company (Bicycle Mounted)
    416 Engineer Company
    416 Signal Company

416 Divisional Troops
416 Replacement Training Battalion
Fortress Infantry Battalion Merzig (Attached)
1024 Fortress Artillery Battalion (Attached)
1025 Fortress Artillery Battalion (Attached)
Jäger Battalion, 5th Parachute Division (Attached)

19th Volksgrenadier Division
Major General Karl Britzelmayer, Commanding
59th Grenadier Regiment
73d Grenadier Regiment
74th Grenadier Regiment
119th Artillery Regiment
119th Fusilier Battalion
119th Engineer Battalion
119th Antitank Battalion
119th Signal Company
19th Divisional Troops

559th Volksgrenadier Division
Major General Kurt Freiherr von der Muhlen
1125th Grenadier Regiment
1126th Grenadier Regiment
1127th Grenadier Regiment
1559th Artillery Regiment
559th Fusilier Battalion
1159th Antitank Battalion
1559th Engineer Battalion
1559th Signal Battalion
559th Divisional Troops

11th Panzer Division (Assigned 17 January)
Lieutenant General Wend von Wietersheim
Lieutenant Colonel W. Drews, Chief of Staff
15th Panzer Regiment
110th Panzer Grenadier Regiment
111th Panzer Grenadier Regiment
119th Panzer Artillery Regiment
61st Motorcycle Battalion
231st Panzer Reconnaissance Battalion

231st Antitank Battalion
231st Panzer Engineer Battalion
341st Panzer Signal Battalion

256th Volksgrenadier Division (Assigned 10 February)[11]
Major General Gerhard Franz, Commanding
Lieutenant Colonel Bernard Kögel, Chief of Staff
> 456th Infantry Regiment
> 476th Infantry Regiment
> 481st Infantry Regiment
> 256th Artillery Regiment
> 256th Fusilier Company
> 256th Reconnaissance Battalion
> 256th Antitank Battalion
> 256th Engineer Battalion
> 256th Signal Battalion
> 256th Divisional Troops

10. This regiment was not an original part of the division, but was formed in November of 1944 after the division arrived in the Saar-Moselle Triangle by incorporating the Jäger Battalion of the 5th Parachute Infantry Division, the 1024 and 1025 Fortress Artillery Battalions, and the Fortress Infantry Battalion Merzig into one infantry regiment, the new 714th. At the time of XX Corps attacks in January, the division numbered in excess of nine thousand men. Lieutenant Colonel Karl Redmer, Chief of Staff, 416th Infantry Division, "Battles of the 416th Infantry Division Between the Moselle and the Saar from October 1944 to 17 February 1945." USAREUR manuscript MS# B-573.

11. This division replaced the 11th Panzer Division in LXXXII Corps order of battle. It was a rebuilt regular infantry division with long experience on both the eastern and western fronts. It contained a high proportion of experienced veterans from both fronts.

SELECTED BIBLIOGRAPHY

There is no one single work on the Saar-Moselle Triangle Campaign. As a result the student of the campaign and the activities of the XX Corps must turn to one of four areas that do bear on that battle. As always when dealing with World War II records, the quality of each record varies with the source and the amount of interest placed in each by those preparing the work. As with all studies of U.S. Army World War II campaigns the major sources are the primary records of individual units involved in the campaign. A second source and an excellent starting point for such studies are the so-called "Green Books," the series by the U.S. Army Center for Military History entitled *The United States Army in World War II*. The volume by noted military historian Charles B. MacDonald is entitled *The United States Army in World War II. The European Theater of Operations. The Last Offensive* (Washington, D.C.: Center for Military History, 1984). The third source is individual unit histories produced by nearly every large U. S. Army unit that participated in World War II. These vary widely in quality and must be regarded with suspicion as to dates, events, and the activities of other allied units. One of the acknowledged best of these fortunately is Laurence G. Byrnes's *History of the 94th Infantry Division in World War II* (Washington, D.C.: Infantry Journal Press, 1948). Finally there are the veterans of the units involved. Many of these have formed associations as a result of their friendships in the army and are quite willing to relate their experiences to an inquiring historian.

Primary Sources

The primary sources for the XX Corps in the Saar-Moselle Triangle are the official records of the units involved. Especially valuable are the records of the 94th Infantry Division, which took the leading role for much of the campaign. The after-action reports of each major unit and particularly the G-3 journal of the 94th Infantry Division were particularly useful. The journals of the 5th Ranger Battalion were also informative. These can be found in the National Archives and Records Service, Military Reference Branch, Record Group 407. Included in the historical reports section and extremely valuable to historians are the combat interviews conducted by teams of historical officers working under the European Theater Historical Section.

There are also narratives written in the field by these historians to complement the interviews. Here, too, the historian must be alert to unit pride affecting the nature of the interview. In the case of the Saar-Moselle battle, there is a situation where a platoon of rangers under Lieutenant Gambosi and another platoon of armored infantry under Lieutenant Mason both fought to clear the town of Irsch, yet neither lieutenant mentions the presence of the other in his combat interview. Finally, and also quite valuable are the series of monographs prepared after the war by U. S. Army historians with German officers who had command positions opposing the allied units in most areas of combat. More than two thousand of these are held by the National Archives and Records Service in the World War II Records Division. As historian Keith E. Bonn has pointed out, if one allows for the natural professional pride and tendency to blame higher authority for all mistakes, these reports are useful in determining the situation on "the other side of the hill." The most useful of these for the Saar-Moselle battle are:

Ingelheim, Ludwig Graf von, "Engagements Fought by LXXXII A. K. during the period 2 Dec 1944 to 29 Mar 1945." MSS# B-066. 1946.

Pflieger, Kurt, "Rhineland Campaign." (416th Infantry Division Commander). MSS# B-090. 1946.

Redmer, Karl, "Battles of the 416th Infantry Division between the Moselle and the Saar from 5 October 1944 to 17 February 1945." (Staff Officer 416th Infantry Division). MSS# B-573. 1947.

Wietersheim, Generalleutnant Wend von, "The 11 Panzer Division in the Rhineland, Part III (from 20 Dec 44 to 10 Feb 45)." MSS# B-417. 1947.

Unpublished Manuscripts

The paucity of documentation on this campaign extends to unpublished manuscripts. I have been able to identify only three that were helpful.

Adair, Robert K., "Letters Home From the Second Platoon, I Company, 376th Infantry, W W II, Europe." Copy provided by the author.

Cantey, Major J., et al, "The 10th U. S. Armored Division in the Saar-Moselle Triangle." The Armored School Research Paper. May, 1949.

King, Dr. Michael J. "Rangers: Selected Combat Operations In World War II." Leavenworth Papers # 11. Fort Leavenworth, Kansas: Combat Studies Institute, June 1985.

Published Sources

Allen, Robert S. *Lucky Forward*. New York: Vanguard Press, 1964.

Blumenson, Martin. *The Patton Papers, 1940–1945*. Boston: Houghton Mifflin, 1974.

Black, Robert W. *Rangers in World War II*. New York: Ivy Books, 1992.

Bonn, Keith E. *When the Odds Were Even. The Vosges Mountains Campaign, October 1944–January 1945*. Novato, Ca.: Presidio Press, 1994.

Bradley, Omar N. *A Soldier's Story*. New York: Henry Holt, 1951.

Bradley, Omar N, with Clay Blair. *A General's Life*. New York: Simon and Schuster, 1983.

Chandler, Alfred D., ed. *The Papers of Dwight David Eisenhower: The War Years*. Vols. 1–5. Baltimore: Johns Hopkins University Press, 1970.

Clarke, Jeffrey J., and Robert Ross Smith. *Riviera to The Rhine*. Washington, DC: Chief Of Military History, 1993.

Codman, Charles R. *Drive*. Boston: Little, Brown, 1957.

Colby, John. *War From the Ground Up. The 90th Division in World War II*. Austin, Texas: Nortex Press, 1991.

D'Este, Carlo. *Patton. A Genius for War*. New York: Harper Collins, 1995.

Doubler, Michael D. *Closing With the Enemy. How GIs Fought the War in Europe, 1944–1945*. Lawrence, Kansas: University Press of Kansas, 1994.

Dyer, George. *XII Corps: Spearhead Of Patton's Third Army*. Baton Rouge, La.: Army Navy Publishing Co., 1947.

Eisenhower, David. *Eisenhower At War, 1943–1945*. London: Collins, 1986.

Eisenhower, Dwight D. *Crusade In Europe*. Garden City, N. Y.: Doubleday, 1948.

Essame, H. *Patton: The Commander.* London: B. T. Batsford, 1974.

Farago, Ladislas. *Patton: Ordeal and Triumph.* New York: Ivan Obolensky, 1963.

Fuermann, George M. and F. Edward Cranz. *Ninety-Fifth Infantry Division History, 1918–1946.* Nashville: Battery Press, n.d.

Harkins, Paul D. *When the Third Cracked Europe.* Harrisburg, Pa.: Stackpole, 1969.

Hobbs, Joseph P. *Dear General: Eisenhower's Wartime Letters to Marshall.* Baltimore: John Hopkins University Press, 1971.

Hutnick, Joseph J. *We Ripened Fast. The Unofficial History of the Seventy-Sixth Infantry Division.* Frankfurt am Main: Otto Lembeck, 1946.

Irving, David. *The War Between the Generals.* New York: Congden and Lattes, 1981.

Kemp, Anthony. *The Unknown Battle: Metz, 1944.* New York: Stein and Day, 1985.

McKee, Alexander. *The Race for the Rhine Bridges.* London: Pan Books, 1974.

Nichols, Lester M. *Impact. The Battle Story of the Tenth Armored Division.* New York: Bradbury, Sayles, O'Neill Co., 1954.

Patton, George S., Jr. *War As I Knew It.* New York: Bantam, 1980.

Pogue, Forrest C. *George C. Marshall:Organizer Of Victory, 1943-1945.* New York: Viking, 1973.

Province, Charles M. *The Unknown Patton.* New York: Bonanza Books, 1983.

———. *Patton's Third Army.* New York: Hippocrene Books, 1992.

Regimental Historical Committee, Information and Education Office. *History of the 376th Infantry Regiment Between the Years of 1921–1945.* Wuppertal-Barmen, Germany: Carl Weddigen, 1945.

Standifer, Leon C. *Not In Vain. A Rifleman Remembers World War II.* Baton Rouge and London: Louisiana State University Press, 1992.

Vannoy, Allyn R. and Jay Karamales. *Against the Panzers. United States Infantry Versus German Tanks, 1944–1945.* Jefferson, N. C. and London: McFarland & Company Inc., 1996.

Wallace, Brenton G., *Patton and His Third Army.* Nashville: Battery Press, 1981 (reprint of 1948 edition).

Weigley, Russell F. *History of the United States Army.* New York: MacMillan, 1967.

————. *Eisenhower's Lieutenants.* Bloomington: Indiana University Press, 1981.

Williams, Mary H. *Chronology, 1941–1945.* Washington, D.C.: Office of the Chief of Military History, 1960.

XX Corps Association. *The XX Corps: Its History and Service in World War II.* Osaka, Japan: Mainichi Pub. Co., 1951.

INDEX